FRENCH HISTORIANS AND ROMANTICISM

Thierry, Guizot, the Saint-Simonians, Quinet, Michelet

Ceri Crossley

London and New York

First published 1993
by Routledge
11 New Fetter Lane, London EC4P 4EE

Simultaneously published in the USA and Canada
by Routledge Inc.
29 West 35th Street, New York, NY 10001

© 1993 Ceri Crossley

Phototypeset in 10/12 pt Garamond by Intype, London
Printed and bound in Great Britain by
T J Press (Padstow) Ltd, Cornwall

British Library Cataloguing in Publication Data
Crossley, Ceri
French Historians and Romanticism:
Thierry, Guizot, the Saint-Simonians,
Quinet, Michelet
I. Title
907.2044.

Library of Congress Cataloging in Publication Data
Crossley, Ceri.
French historians and romanticism/Ceri Crossley.
p.   cm.
Includes bibliographical references and index.
1. France–Historiography. 2. France–History–Revolution.
1789–1799–Influence. 3. Historians–France–Attitudes.
4. Romanticism–France. I. Title.
DC36.9.C76 1993
944'.0072–dc20   92-36697

ISBN 0–415–02118–9

University of Hertfordshire

Wall Hall Campus Library
Aldenham Watford Herts WD2 8AT
Tel (0707) 285743 Fax (0707) 285744

This book must be returned or renewed on or before the
last date stamped below. The library retains the right to recall
books at any time. A fine may be charged for overdue items.

Contents

Acknowledgements

The present book is the result of much time spent exploring French Romanticism, especially its religious and political dimensions. I have learnt a great deal from the scholars and critics cited in the Notes and Bibliography. I have also drawn considerable benefit from discussions with friends and colleagues. I would particularly like to mention Frank Paul Bowman, Donald Charlton, Michel Crouzet, Jean-Yves Guiomar, Peter Jones, Paul Viallaneix, Christopher Warne, Dennis Wood, Anthony Zielonka. I owe a particular debt to Simone Bernard-Griffiths of the Centre de Recherches Révolutionnaires et Romantiques of the University of Clermont-Ferrand. I would like to record my thanks to the British Academy for the award of a research grant. I have received support on a number of occasions from the Faculty of Arts of the University of Birmingham. I am grateful to the Dean, Professor Leon Pompa, for the consistent encouragement he has given to research in the humanities. Translations from the French are either my own or based upon the published translations listed in the bibliography.

Abbreviations

The following abbreviations are used in the text. A full bibliography is given on pp. 270–80.

Chapter 2 Works by Augustin Thierry

DAEH   *Dix ans d'études historiques* (Brussels: Gregoir & Wouters, 1839)

EHFP   *Essai sur l'histoire de la formation et des progrès du tiers état* (Paris: Firmin-Didot, 1883)

HCA   *Histoire de la conquête de l'Angleterre par les Normands* (Paris: Jouvet, 1882)

LHF   *Lettres sur l'histoire de France* (Brussels: Gregoir & Wouters, 1839)

R   *Récits des temps mérovingiens précédés de considérations sur l'histoire de France* (Brussels: Société belge de librairie, 1840)

Chapter 3 Works by François Guizot

DF   *De la démocratie en France* (Paris: Masson, 1849)

DGF   *Du gouvernement de la France depuis la Restauration et du ministère actuel* (Paris: Ladvocat, 1820)

DHRA   *Discours sur l'histoire de la révolution d'Angleterre* (Brussels: Meline, 1850)

DMG   *Des moyens de gouvernement et d'opposition dans l'état actuel de la France* (Paris: Belin, 1988)

EHF   *Essais sur l'histoire de France* (Paris: Perrin, 1884)

HCE   *Histoire de la civilisation en Europe* (Paris: Hachette, 1985)

ABBREVIATIONS

HCF	*Histoire de la civilisation en France depuis la chute de l'Empire romain jusqu'en 1789* (Brussels: Vandooren; Paris: Pichon & Didier, 1829–32)
HOGR	*Histoire des origines du gouvernement représentatif et des institutions politiques de l'Europe* (Paris: Didier, 1880)
M	*Mémoires pour servir à l'histoire de mon temps* (Paris: Michel Lévy, 1858–67)
MEM	*Méditations et études morales* (Paris: Didier, 1852)
MPH	*Mélanges politiques et historiques* (Paris: Michel Lévy, 1869)
TG	*Trois générations. 1789–1814–1848* (Paris: Michel Lévy, 1852)

Chapter 4 Works of Saint-Simon and the Saint-Simonians

O	*Œuvres* (Geneva: Slatkine, 1977)
DSS	*Doctrine de Saint-Simon. Exposition. Première année. 1828–1829* (Paris: Au bureau de l'*Organisateur*, 1831)

Chapter 5 Works by Edgar Quinet

A	'Ahasvérus', *Revue des deux mondes* (October 1833)
DLA	'De l'avenir des religions', *Revue des deux mondes* (July 1831)
DLAER	*De l'Allemagne et de la Révolution* (Paris: Paulin, 1832)
DLN	*De la nature et de l'histoire dans leurs rapports avec les traditions religieuses et épiques* (Paris: Levrault, 1830)
DLR	'De la Révolution et de la philosophie', *Revue des deux mondes* (July 1831)
I, E	*Introduction* and *Etude sur le caractère et les écrits de Herder* (Paris: Levrault, 1827–8)
LPDA	'Le pont d'Arcole', *Revue des deux mondes* 3 (1832)
LR	*La Révolution* (Paris: Librairie Internationale, 1865)
OC	*Œuvres complètes* (Paris: Pagnerre, 1857–8)

Chapter 6 Works by Jules Michelet

DJ	*Des Jésuites* (Paris: Pauvert, 1966)
DP	*Du prêtre, de la femme, et de la famille* (Brussels: Meline, 1845)

ABBREVIATIONS

HRF	*Histoire de la Révolution française* (Paris: Maron and Flammarion, 1868)
J	*Journal*, vols 1 and 2, ed. P. Viallaneix (Paris: Gallimard, 1959–62); vols 3 and 4, ed. Cl. Digeon (Paris: Gallimard, 1976)
LE	*L'Etudiant*, ed. G. Picon (Paris: Seuil, 1970)
LF	*La Femme* (Paris: Flammarion, 1981)
LP	*Le Peuple* (Paris: Flammarion, 1974)
OC	*Œuvres complètes* (Paris: Flammarion, 1971)
LVR	Viallaneix, Paul, *La Voie royale. Esssai sur l'idée de peuple dans l'œuvre de Michelet* (Paris: Flammarion, 1971)

1

Introduction: history and the post-revolutionary context

The philosopher R. G. Collingwood once observed that the past as past was wholly unknowable. What was knowable was something different: the elements of the past which had been residually preserved in the present.[1] In other words, what we take to be knowledge of past reality derives in fact from those texts, artefacts, buildings, belief systems, memories and traditions which have somehow survived and are amenable to investigation – and interpretation. History can only be written from the standpoint of present reality and can never encompass either the totality of events or the fullness of meaning. The historical consciousness inevitably selects and orders its material in accordance with contemporary concerns which consciously or unconsciously determine the frame of reference of its operations. However, while the being of the past may be unknowable in an absolute sense its effects remain relentlessly present; its traces surround us and form the theatre of our actions; it is through our relation to history (personal, family, collective) that we acquire an individual identity within culture. The activity of the individual self is inscribed within groups and cultures, themselves historically constructed, and these in turn legitimise certain forms of social relations. Unknowable the past may be, but the discourse on the past possesses a truth value in so far as it acts as a principle of legitimation, sanctioning political power, justifying social hierarchies, determining rights and responsibilities. The past, retrospectively reconstructed as history, functions as a source of authority, overtly in the shape of jurisprudence and covertly in the form of the ways of feeling, the attitudes of mind, the norms of behaviour which are transmitted to future generations and are internalised by them through the process of socialisation.

1

My aim in this book is to describe the major components of
the French Romantic construction of the past, with its dominant
sense of purposeful movement, energy and potentiality. My point
of departure is the notion that foremost among the cultural attri-
butes which are the defining characteristics of collective entities is
the relation which a given culture entertains with the passing of
time. A culture's self-definition is inscribed within its understanding of the collective past, of how it came to be what it is, and
how it conceives of its development. I shall look at some of the
ways in which the past was rediscovered, retrieved and represented
in French thought broadly between 1815 and 1851 through the
writings of Guizot, Thierry, Cousin, Quinet, Michelet and others.
I shall be concerned with the assumptions which governed their
different readings of the past and with the ways in which their
theory and practice of history were themselves influenced by historical circumstance.

History continues to occupy a remarkably central position in
French cultural life, more so certainly than in the United Kingdom. In France the discourse on the past is an essential component
of the discourse on society and politics in general. Why should
this be so? In my view this desire to use the past as a point of
reference illuminating present reality has to do with the fact of
the Revolution and its still unresolved consequences. Arguments
over the meaning and value of the Revolution persist despite the
decline of orthodox marxist readings and the dominance of
François Furet and his disciples. What needs to be emphasised
here is the degree to which the Revolution problematised the
whole relation to the past while at the same time setting the agenda
for modern political culture. The Revolution initially created in
France an awareness of the uniqueness of the present. The past
was rejected. New institutions were to be established which would
correspond to genuine human needs and actualise the universal
rights of man. This mood of renewal was recaptured by Michelet
in his lyrical evocation of the great Fête de la Fédération of 1790;
the event seemed to stand outside time, an eternal, a timeless
moment of hope and potentiality. However, while it is no exaggeration to say that in the wake of the French Revolution the nation
stood in a new relation to time – the rhetoric of renewal taking
concrete form in the revolutionary calendar – events demonstrated
the power of the past to overwhelm the promise of the present.
The hope of 1789–90 was followed by division, civil war, the

2

Terror, the despotism of Napoleon and finally defeat at Waterloo. The old centres of spiritual, political and moral authority were destroyed but no stable new order emerged. After 1815 the desire to understand the recent period of instability developed into a more general reflection on the past, its direction and its meaning.

As the nineteenth century unfolded the English idea of progress, like the Whig interpretation of history, became identified by many with a belief in the inevitability of gradual improvement. In France, by the very nature of things, the idea of progress was more directly linked to political struggles for individual and collective freedom and to the seemingly inevitable oscillation between revolution and reaction. British history is reformist whereas French history is revolutionary.[2] For Frenchmen, the grandeur – or the horror – of 1789 lay in its repudiation of the past, in its attempt to create a new world of values, boldly to actualise a heroic ideal. In this way the relation of post-revolutionary France to 1789 can be viewed as the relation to a founding origin. The Revolution was more than a revolt, more than the outbreak of violence against authority. It created a new relation between before and after, a temporal disjunction which called into question the nature and purpose of human action. The Revolution was a violently transgressive act of regicide which sundered the nation from its past, an act of collective parricide which nevertheless inaugurated a new order and established the nation-state.[3] But while the Revolution transformed the relation to the past this relation was experienced and theorised in different ways as the nineteenth century unfolded. The work of the Romantic historians is to be seen in this context. Their writing is worthy of searching study because it reveals the degree to which the recovery of national history was coextensive with the attempt to understand and account for the French Revolution.

Ideas of the past – and the future – are not fixed. They are historically and culturally formed. Historians do more than conserve the object of their attention; they endow history with meaning as their narrative unfolds. The work of Hayden White has done much to open up this area by describing the different tropes which govern the plotting of the historical field.[4] In the present study, however, my main concern does not lie with the literariness of historical discourse, with the extent to which it conforms or does not conform to particular structures or forms of textual organisation which in turn govern the production of meaning.

Most of my attention will involve more traditional methods of analysis and be devoted to matters of intellectual history and social and political theory. This Introduction aims to present the reader with a view of the different currents of historical explanation which dominated intellectual debate in France from the Directory to the end of the Restoration. Subsequent chapters will, for the most part, concentrate upon individual writers and thinkers. My aim is to show how a new set of governing ideas concerning the nature of history altered the understanding of the relationship between individual and social reality, and led in some instances to a new sense of the sacred.

The central concern of liberal French intellectuals after 1815 was the relation of the present to the inheritance of the Revolution.[5] The leaders of the Revolution had believed that human nature could be remade, refashioned, and that the past could in effect be rejected, disowned. Looking back over French history in his *Politique libérale* (1875) Charles de Rémusat saw in this rejection of the national past an essential component of the French revolutionary spirit. In Rémusat's eyes France represented the unique case of a country which had turned against its past to the extent of denigrating and disowning the collective memories of a thousand years. No other nation had gone so far in attempting to eliminate and eradicate the sense of the past. No other nation, concluded Rémusat, 'had made so great a sacrifice of its past to its future'.[6] Rémusat's stance was in fact that of the liberal intellectuals of the years 1815–30 who rapidly abandoned the outright rejection of the past professed by the revolutionaries. They recognised that the disavowal of the collective past was an error which had in effect confirmed the reactionary view that the Revolution was an aberration, a disruption of the natural order of things. Restoration liberal historians set out to appropriate the historical field, to discover and celebrate precursors of their cause. As we shall see, it was with this aim in view that Thierry, Guizot and Mignet described the emancipation of the Communes and the rise of the Third Estate. Their writing was in tune with the times for it largely accorded with the interests and aspirations of the middle classes who would seize the political initiative in 1830.[7] History furnished them with a sense of collective development which allowed them to disentangle the constitutionalism of 1789 from the radical republicanism of 1793. Following the lead given by Madame de Staël in her posthumously published *Considérations sur la Révolution française* (1818), liberals argued that the disruption of history caused by 1789 took on meaning when set within a more general movement of national history. They explained that liberty was not invented in 1789; its presence could be found in earlier centuries. In their view history embodied not submission to authority but resistance to arbitrary rule.

In this way history became integral to liberal doctrine. Henceforward it was to be the reference to history – rather than any appeal to abstract rights (which smacked of the revolutionary republic and the destruction of freedom in the name of democracy) – which furnished liberals with persuasive arguments in favour of reform and civil equality. The writing of history was a mobilising project which ascribed authority and legitimacy to the revolutionary nation-state and which contained an implicit critique of social and political reality. The Restoration witnessed the displacement of politics into history. The strength of such history, written against the established order (albeit in defence of the constitutional monarchy), was that it was predicated upon an idea of the future. The collective dynamic discovered in the past was also at work in the present, creating the future. The discourse on the past which emerged was a direct response to conditions prevailing in France in its new post-revolutionary cultural configuration. Such discourse was symbolic in character, carrying not only facts and memories but values, recognitions and aspirations. National unity needed an idea of tradition and continuity which somehow explained the Revolution and invested it with meaning. The collective memory was no longer to be jettisoned in favour of the claims of political theory.

The years between 1815 and 1830 corresponded to a period of intense historical activity in France. The reason for this, as Stanley Mellon has explained in a seminal study, was that during the Restoration history became in effect the language of politics.[8] The Charter of 1814 sought to bring about a degree of reconciliation by dividing sovereignty between the king and the nation. Liberals who argued in favour of the extension of rights and freedoms defended this constitutional compromise which they saw as incorporating the true spirit of the Revolution. Against them were ranged the conservative monarchists, the Ultras, the returning émigrés whose objective was a complete reversion to the Ancien Régime. In their vengeful eyes the Revolution was a criminal act. It was to be rejected as a block. They were suspicious of all liberal calls for reform since in them they detected a covert resurgence of Jacobinism. The intellectual cohesion of the Ultras was provided by the writings of the traditionalist school: Joseph de Maistre (1753–1821), Louis de Bonald (1754–1840) and Félicité de Lamennais (1782–1854). The central element of the traditionalist critique of Enlightenment philosophy was that the *philosophes* had mistakenly ascribed priority and superiority to the individual over society. In the eighteenth century sensationalist psychology had combined with moral relativism to produce an abstract notion of the individual which had subsequently been manipulated by the universalist rhetoric of the Revolution to support the causes of freedom, equality and democracy.[9] In the opinion of de Maistre eighteenth-century rationalism was an abomination; it eroded the social fabric and led directly to the dislocation of 1789. That was also Lamennais's thesis in the *Essai sur l'indifférence* (1817–23). According to Joseph de Maistre the great error of the Enlightenment had been to believe that men had the power to create laws and invent institutions. In reality society was not a construction of the rational will of individuals but rather the manifestation of a power which both transcended and sustained the collective entity concerned. Individuals were formed by society and only existed in and through social relationships. At the very heart of social reality lay religion. In the *Génie du christianisme* (1802) Chateaubriand argued persuasively that human beings had genuine religious needs. Religion was inseparable from collective life; it lent duration, continuity, identity and meaning to society.

The Revolution, on the other hand, was the agent of the forces of unbelief; it had disrupted the natural processes of history. For de Maistre the Revolution was radically evil, satanic. But at the same time it possessed an awesome power and energy.[10] In his *Considérations sur la France* (1797) he wrote that the Revolution was a divinely ordained punishment meted out to the French nation for failing to serve the cause of throne and altar. History was at once the unfolding of a divine purpose and a story of blood and violence, explicable by reference to the theory of reversibility according to which the sufferings of the innocent atoned for the sins of the guilty. History was not explicable in purely human terms. This darkly uncompromising providentialist interpretation of history – which none the less accommodated the idea that France had a special mission to fulfil – had analogies with some of the republican theories I shall be examining later. However, de

Maistre's views were clearly incompatible with a truly developmental philosophy of history. All positive valorisation of change
as progress was avoided. The objective of the Ultras was the
restoration of throne and altar and not the establishment of a
different order (which by their definition would collapse into
impurity). Neither was this conservative metaphysic of history
which rejected constitutions in favour of reverence for tradition
really identical with the superficially similar understanding of the
power of custom and organic processes proposed by Burke.

The keynote was the rejection of the liberal notion of rights in
favour of submission to an intransigent and intolerant authority.
The Reformation's appeal to individual conscience had been
crushed in the course of the wars of religion and by the Revocation
of the Edict of Nantes. However, the Revolution had given rights
to Protestants – and to Jews. Authoritarian Catholicism, on the
other hand, was hostile to both groups. Traditionalism regarded
liberal freedoms in general (freedom of the press, of worship) as
unacceptable challenges to the sacred nature of an organic society
which was grounded in truths transmitted from the collective past.
Difficulties arose because Restoration political life rested on the
Charter of 1814 which represented a compromise of sorts between
royalism and liberalism. There was also the problem that divisions
existed within the political Right: between the Ultras and more
moderate conservatives, between the émigrés returning after 1815
and those who had come back during the Empire, between outright monarchists and those who defended the role of the aristocracy (such as Montlosier who revived Boulainvilliers's explanation
of French history as a conflict between Gauls and Franks). There
was the additional and inescapable fact that the monarchy had
only fully regained power in the nineteenth century thanks to the
invasion of French territory by foreign armies. Nevertheless, the
Ultras felt they had right and history, as well as God, on their
side and the political project of the Right rested on the paradoxical
belief that it was possible to organise a return to an ordered
monarchy in which social relations would once again be governed
by largely unconscious beliefs and practices. The causes of the
Revolution were explained with reference back to the Reformation
and to Enlightenment philosophy but these subversive intellectual
currents were castigated as errors, not seen as manifestations of
an alternative tradition. The Revolution was held to be evil but it
was above all seen as an aberration. The argument which Barruel

had advanced in 1797 to the effect that the Revolution was a criminal conspiracy against throne and altar was revived. The profound changes which France had undergone during the Revolution and Empire could seemingly in large measure be reversed by force. The Right maintained its outright hostility to the Revolution in all its forms.[11]

A new generation of writers emerged, influenced by the *Génie du christianisme*, and in their work feeling for nature joined with historical sensibility to produce texts which reinforced the spirit of reaction, albeit in a mood tinged with melancholy and a sense of loss. French Romanticism in its early legitimist phase looked back to an idealised vision of the Middle Ages. For the Right the monarchy had been the constant ordering and unifying principle throughout French history until 1789. The society of the future was to be a return to a lost past symbolically organised around the king and the church. The future would be the perpetuation of the past. Such a view drew strength from its power to integrate individuals into social life (while denying them participation and rights) and from its sense of the importance of the past. But it was essentially a static vision which ultimately valorised sameness. Liberals came to a different accommodation with the collective dimension and inscribed it in a developmental theory of history. Traditionalist thought contained elements susceptible of a more dynamic interpretation – for example Lamennais's reliance on the notion of universal consent – but, as Lamennais's own evolution indicated, history as progress soon became heterodoxy. Catholic royalism, convinced of the absolute truth of its dogmas, proceeded in the manner of the Counter-Revolution, by excluding from its definition of France and Frenchness all who disagreed with its central tenets. Traditionalist Catholicism appealed to a lost sense of ontological security and branded as loathsome the post-traditional order of modernity which seemed devoid of any enduring metaphysical principle. De Bonald, for example, was not interested in the formation of self-identity. What mattered to him was the reconstruction of the ontological framework which determined social norms and human conduct. This patterning underpinned the distribution of power and guaranteed the principle of authority which preserved social cohesion despite the pressures of conflicting individual wills.

At first sight de Bonald's affection for an idealised feudal monarchy suggested a significant interest in the past; after all, it provided a useful prop for the Catholic identity in the present. He also elaborated a cyclical theory of political change which had analogies with Vico: power was originally personal (the monarchy), then public (the feudal monarchy) and finally popular (this last condition eventually produced the Revolution; de Bonald hoped that the reimposition of personal authority by Napoleon signalled a return to the first stage, hence the start of a new cycle). However, it is important to note that de Bonald did not make history a bearer of values. He conceived of the truth as something immutable, fixed in unchanging structures. Truth was not emerging; it had been disclosed to humanity by revelation and transmitted by language (which was divine in origin). De Bonald perceived the interconnections between the political and the historical but his object was to anchor politics in the metaphysical order. Religion alone, because it drew its authority from God – not from a historically definable moment of foundation – was capable of unifying society. De Bonald wanted France to organise power in the manner which was authorised by tradition. Change was not to be denied but what mattered was making reality conform to the law, to fundamental metaphysical principles. In the name of God de Bonald resisted the expansion of history's authority and its consequent perils – moral relativism and political pluralism. History in his eyes was neither a dialectical process nor the self-development of reason. What was valued was the ideal structure of meaning which guaranteed law but stood outside phenomenal reality. Hence de Bonald did not display a sense that historical knowledge was something essential to the completeness of existence.

The events of the past were not irradiated by de Bonald's charmless prose. Indeed, he shared with his adversaries, the Idéologues, a definite scepticism concerning the status and importance of history. It was fine to look to history for examples but it was the triadic structure of power relations which was of greater importance because it was inherent within the nature of things and had the status of a transhistorical given. Rather than give assent to development as a good, de Bonald asserted the value of the immutable, of the whole which was greater than the sum of its parts, of the eternal which stood outside time. His science of society was a political theology rather than a historical sociology (although he was to exert a real influence over thinkers such as Auguste Comte and Saint-Simon).[12] However, Catholicism in less intransigent forms than those proposed by de Bonald or de Maistre did manage to engage with the idea of history as development. Some inserted the Revolution within a wider philosophy of history – Ballanche's general understanding of history in terms of initiation and expiation was a case in point. And in general terms the types of social Catholicism which came to prominence after 1830 were much more sensitive to the idea of history as progress. Indeed, certain Catholic socialists, such as Buchez, went much further and came to view history itself as the incarnation of the logos and to represent the Revolution as fundamentally Christian in nature.

Conservatives felt secure in their representation of the past. History was an invaluable point of reference, stabilising the present, defining the only alternative. The reconstruction of social order was envisaged from the perspective of the past. The lessons drawn from the past served to confirm received truth. The Ancien Régime emerged less as a historically determined society than as an idealised, hierarchically organised community in which everyone knew his or her place, an unchallengeable system of castes and power relationships. From the conservative vantage point, the content of the past was known, its meaning was stable and assured. There was no doubt that the disruption of the social order and the collapse of authority had been ushered in by individualism, science and unbelief. Liberals, for their part, had to face the fact that the meaning of individualism had been compromised by revolutionary virtue. Hence their strategy was of distinguishing between the constitutional spirit of 1789 and the violence of 1793. They shared the conservatives' revulsion from the violence of 1793–4, but they argued that the Terror was not the inevitable consequence of 1789. Liberals held that the Revolution, by bringing about civil equality, had introduced an irreversible positive change. In their mind the Restoration had to come to terms with the gains of the Revolution: equality before the law and a restricted form of representative government.

THE INHERITANCE OF ENLIGHTENMENT LIBERALISM: THE IDEOLOGUES

The texts I shall be concerned with in this book reflect the change from Enlightenment to Romantic modes of social and historical explanation. The period 1815–30 witnessed the emergence of the new history – Augustin Thierry's examination of the Norman Conquest appeared in 1825 – but in order to understand these developments we need first to attend to the direction in which liberal thinking had been moving since the closing years of the revolutionary decade. Classical liberalism of the eighteenth century placed individuals in isolation and viewed them as self-sufficient units pursuing happiness. Human conduct was explained in terms of individual wishes, desires and calculations but it was also held that, taken as a whole, the self-directed actions of individuals contributed to general improvement and material progress. However, the events of the Revolution altered the perspective in which liberalism was to be judged. First, 1789 redefined collective identity as the nation but it did so by excluding from the national community groups which were considered hostile to its constitution – the nobility and the clergy – and this inevitably cast doubt upon the universal application of natural rights. Second, as events unfolded the potential for dictatorship contained within the theory of the general will was progressively revealed. Third, the Revolution demonstrated the crucial role played by the people – the unenlightened, propertyless urban and rural masses – in forcing change. Had aristocratic and middle-class intellectuals unleashed a force which they could no longer control? After Thermidor and under the Directory and the Consulate the objective of liberals was to preserve what was valuable in the revolutionary inheritance. At that juncture the cause of moderate republicanism was defended by the Idéologues, the group of intellectuals, philosophers and scientists which included Destutt de Tracy, Volney, Daunou, Garat, Ginguené, Cabanis, Bichat and Broussais.[13] They exerted a direct influence on government policy – notably in the field of education reform – and their ideas reached a wider audience via their influential journal *La Décade philosophique* (1794–1807).[14]

These were men who remained loyal to the ideal of scientific method as defined by the eighteenth century. They had suffered under the Terror. Daunou, Volney and Destutt de Tracy were imprisoned. Condorcet died in prison in 1794, probably by his own hand. Although the long shadow of the Terror fell across the present they steadfastly refused to repudiate the critical rationalism which had produced the Revolution. They remained convinced that analytical reason could discover truth, improve society and increase the sum of human happiness. Despite the Terror they believed that scientific knowledge could be applied to remodel society on a rational basis. A scientific morality and a scientific politics were possible, indeed achievable. It is fair to say that in general their work inclined towards materialism and that anticlericalism was part of their make-up. They followed Condillac in explaining mental phenomena in terms of man's physical nature. The moral life was viewed as rigorously dependent upon external sensations. Man was viewed essentially as a sentient being, the product of his environment. The pursuit of pleasure and the avoidance of pain were the mainsprings of human actions; co-operation within society was understood as the mechanism which facilitated the actualisation of individual desires.

The importance of the Idéologues for this study lies in the fact that they represented a form of liberalism which did not focus upon an appeal to history.[15] Indeed they tended to be suspicious of history when they did not dismiss it out of hand as if it were a dustbin containing outmoded ideas, prejudices and superstitions. Whereas Restoration liberals would soon be turning to the past in support of their arguments, the Idéologues did not feel the need to appeal to historical rights or to unearth an alternative tradition of freedom. The rights and responsibilities of the individual could, they judged, adequately be defined by the correct application of reason to the study of the origin of ideas. The movement from Ideology to Restoration liberalism – from Destutt de Tracy to Cousin – corresponded to a significant shift in sensibility and to a change in epistemology. In order for the discourse on the past to become central to the definition of what constituted the human sciences a break had to be made with Enlightenment modes of thought, with eighteenth-century representations of the mind–body relation, with natural law and with the main tenets of social contract theory. The Idéologues still wanted to refashion society in accordance with the dominant ideas of sensationalism. Their prime concern lay with the origin of ideas, with establishing the facts of psychology in a clear, objective, scientific manner. Knowledge of man and of the world were held to arise from experience and not from revelation, innate ideas or any process of intuition. The faculties, including memory, were explained in terms of the combination and comparison of sensations. Clear and accurate knowledge was arrived at by decomposing complex objects into their constituent elements. They formulated the project of a human science which was consistent with sensationalist epistemology and largely independent of reference to history. To be sure they believed in progress, in gradual improvement, in an increase in scientific knowledge; in a word, in the historical scheme outlined by Condorcet in his posthumously published *Esquisse d'un tableau historique des progrès de l'esprit humain* (1795); but they did not relate the development of human reason to the self-development of a higher power.

More mystical views of the collective destiny of humankind were of course not absent from the eighteenth century – but for these we would need to investigate the occultist and illuminist traditions.[16] As far as the Idéologues were concerned, it was the natural sciences or mathematics which provided valid models for the science of man. The phenomena of individual and social life were to be observed and classified; general laws would then be formulated which would account for human behaviour. Many – including Saint-Simon – were intrigued by the psycho-physiological explanations of the health or sickness of society which emerged. However, the salient point for our purpose in this study is that the human science of the Idéologues did not foreground history.

The Idéologues aspired to a world which was secular and rational. Religions were at best transformations of scientific ideas (a warm welcome was extended to Dupuis's famous explanation of all religions as variations on sun worship) and at worst – and this was the norm – agents of oppression. The past, which was replete with ignorance, prejudice and superstition, could usefully be ignored.[17] In his *Eléments d'Idéologie*, Destutt de Tracy (1754–1836) left no room for the science of memory or, for that matter, for the imagination.[18] Condorcet, despite the utopian tenth chapter of the *Esquisse*, viewed history not as a process of becoming but as the emergence of increasingly complex combinations of sensations and ideas.[19] History charted increasing human mastery over nature but it also drew attention to the factors which hindered the advance of freedom and reason.[20] Why attend overmuch to history when it contained so many errors, dead ends, unfulfilled promises? What expectations could be had of history?

As Emmet Kennedy has remarked, the history of philosophy held no great attraction for the Idéologues since in their eyes it marked a 'vision of linear progress from error to truth'.[21] Destutt de Tracy described the progression from despotism to representative government but the legitimacy of the latter rested on reason, not history. This was all very much at variance with the views soon to be articulated by Cousinian eclecticism which held that history contained 'truths scattered among all previous systems'.[22] The opinion of the Idéologues was different: on the one hand, historical knowledge was deemed largely irrelevant since it diverted attention from the urgent concerns of the present; on the other, it was potentially subversive of the project of building the rational society on account of the catalogue of errors which formed most of its content. Far better for the intellectual elite to devote its energies to building a society which embodied the scientifically verifiable principles of rational morality. In a government circular of 1799 which helped establish the curriculum of the new *écoles centrales*, Destutt de Tracy declared his wish that pupils acquire knowledge of the events of world history, but he made clear that the purpose of studying the past was to discover and understand the relationship between 'men's happiness and the extent and accuracy of their ideas'.[23] Social development was a reality but it was related to the development of the linguistic systems which allowed the increase in knowledge to take place. Social unity would be actualised by attributing power and authority to scientific reason and by establishing institutions which would protect the individual subject. Ideology wanted to steer a course which avoided both the Scylla of Jacobin authoritarianism and the Charybdis of counter-revolutionary irrationalism. Politics had primacy over history when it came to providing society with a rational organisation.

And yet, despite this scepticism regarding the usefulness of the past, Ideology did contain historians within its ranks. A valuable contribution was made by Volney (1757–1820), who examined the methodology of history and who, while lending weight to the Idéologues' distrust of the past, did so in a manner which paradoxically opened up fertile new areas of enquiry.[24] Volney was a loyal man of the Enlightenment. He served the revolutionary cause by publishing *La Loi naturelle ou cathéchisme du citoyen français* (1793). He is best remembered for an earlier work, *Les Ruines ou méditations sur les révolutions des empires* (1791), in which he described the errors of past centuries from the standpoint of the rationalist critic of religion. In 1795 Volney delivered at the Ecole Normale a course of lectures which dealt with questions of methodology and historical truth.[25] In these *Leçons d'histoire* he explained that history could not aspire to the high degree of certainty achieved in the natural sciences; the facts with which history was concerned were not given directly in sense experience but were mediated through language and presented in discourse. The student of history encountered a 'fantastic picture of vanished facts of which but a shadowy image has remained' (p. 570). Historical facts were held to be uncertain since they either reflected deliberate bias or were coloured by the perceptions of a particular individual or culture. It was the duty of the responsible historian to scrutinise his sources and to evaluate the credibility of earlier historians. Volney reflected the debunking approach of much politically committed Enlightenment historical writing. For example, he viewed myths and legends as primitive and unsophisticated expressions of an irrational mind rather than as telling manifestations of a mythopoeic collective imagination. However, he drew closer to the concerns of later generations when he suggested that history should envisage humankind 'as one society and the peoples as individuals' (p. 513). Likewise he prefigured the Romantic wish to discover the deep structures of national history imprinted in language: 'Each language is a complete history since it is the register of all the ideas of a people' (p. 598).

The *Leçons d'histoire* brought together two contrasting attitudes. In the first place Volney allied himself with the Idéologues' historical scepticism. Only limited value was to be placed upon a discipline which could aspire to probabilities, not to certainties. History amounted to a huge collection of 'moral and social experiments which mankind has conducted upon itself unwillingly and with reckless extravagance' (p. 554). Volney considered that it was a good thing for all citizens to acquire knowledge of reading, writing and arithmetic, to understand matters of biology, physics and geography. These were useful kinds of knowledge which had a bearing on the practical business of living. History, however, did not fall into this category. It was deemed to be an inappropriate subject for the immature minds of young children at primary school. And why should an artisan or a merchant bother himself with the existence of Alexander the Great?

Nevertheless, this questioning of the value of historical knowledge did not tell the whole story. Volney proposed the construction of a new universal history written by teams of scholars. He prefigured the Romantics' view of collective entities, viewing them as active agents living in a relationship with their natural environment. He observed that history was useful for developing the '*physiological science*' of governments (p. 572) by which he meant the comparative study of the rise and fall of different political systems. History was thus valuable after all – but this was history as a serious intellectual discipline, secure in the hands of an elite. In Volney's view, the Revolution demonstrated just how an idealised but mistaken view of the past could take hold and wreak havoc in the present. He attributed the errors of 1793 to a misguided attempt, by men whose passions had been inflamed by their Classical education, to imitate the ancient republics; a false idea of history had sabotaged the attempt made by Enlightenment reason to establish a society of peace and tolerance. Volney responded by challenging the prestige of the Classical world – in his opinion the Greeks resembled barbarians, and the Spartans bore a distinct likeness to the Iroquois. In this way, despite his many sideswipes at the inadequacies of history, Volney was not seriously advocating its abandonment. The truths of history were limited but were no less necessary for the well-being of society.

The case of Volney illustrates nicely both the Idéologues' suspicion of history and their concern at its power to undermine the rule of reason. History constituted a significant branch of human knowledge but the difficulty of establishing historical truth rendered this form of knowledge disturbingly unstable. Hence the wish that history, as an inherently imperfect science, should remain the province of an elite. Nevertheless, it is worth recalling that the Idéologues' wariness about history as a discipline did not lead them to question their general belief in human perfectibility, a belief which – in most cases – they managed to reconcile with their admiration for the achievements of Classical antiquity (and with their corresponding disregard for the Middle Ages). The Idéologues' sense of historical change could quite easily accommodate periods of decadence and decline because they viewed history as the consequence of unpredictable human actions and decisions rather than as a process driven by a truly developmental metaphysic.

In practice, writers and intellectuals associated with the Idéologues did produce a number of texts which were founded on a broad framework of historical explanation. Knowledge of other cultures inevitably required that attention be paid to origins, continuities and fractures. Literary history was tackled by Ginguené in his ambitious nine-volume *Histoire littéraire d'Italie* (1811–19). Such texts were impressive in their erudition but distinctly dry and analytical in tone. They lacked the invigorating sense of culture as an active force which we find for example in Mme de Staël's *De la littérature considérée dans ses rapports avec les institutions sociales* (1800). Most Idéologues who were interested in history were intellectually and temperamentally at odds with the re-evaluation of the Middle Ages which characterised the early nineteenth century; they were equally at odds with the aesthetics of Romanticism which in their opinion expressed an uncompromisingly reactionary political culture. They took history seriously, no longer viewing it simply as a rhetorical exercise, but in their approach they remained true to Classicism's focus on moral truth and clarity of form.

The most influential representative of Idéologue history was Daunou (1761–1839). He was active in a number of fields, pursuing political, academic and administrative careers. He was elected to the Convention, helped to draft the Constitution of the Year III, was responsible for the education law of 1795 and served as a deputy under the Restoration and the July Monarchy. He was head of the Archives under the Empire, held a chair of history at the Collège de France during the Restoration and returned to the Archives under the July Monarchy (where he was Michelet's immediate superior). He wielded considerable power and influence within academic institutions and in organs of learning such as the *Journal des savants*. In 1810 he published his *Essai historique sur la puissance temporelle des papes* and in 1819 he reaffirmed his liberal credentials by bringing out an *Essai sur les garanties individuelles que réclame l'état actuel de la société*. Daunou's lectures, his *Cours d'études historiques*, were published after his death and comprise twenty weighty volumes. They give us a clear sense of what, in the eyes of a leading Idéologue, constituted the proper way of doing history. Daunou's work was sober and analytical. In Cheryl Welch's phrase, he 'illuminated man's nature through historical example'.[26] Daunou believed that sense could be made of history without having recourse to mysterious forces or to some superior necessity. History was unpredictable precisely because it was the product of conflicting human projects. It was a reflection of man's fundamental needs and desires. In Daunou's mind it was a dangerous error to attempt to explain the facts of experiential reality by relating them to the activity of a higher power. He implied that whatever standpoint the historian adopted, the events of history could never be induced to mirror the order of nature.

The historian's prime duty was to use reason to establish the facts. Daunou stuck by the methods and values of the Enlightenment, praising Barthélemy's *Voyage du jeune Anacharsis* (1788) and remarking that in Condorcet's work 'everything bore the imprint of true philosophy, of the philosophy which observes, tests, analyses and employs the results of its researches in the service of society's needs' (p. 364).[27] Too often, in his view, the new Romantic historiography abandoned serious enquiry in favour of the enchantments of the imagination. Guizot, Victor Cousin (1792–1867), Prosper de Barante (1782–1866) and Michelet were all criticised. For Daunou, the true historian represented the critical intelligence. The study of history required the application of reason and method. Only at a later stage could the imagination be allowed to intervene: 'whereas enthusiasm appears sometimes to have been useful [in writing history], this has occurred when it has taken the form of an ardent, even passionate commitment to truths which had been previously studiously researched by reason and established after mature reflection' (p. 21). As these words suggest, Daunou was distinctly cool when it came to ascribing any real legitimacy to the imagination. He clearly felt that to privilege the imagination was to disdain scientific method and run the risk of compromising truth. He was unhappy with what he judged to be his contemporaries' ill-considered admiration for the supposedly naïve beauty of the Middle Ages.

Daunou was profoundly hostile to history as system. In his view the historian should concern himself with the direct causes of events and not try to relate historical facts to a hidden, ideal patterning. Daunou did not dispute the fact of progress but he wanted it defined in a manner which did not deprive men of their freedom. In his mind the introduction of system and philosophy into history led to determinism, to what was then termed historical fatalism. He had no time for 'ideal history' as had been proposed by the Neapolitan philosopher Giambattista Vico (1668–1744). In Kant's *Idea of a Universal History* he found a notion of continuous and necessary progress which he described as a hypothesis difficult to reconcile with positive history (p. 416). He agreed that history exhibited patterns of causation but he was absolutely opposed to what he saw as the determinism inherent in the totalising aspirations of the philosophical historians:

Universal fatalism denatures and falsifies history, which, after all, has as its sole subject matter objects in movement and which conceives as true nothing which exists beyond the real; the only causes known to history are those which occur positively and are themselves facts.

(p. 415)

The rehabilitation of the medieval period was held up as an example of the nefarious power of historical determinism at work:

I know that today people say that the Middle Ages were progressive, that the period was necessary and extremely useful. But despite all the trouble that has been taken to get history to come to this conclusion, it is, I believe, so thoroughly contradicted by the facts that no one can seriously hope to establish it as correct.

(p. 418)

Daunou had no time for mysticism or illuminism, no time for the extravagances of Swedenborg. However, his main enemy was the Platonic desire to explain the world of contingency in terms of a hidden intellectual reality, to relate the diversity of the real to the oneness of the true. In contemporary terms this meant that Daunou repudiated the application of the idealist metaphysics of Victor Cousin to the study of history.

THE LIMITS OF ENLIGHTENMENT LIBERALISM: ROYER-COLLARD AND BENJAMIN CONSTANT

The Idéologues transmitted to the nineteenth century the critical, individualistic liberalism of the eighteenth century with its attendant faith in science and impatience with all forms of positive religion. Such a doctrine, sceptical and analytical, was inherently subversive of authoritarian political structures. It was unlikely to be tolerated for long by a regime such as the Empire which sought an accommodation with the church and wanted to use religion as a means of social control. In 1803 Napoleon moved to suppress the influence of the Idéologues by closing the Second Class of the Institute, the Class of Moral and Political Sciences, which was a bastion of liberalism and sensationalist philosophy. Individuals such as Daunou and Destutt de Tracy subsequently pursued administrative and political careers under the Empire and the Restoration but they held fast to the empiricism and sensationalism which underpinned their liberalism. However, among other thinkers associated with the Idéologues we detect a change of mood, a movement away from strict sensationalism with its representation of the human mind as essentially passive. Gérando displayed a considerable interest in contemporary German currents of thought. Laromiguière drew attention to the limitations of sensationalist epistemology.[28] And most notably there was the case of the philosopher Maine de Biran who progressively abandoned the scientific materialism of Cabanis in favour of spiritualism and a philosophy of consciousness.[29] These developments reflected a broader intellectual realignment. It is fair to say that by the early 1800s the Idéologues were out of step with the spirit of the times. Their tendency to dismiss religion did not sit well with a post-revolutionary mood which exulted in the feeling for the infinite and discovered the presence of the divine in the beauties of the natural world. The France of the early nineteenth century was responsive to Chateaubriand's cocktail of Catholicism, royalism and Rousseauism. The author of the *Génie du christianisme* unashamedly stole his opponents' clothes by proclaiming that not philosophy but the Christian religion was the real civilising power. Instead of viewing the Catholic Middle Ages as a time of ignorance and obscurantism, Chateaubriand praised the church for protecting knowledge, developing agriculture and fostering commerce. Scientific materialism was out of fashion. Religion was not just true, it was beautiful and useful as well. Henceforth there would be room for mystery, for revelation and for truths disclosed by feeling and bodied forth by the imagination. It no longer seemed foolish to debate the destiny of the soul or discuss the spirituality of the inner life.

Sensationalism, which portrayed man as the product of his environment, offered little to a generation which was turning to currents of thought that represented consciousness as a unifying, active force in contact with an underlying spiritual reality. Similarly, the Idéologues' commitment to a narrow rationalist account of human nature was unlikely to strike a chord with those who considered that man's spiritual needs were legitimate and who recognised that religion amounted to much more than a priestly conspiracy. The definition of the individual transmitted by the Idéologues was inadequate, if not severely flawed. Nineteenth-century liberals proposed a substantive revision of eighteenth-century liberalism, a revision which eschewed scientific

INTRODUCTION

materialism. This new current accepted the centrality of religious experience (although sometimes reinterpreting the meaning of religion in ways unacceptable to orthodox believers). It valorised interiority and embraced history. Although it is always difficult to draw hard and fast distinctions in such areas, the grouping to which I shall now turn included three survivors of the revolutionary decade, Royer-Collard, Mme de Staël and Benjamin Constant.

Pierre Paul Royer-Collard (1763–1845) spoke for the generation which had lived through the turbulent years of change when he declared 'we want to end the Revolution' (I, p. 175).[30] But this was a common refrain and one amenable to a range of interpretations. For Royer-Collard himself, ending the Revolution meant repudiating the individualism which had produced an atomised society whose lack of cohesion had allowed arbitrary rule, centralisation and dictatorship to take hold. Revolutionary individualism was presented as a negative force, a dissolving agent, a threat to the stability of society. Liberal individualism was different because it rejected popular sovereignty and participatory democracy in favour of legal equality and representative institutions. Under the Directory Royer-Collard had already been giving advice on the state of France to the future Louis XVIII. After 1815 he argued the case for the constitutional monarchy but he recognised that the Revolution, by bringing about civil equality, had introduced a positive, irreversible change. In his view the crucial task facing the Restoration was how to come to terms with this new reality while reinstating the principle of legality which accompanied the legitimate monarchy. The Charter was seen as offering a defence against the temptation to rule in an arbitrary fashion which affected French politics on the Left and on the Right. What was required was a framework of legality which guaranteed essential rights and protected the individual from encroachments by the state. The defence of the private sphere of life was now viewed as essential for social stability. Royer-Collard described his times as democratic. However, in so doing he was not referring to a political system but to the defining characteristics of a society in which the middle classes, by dint of their enterprise and labour, now occupied a central position. He concluded that it was futile to try and reimpose on France a set of inherited privileges for to do so would be to reverse the process of civilisation by which a greater proportion of society gained in wealth and knowledge, and fulfilled a role in public affairs. In this way Royer-Collard

21

related liberal theory to the movement of historical change. He also scoured French history for precedents of the Charter of 1814.

Royer-Collard repudiated eighteenth-century sensationalist philosophy which he claimed made man a passive product of his environment. He argued instead in favour of an initial activity of mind and presented consciousness as an organising force. He asserted that our ideas of existence, duration and energy did not derive from the external world but from ourselves; we have these ideas 'because we exist, because we endure, because we are a cause' (I, p. 118). Clearly Royer-Collard was closer to Kant and Maine de Biran than to Locke or Condillac. He posited an initial activity of mind: 'the *self* has duration, because it acts. . . . To think is to will; thought is active by its very nature' (I, p. 121). This foregrounding of consciousness as an active, spiritualistic agent became the philosophical foundation of post-revolutionary political liberalism. Liberal freedoms amounted to more than beliefs in individual rights, property and the market. Liberal freedoms allowed the self fully to realise itself. Thus while liberals rejected the traditionalists' emphasis on submission to authority they recognised that the conduct of individuals could not adequately be explained in terms of the morality of enlightened self-interest.

Royer-Collard, as we have seen, pointed to an initial activity of mind which organised the perception of reality. In *De l'Allemagne* (1810) Mme de Staël criticised Enlightenment epistemology and rehabilitated the notions of duty and self-sacrifice, devoting a famous chapter to 'enthusiasm', understood as the indwelling of spirit in man. Under the influence of Kant and Jacobi, she argued that human beings, by turning inward and listening to the voice of conscience, could gain access to the truth. The idea of the infinite could be grasped by feeling and by the imagination as well as by reason.

Benjamin Constant likewise sought to reveal the complexity of the self. He drew a distinction between the plane of transient sensations and the inner world of deep feelings which corresponded to the voice of conscience and moral duty. Constant recognised the need to rescue the principle of liberalism from the eighteenth-century morality of self-interest. By so doing he associated himself with the general nineteenth-century rejection of contractual theories and allied himself with those who considered laws, institutions and religions as both external embodiments of ideas and expressions of social life. In his novel *Adolphe* he offered a diagnosis of what he called one of the principal moral sicknesses of his age. The main protagonist discovers the intractable inadequacy of living on the plane of shifting sensations but he is prevented by his arid intellectualism and his lucid indifference from transcending his solitude. Constant's portrayal of Adolphe reflected both the critique of the artificiality of society adumbrated by Rousseau and the moral individualism articulated by Kant and his disciples. To define the individual as a bundle of sensations was to deprive him of the truth of his being. The isolated self was fragmented, it lacked moral strength, and this weakness, Constant believed, characterised his times: 'Fidelity in love is a force like religious belief, like the enthusiasm for liberty. However we no longer have any strength. We no longer know either how to love, believe or will.'[31] The rediscovery of the inner moral life, of the power of consciousness, marked the inception of the reconstruction of both selfhood and social relations. For human beings to unite in society, something more than self-interest was required, a sense of duty and devotion to a moral ideal. Constant, however, drew attention to the largely unconscious processes of collective life, to the fact that human needs – including the need for freedom – were expressed through an evolving series of political and religious institutions.

Constant's thought is complex. In one sense men are victims of the tragedy of their social condition; in another it is society and its conventions which are the conditions of improvement. On the one hand, Constant accepted that an idea of the future could not be actualised in the present by the application of abstract political theory; on the other, he noted the need for a precise constitutional framework which formed a necessary contract between government and the governed. Constant believed in progress but he valued duration and continuity more. He felt that without duration there could be no genuine moral sense, no real freedom. He considered that the political and religious institutions which provide a necessary framework for life grow and develop through time. The disruption of these processes, as in the Revolution, was a reckless act.

Constant, who was well versed in speculative German thought as well as in the ideas of the Scottish Enlightenment, brought to liberalism a deep sense of history as a meaningful process.[32] Change was held to be purposeful and irresistible; the general movement of history testified to the progressive emancipation of individual conscience. As part of this process political and religious institutions were transformed – or discarded if they failed to accommodate new developments in the human spirit. This process was rational, but it was also revelatory of a higher purpose.[33] To turn to history was to become aware of humankind's legitimate dissatisfaction with present reality. However, Constant forswore the communitarian dream of overcoming alienation through politics and he rejected the volcanic dynamism of those who placed revolutionary freedom as the moving force of history.[34] The values which Constant held dear and which corresponded to his idea of human perfectibility were bodied forth in mysterious historical processes which ultimately escaped human control. Indeed at times Constant's thought displayed a decidedly quietistic dimension. Sudden disruptions in the movement of history were unlikely to contribute to the nurturing of the essential private freedoms. Values were not invented or arbitrarily imposed.

Constant argued that the revolutionaries had confused ancient liberty with modern freedom. In their enthusiasm for the Classical republics they had failed to recognise that modern freedoms extended beyond the public domain of politics to encompass the defence of a rigorously private space. They had also made the error of wanting to impose their conception of law as the expression of the general will, of seeking to make it triumph over 'all other powers, even that of memory and time'.[35] Here Constant was articulating an idea which lay at the centre of the liberal historical project, the close bond between memory and morality. The new liberalism was as committed to the defence of the individual subject as had been the liberalism of the eighteenth century. However, that defence was now supported by a sense of history as a purposeful process of becoming. Knowledge of the past was of vital importance because history offered a ground of value, a foundation of meaning. The Revolution had transformed people's expectations of themselves. Instead of defining the individual as separate and isolated, post-revolutionary liberalism sought to overcome the sense of disconnectedness by representing the subject as embedded in a network of relationships, as a participant in a process of unfolding.

LIBERAL THOUGHT IN THE 1820s:
INDUSTRIALISM, REVOLUTIONARY HISTORY, METAPHYSICAL IDEALISM

The 1820s witnessed the consolidation of liberal history. Its two most important representatives, Thierry and Guizot, will be examined in detail in separate chapters. The interest in history was not just a fashion – Romantic medievalism, Walter Scott, etc. – it was a response to the impact of 1789 and the domination of the country by the personality of one man, Napoleon. Liberals in the main supported the Charter of 1814 which promised the possibility of excluding extremes while holding in play contending forces. Liberals aspired to a unified nation no longer threatened by the presence of avenging factions. Their recipe was a constitutional monarchy with representative institutions.

However, the intellectual climate had moved on from the heyday of the Idéologues. By the 1820s history had become a necessary component of any serious reflection on the state of French society. Liberal freedoms needed to be provided with a historical foundation which marked them out from the enduring memory of Jacobinism – there seemed no chance of the Revolution petering out in silence. Hence the need to refashion national history so as to justify 1789 while portraying 1793 as an idea refuted by historical experience. Henceforward, it was hoped, reasonable people, those who believed in compromise and moderation, would find succour and useful precedent within the national past. However, there were many strands within what we broadly term Restoration liberalism. Opposition to any return to the Ancien Régime united individuals who were in substantial disaccord when it came to analysing what was deficient in the present organisation of society. Thus, in contrast to the political liberalism of the 'doctrinaires', the group including Guizot and Royer-Collard, we have those thinkers who represented primarily economic liberalism after the manner of Jean-Baptiste Say. These were the theorists of 'industrialism' and they are of significance for our subject for three reasons. First, it was within their intellectual milieu that Augustin Thierry formulated his views on French history. Second, Saint-Simonianism represented both an elaboration and a critique of the idea of industrialism. Third, industrialism articulated a view of history which supported some aspects – but significantly not all – of the interpretation of history offered by a 'doctrinaire' historian such as Guizot.[36]

Charles Dunoyer (1786–1862) can be taken as representative of this tendency. In collaboration with his friend Charles Comte (1782–1837) he brought out an influential opposition journal, *Le Censeur*, later *Le Censeur européen*, which appeared irregularly between 1814 and 1825. Dunoyer defended the modern bourgeois economy with its reliance on the strength of private interest. He received prison sentences in 1817 and 1819 on account of his anti-government views. The July Monarchy recognised his talents: after 1830 he was appointed Prefect of the Allier, the Mayenne and then of the Somme. His writings focused on economic matters and are most usefully viewed as an extension of the ideas of the Idéologues (Destutt de Tracy helped advance Dunoyer's career). Dunoyer was not concerned with inner spirituality. He placed emphasis upon the value of productive work and viewed man as an individual pursuing personal desires. However, he was more inclined than the Idéologues to provide his thought with a historical framework. This included an analysis of the origins of class conflict and a justification of the division of labour in terms of social evolution. Dunoyer and like-minded economists discerned in history the presence of forces which led inexorably to the dissolution of stratified traditional society and to the emergence of the modern, liberal identity.

Dunoyer's *L'Industrie et la morale considérées dans leurs rapports avec la liberté* (1825) provides a helpful illustration of the position of the liberal economists.[37] The burden of Dunoyer's argument was that wealth was a good thing, not a corrupting influence which weakened the moral sinews of society. We are told that Rousseau and Raynal had plainly been wrong in contrasting freedom with civilisation; in reality the development of civilisation (growth in knowledge, civility, sociability and material well-being) corresponded to an increase, not a decline, in freedom. Wealth, Dunoyer argued, derived from individual endeavour and from the application of new scientific knowledge. He set out to show that liberty and happiness for the greatest number arose from the freeing of individual energies. He was a supporter of the Revolution which he praised for sweeping away those inherited privileges and social stratifications which impeded the development of industry and commerce. Why then had the Revolution failed fully to usher in the new competitive industrial world? Dunoyer's answer was that while 1789 destroyed the society of orders and privileges its emphasis on rights had been misleading because it paid insufficient heed to natural inequalities. The Revolution should have inaugurated industrial society, a competitive world of individual producers pursuing their own self-defined goals. Instead, the Revolution opened up to all citizens the dream of access to a new life of privilege, in the form of disguised patronage dispensed by the state. Under the Ancien Régime political power and influence had lain in the hands of a small minority; the Revolution misguidedly gave the majority the illusion that what previously had only been conceivable for the few was henceforth open to all. So instead of the newly liberated energies being used productively, citizens sought to follow careers as functionaries of the state. This process, continued Dunoyer, became further entrenched under the Empire; industrial progress was held back as the resources of the nation were drained in order to fund a bloated bureaucracy which in turn restricted individual enterprise.

Dunoyer's argument was that the capitalist economy's reliance upon innovation and the market made it a force for freedom and a servant of civilisation. He admired the United States. Little government was good government. He wanted the passion for work to replace the desire for power, he wanted primacy to be given to economic over political factors. This did not amount to a denial of politics but to a desire to see the sphere of politics circumscribed and the energies of producers released. Dunoyer genuinely believed that industrialism would of itself produce a better society. Here the voice of utopian capitalism rang out, proclaiming that industry would put an end to oppression and destroy the master–slave relationship for ever (p. 349). In a truly industrial form of social organisation, Dunoyer claimed, production and commerce would replace wars of conquest; individual producers would unite in their wish to 'propagate the doctrine' (p. 357). However, when Dunoyer spoke in this vein or used words such as 'association' he meant something different from the Saint-Simonians when they used the terms. Dunoyer foresaw a society of producers – of 'industrialists' in Saint-Simon's usage – but he did not feel moved to respond to the possibility of overproduction or to the feelings of insecurity experienced by individuals who were left exclusively reliant upon their own resources. The consequences of the division of labour did not trouble him. Neither was he disturbed by the prospect of unemployment within the bourgeois economy. He felt sure that inequalities of wealth would be reduced as industrialism gained ground. However, he did not anticipate that poverty would ever permanently disappear. In fact he drew starkly Malthusian conclusions, rejecting the very idea of welfare: if the poor were helped they would only have more children. The aim of industrial society was to redistribute inequality, not do away with it.

Dunoyer gave his economic liberalism a historical dimension which supported his view of the industrial society of the future. The basic meaning of history was held to lie in the development of man's productive capacities. Man moved from a stage of primitive barbarity (cannibalism), through a nomadic state of existence (hunting) to a settled, agricultural society. The period from antiquity to the nineteenth century was divided into epochs which corresponded to changes in modes of production (as opposed to moments in political, religious or intellectual history). As this process unfolded the lot of the oppressed members of society improved.[38] For Dunoyer the end of history corresponded to the moment when the labouring classes would fully replace the dominating classes (p. 410). In schematic form the process ran as follows: the labouring classes (men of industry) who were slaves in antiquity became serfs in the Middle Ages; they achieved emancipation with the Communes and then formed the Third Estate which subsequently became identified with society in its entirety (p. 236).

In his treatment of the rise of the Communes Dunoyer was close to Guizot, Thierry, Mignet and liberal historiography in general; however, in his case the emphasis was placed unambiguously upon economic determinants: 'in the Middle Ages it was industry which freed the Communes from the tyranny of the feudal lords' (p. 13). Dunoyer's interpretation of history was predicated upon the belief that man fulfilled his true destiny when he worked as an individual producing goods within a social system based upon the value of exchange. In his opinion history did not correspond to the actualisation of a metaphysical principle or a providential plan. Unlike Constant or Guizot he paid little heed to the role played by religious ideas in bringing about change; indeed he scoffed at the traditional topos of Christian apologetics that the coming of Christ put an end to slavery.[39] In his view Christianity had been content to accommodate the reality of slavery for many centuries; the abandonment of slavery reflected something quite different from religious conviction – a change in social conditions and modes of industrial production. It is evident in the light of such comments that whereas the Romantic historians placed ideas at the centre of history, Dunoyer related the intellectual superstructure directly to the material base. Human history was not determined by the mysterious actualisation of the ideas of reason, liberty and justice. Dunoyer disabused his readers on this score, reminding them that history was not a novel (p. 240). Progress, moral as well as material, was real but it occurred when a particular way of life yielded to irresistible material forces. Thus we learn that the nomadic way of life was abandoned when there were no more lands left to ravage. However, Dunoyer was not consistent in his determinism; for example, he found no difficulty in making the somewhat contradictory assertion that the oppressed classes have usually progressed only when they have had recourse to the use of force.

Nevertheless, there can be no doubt that Dunoyer considered that history was moving in the correct direction, in the direction of increased freedom, production and competition. Joseph de Maistre despised and feared the unsettling world of liberal capitalism with its anarchic individualism. Dunoyer disagreed. He debunked the myth of the Ancien Régime as a model of organic order, claiming that the system of corporations and fixed social groupings in fact encouraged social disharmony, mutual hostility, envy and discord. He argued the opposite case, that industrial society, founded on individual initiative and self-reliance, would take an orderly, stable and peaceful form – so long as the will to political power was contained and did not get in the way of the desire for enterprise and wealth creation. Only industrial society, we are told, encouraged the full flowering of the faculties. The harsh reality of the working conditions endured by those labouring in factories did nothing to dent this optimism. Like Saint-Simon, Dunoyer contrasted the industrial classes with the idle rich. However, Dunoyer tended more to moral censure, blaming men for being naturally lazy. His interpretation of history offered what amounted to a version of the cunning of reason which managed to reverse man's natural disinclination to work productively. Over the centuries oppressors and oppressed had seemingly collaborated in a conflictual process, the upshot of which was the emergence of individualism and industry. The sufferings recorded in history were retrospectively justified as part of the sequence of events which enabled humankind to transcend its condition of idleness. Dunoyer's thought thus marked a significant accommodation between the materialism of the Idéologues and the prevailing sense that values needed to be grounded in history.

The idea that historical change was inevitable, that the French Revolution had not been an aberration but the necessary consequence of earlier developments within French society, was crucial to the political debates of the Restoration. Royalist historians maintained their total rejection of the Revolution, often using apocalyptic language to hold up to scorn the criminal acts and atrocities which scarred the recent past.[40] Liberal historians, in addition to disinterring a tradition of liberty within the national past, began to scrutinise the events of the Revolution itself. By the 1820s, large amounts of material relating to the Revolution were being published. There was an avalanche of memoirs and other documents, some genuine, some fictitious. Sufficient time had now elapsed for historians to take, if not a disinterested, at least a somewhat more dispassionate view of the revolutionary decade. The very project was of course anathema to the Ultras. Liberals, on the other hand, began to look in detail at the years 1789–99, tracing patterns of cause and effect, relating individual actions to broader issues of class conflict, in a word fashioning a new reading of the revolutionary decade which, although it had to deal with difficult problems such as the origins of the Terror and the Dix-huit Brumaire, started from the premise that the historian could get to the truth of the Revolution by explaining the course of events in terms of the working out of a new social principle.

Between 1823 and 1830 Adolphe Thiers brought out his *Histoire de la Révolution française* in ten volumes.[41] In 1824 François Mignet published his *Histoire de la Révolution française depuis 1789 jusqu'en 1814*.[42] The two men were friends, both from Provence and both active in Parisian opposition journalism. Their histories were written from a liberal perspective which endorsed the bourgeois order that had taken shape in 1789 and needed to be defended against the reactionaries of the Restoration. In an important sense their approach set the agenda for the debate on the Revolution for the next thirty years. Thiers's work was popular and immensely readable, full of the drama of political history. By 1833, 150,000 copies had been sold. Mignet, in a much more compact work, was more reflective, placing emphasis on social and economic factors but still writing narrative history. Thiers claimed to be impartial but he was clearly not a neutral observer. He was a journalist on the liberal and anticlerical *Constitutionnel*, and his history placed him firmly in the opposition camp as far as Restoration politics were concerned. Both men saw the Revolution as the inevitable consequence of the transformation of French society and the development of the Third Estate. In Mignet's words the Estates General only decreed a revolution which had already taken place (I, p. 38).[43] Violence occurred because conservative forces failed to recognise and accommodate irresistible economic and social changes. According to Thiers the violence of 1789 had been necessary in order for legal equality, eligibility for offices, press freedom and annual representation to become realities in France. Neither historian was about to apologise for the Revolution, the event which in Mignet's words began a new era in European society, one which transformed totally the 'inner existence of the nation' (I, p. 2).

The philosophy of history which underlay Thiers's and Mignet's approach to the Revolution was implicit rather than explicit. It amounted to a form of historical determinism and was referred to by contemporaries as 'le fatalisme historique', historical fatalism. The critics of the two historians accused them of an absence of moral judgement, of failing to condemn evil, of offering a discreet but real apology for the Terror. On this score Mignet's Introduction set the tone, for, after having declared that the Revolution brought about great reforms, he added the comment that it none the less produced 'passing excesses' along with its 'enduring benefits' (I, p. 3). Mignet's great achievement was that he extended the meaning of the Revolution by making it understandable in class terms, in a way which was distinctly novel in 1824. Mignet's approach was influential and innovative because it drew attention to class divisions within the Third Estate itself. In Mignet's opinion there were two Revolutions, the middle-class Revolution of 1789–91 and the popular revolution against the middle class of 1792–5. The latter was caused by the conditions of the war. For Mignet as for de Maistre, the Revolution seemed to possess a momentum of its own. However, Mignet clung to the idea that beneath the shifting, unpredictable surface of events forces were at work constructing a new order, that the spectacle of violence and disillusion was not the whole story, that in a mysterious way disintegration confirmed the national will. Having reached the Directory he drew some conclusions:

> The French Revolution, which had destroyed the old government and completely overturned the old society, had two quite distinct objectives, that of a free constitution, and that of a more perfected social state. The six years which we have just gone over were the search for government by each of the classes which composed the French nation. The privileged classes wished to establish their regime against the court and against the bourgeoisie by preserving the orders and the Estates General; the bourgeoisie sought to establish its regime against the privileged classes and against the multitude by the constitution of 1791; and the multitude wanted to establish its regime against all the others, by the constitution of 1793. None of these governments could consolidate itself, because they were all exclusive. But during their attempts, each class, in power for a time, destroyed all that was intolerant or calculated to oppose the foundation of the new French society which rested upon equality of rights and the most equitable arrangements. When the Directory succeeded the Convention the class struggles were greatly reduced . . . the mass of the nation which had been so profoundly shaken between 1789 and 1795 sought rest and agreement in accordance with the new order of things. This period witnessed the end of one movement and the commencement of another. After the agitation, the immense labour and the spirit of total destruction which had filled its first years, the Revolution took on a new character of inner repose and civil organisation.
>
> (II, 175–7)

Mignet distinguished between the different phases of the Revolution but bound events together in such a way as to suggest that an impersonal necessity, 'la force des choses', was at work. His explanation of events made them appear inevitable and this struck many as offering a justification for the Terror. A similarly deterministic mode of explanation underlay Thiers's writing although in his case the broader philosophical implications were less clearly articulated. Thiers, like Mignet, was a liberal in economic as well as in political terms. Neither man was nostalgic for Jacobin centralised control of the economy and neither wanted a return to authoritarian democracy. The second revolution, the popular revolution of 1792, was explicable for social, economic and political reasons but it remained inferior to the revolution of 1789. Thiers scorned the 'populace' and Mignet regretted the acquisition of power by the 'multitude'. However, both historians seemed willing to condone excesses as the consequence of the pressure of circumstance. Despite the antipathy he felt for Robespierre, Thiers rehabilitated the Convention, and took pride in the energy deployed in the defence of the nation. Mignet extended his deterministic mode of explanation to all of French history, viewing the rise of feudalism and the triumph of absolutism as equally necessary. Conservatives were outraged by the interpretation of the Revolution. But liberals too had misgivings. Benjamin Constant for one was angry at what seemed a betrayal of principle, a willingness to provide the criminals of the past with a retrospective amnesty.

For Thiers and Mignet the Revolution was necessary. It was bound to happen given the obstacles placed in the way of the advance of the Third Estate. From the standpoint of the 1820s its gains outweighed its losses. The idea of historical inevitability, the tracing of economic and social causes and effects, made the Revolution an intelligible phenomenon, manageable by mind, a sequence of events held together in a special kind of coherence. The disturbing aspects of the Revolution were not elided but their impact was softened so that they did not destabilise the reader's response. Memory was reordered to recall the achievements of the Revolution, including those of the Convention. The actions of individuals were defined by their roles and their roles were defined by the external pressures of social change. In the final analysis the return to order under Napoleon was deemed as necessary as 1789 itself. The objective of a historian such as Guizot was to distinguish between 1789 and 1793. Mignet and Thiers were no less convinced than Guizot that in the post-revolutionary world of modernity power was to be entrusted to the middle classes; however, their argument suggested that the Revolution commanded loyalty in its entirety. The textualisation of the Revolution which they undertook did not ennoble a communal identity in the manner of Michelet but it did strike a deep chord of recognition within the liberal opposition of the Restoration. Its message was that not only the long centuries of the French past but the Revolution itself could be reassessed and viewed as legitimate. The excesses of the Republic could be explained and justified since the outcome of the process was modern society with representative institutions and liberal political and economic freedoms. These freedoms remained insecure under the Restoration. After 1830 they seemed fully established.

Thiers then pursued his political career and Mignet his historical researches. In 1873, looking back on the July Monarchy, Mignet described it as the best government France could have had as far as rights and prosperity were concerned.[44] But was there not some substance in the charge that these liberal histories subverted morality, that they avoided making difficult moral judgements? After all, the Revolution was a great moral and religious crisis as well as a period of historical turmoil. Perhaps commitment to freedom required something more than assent to the past, perhaps it placed historians under an obligation to sacrifice the comforts of historical necessity? Other historians – Barante, Quinet, Louis Vitet (1802–73), Michelet – came to question the assumptions of Thiers and Mignet which, they felt, compromised the future by justifying the past. Was the moral and political condition of France helped in the long run by histories which yielded to the temptation of quiescence before an impersonal necessity while at the same time voicing support for liberal freedoms?

The propensity to align liberal freedom with historical inevitability is once again present in the work of Victor Cousin (1792–1867), the most prominent philosopher of the Restoration.[45] Cousin stood by the Charter of 1814 which in his judgement marked the 'real fusion of the king and the people' (I, 13, p. 400).[46] In his view the Revolution was justified on account of the decadence of the monarchy and the general decline of French society in the eighteenth century. It had been unfortunate, however, that the excesses of the Ancien Régime had been replaced by the temporary triumph of popular sovereignty. Cousin's main concern lay with the process of post-revolutionary reconstruction. He stood by the liberal position that the Charter represented the best line of defence against the Ultras because it marked the inception of a constitutional order which avoided extremes, sought conciliation and moderation, and preserved both the monarchical principle and private freedoms. What was needed was a philosophical counterpart to the Charter. In a lecture of 1817 he commented: 'The eighteenth century was the age of criticism and of destructions; the nineteenth century must be the age of intelligent rehabilitations'.[47] In his view philosophy had a key role to play as a unifying agent, as the source of a set of beliefs which would underpin the new social cohesion. Initially in accord with sensationalism, Cousin moved in the direction of spiritualism under the influence of Royer-Collard and Maine de Biran. Far from rejecting religion in the manner of the scientific materialists of the Enlightenment, Cousin gave it considerable prominence. His spiritualist philosophy sought an accommodation with faith. He considered that what France needed was a new synthesis uniting king and nation, faith and reason, religion and philosophy. However, while conciliation was the order of the day it proved hard to achieve. The church was in no mood to make concessions and Cousin, for his part, stood by his commitment to intellectual freedom, toleration and liberty of expression. His argument that philosophy and religion were different modes of apprehending the same fundamental reality was unsatisfactory since it came down to presenting religion as philosophy for the poorly educated, a solution which appealed as little to orthodox believers as it did to Cousin's critics on the Left who accused him of making philosophy the poodle of the church.

Cousin's hostility to the eighteenth century marked him off irrevocably from most of the surviving Idéologues and left-republicans. His philosophy had an idealist core which they could not accept. However, the philosophy of reconstruction which he proposed under the name of eclecticism amounted to something more subtle than an outright repudiation of eighteenth-century thought. Cousin's aim was to examine different philosophical systems in order to extract from them what was true and discard what was false. His argument moved from psychology to history and to ontology. He held that the human mind could only develop four points of view: sensationalism (which he called sensualism), idealism, scepticism and mysticism. The history of philosophy, which was the 'manifestation of the human mind', was of crucial importance to his argument because it demonstrated how these four stages followed each other in sequence (II, p. 2). For Cousin this process had the status of a scientific law and could be used predictively. History, primarily in the form of the history of philosophy, gave expression to the fourfold ways in which the human mind grasped reality. The philosopher of the nineteenth century could draw together the elements of truth discovered in the experience of the past and construct out of them a new synthesis, a new set of ideas which could offer meaning and belief to post-revolutionary man. History obviously amounted to more than chronology. History was no 'mere literary amusement addressing itself solely to the imagination' (II, p. 58). It was a discipline organised by reason which went beyond retracing the succession of events. The influence of German Idealism was clearly at work in Cousin's approach. In an essay of 1823, *De la philosophie de l'histoire*, he gave priority to the inner world of spirit. History had, so to speak, an inside (ideas) and an outside (events and actions). What mattered were the divine ideas which actualised themselves in history and which ultimately endowed the whole process with meaning. For Cousin events were symbols:

> The real only becomes knowledge in virtue of its relationship to the truth which it reflects, to which it conforms. It is in virtue of this conformity that the real possesses truth; the world which passes contains another world which does not pass and which constitutes its essence, truth and dignity.[48]

Cousin held that reason was impersonal and granted knowledge of the truth. What was new in his approach was the insistence that self-knowledge could become a guide to historical knowledge: the facts of human nature which were present within individuality were also repeated within the life of humankind. History was defined as the 'large-scale representation of human nature' (I, 2, p. 8). 'What reflection is to the individual', observed Cousin, 'history is to mankind' (I, 7, p. 11).

Cousin considered both history and nature as aspects of a greater totality. He believed that the Idea which was present in unconscious nature, manifesting itself hierarchically (but without any genuinely evolutionary force) in the mineral, vegetable and animal kingdoms, achieved self-knowledge within human consciousness. History and freedom were coextensive, for without freedom there could be no development. The universe had not been created out of nothingness. It would be more accurate to say that God created, indeed continued to create, the universe out of himself and that the processes of universal life were a consequence of the divine nature. God was not simply mind and substance; he was also causation and force, the expansive dynamics of universal life. As the embodiment of freedom and consciousness man stood in opposition to nature; but at a deeper level mind and nature shared a common origin in the Absolute. Cousin followed Hegel in dividing history into three great epochs: the orient, ancient Greece and the Christian west.[49] Each marked a different way of conceiving the infinite, the finite and their relationship. In the orient man was unfree, religiously and politically; he had no real self-consciousness, hence no history. This first stage in human history was characterised by unity, infinity and eternity. The orient represented nature as infinite and inclined to pantheism. In Greece, in a less oppressive natural environment, anthropomorphism replaced pantheism, liberty increased and freer political forms replaced oriental despotism. The Classical world was the civilisation of the finite. Finally, with the coming of Christianity, the presence of the infinite within the finite was fully acknowledged. Such was Cousin's overview of the three stages of world history. The new philosophical history, as he conceived it, had as its task to trace the manifestations of the Idea, to follow the ways in which collectivities actualised a hidden ideal content. Cousin singled out metaphysics as the most adequate expression of the ideal essence of a collective entity. The history of philosophy became more central than either political or religious history; in the final analysis it was the only true history, 'la seule vraie histoire' (I, 3, p. 28).

History revealed a catalogue of errors but Cousin contended that it was possible to look beyond succession, diversity and difference, and discover unity and truth. The errors of history contained incomplete truths. On the one hand, history told of the growth of freedom and consciousness. On the other, it actualised the three underlying ideas which structured reality: the infinite, the finite and their relation. Cousin held that once the governing idea of an epoch had been fully grasped, its consequences in the world of fact could be predicted with confidence; history would then become an inflexible, sublime, living geometry obeying laws which mirrored the laws of nature. History was progressive and never regressed. Everything took place for the best. Cousin proudly professed what he called his 'elevated historical optimism' (I, 7, p. 39). The judgements of history were the judgements of God, and Cousin was in no way disquieted by the harshness of history's verdict: 'the party of the vanquished is always the party of the past' (I, 10, p. 37). He explained that conflict between peoples was inevitable because each collective entity believed that the idea which it was seeking to actualise corresponded to the truth. In reality, however, it was but one imperfect embodiment of the truth. The violence and suffering which arose from such conflicts did not concern Cousin, who believed that war was useful and necessary. Right was always on the side of the victor: 'the strongest idea in an epoch is necessarily that which is in closest relation with the spirit of the epoch in question' (I, 9, p. 29).

Unlike the liberal economists who envisaged a future where commerce replaced war, Cousin believed that war served the advance of civilisation. Conflict was a necessary part of progress and to dream of perpetual peace was to accept the possibility of a dangerous immobilism. Even Waterloo was explained away by Cousin: we are told that the real conflict did not so much take place on the battlefield as in the mind. The real struggle was a clash of ideas between France (the philosophical leader of southern Europe) and Germany (the spirit of the north). Ever the optimist, Cousin concluded that European civilisation emerged the victor from this bloodletting. Somewhat surprisingly, the printed text of Cousin's lectures informs us that such comments on the defeat of France were greeted with applause from his audience.

The Idea – ultimately divine in origin – was manifested in nature and then actualised by collective entities. It became the living substance of a people. But it was not an essence in repose; it was, like the divine nature of which it partook, an active, expansive principle. Those peoples and social groups which did not represent a substantive idea were held to lack meaning and value – and were thus of no interest to the historian. If a people did not embody an idea its existence was declared to be 'unintelligible' (I, 9, p. 7) and its collective destiny, we assume, was deemed to be worthless. However, in addition to its embodiment in collective entities the Idea was also incarnated in great individuals, in those figures whom Hegel described as world-historical. Great men were instruments of God, of the Idea which circulated throughout all the activities of a culture. They were the 'representatives of those who do not appear in history' (I, 10, p. 13) in the sense that although ordinary citizens themselves only managed to give limited expression to the Idea, they none the less were able to recognise in the great man the actualisation of the collective essence. However, these ordinary members of society were to be distinguished from a separate group which Cousin treated with disdain. This latter group was made up of those who remained preoccupied with their own transient existences. Such 'individuals who are only individuals' were viewed by Cousin as self-centred, bothersome and hostile to authority, the flotsam and jetsam floating on the tide of history, leaving no enduring trace behind them (I, 10, p. 11). What interested Cousin was the ideal content of history, the reality which lay behind appearances. Great men mattered because they embodied general ideas. On the other hand their private selves and their personal characteristics were of little interest: Cousin dismissively remarked that biography and memoirs dealt adequately with the superficial aspects of the personality. The proper concern of the philosophical historian lay elsewhere, with the progressive unfolding of the life of Spirit. True history would be an inclusive, philosophical universal history, a master discourse of governing ideas which was also a totalisation of the various histories of different aspects of social life.

Cousin told his audience that universal history was a relatively recent development in European cultural life, having begun only in the seventeenth century. He listed Bossuet, Vico, Voltaire, Herder, Ferguson, Condorcet and Turgot as precursors but he found fault with all of them on different grounds. Condorcet's work fared particularly badly: the *Esquisse* was not a serious piece of scholarly work at all and was best considered an elegant trifle, suitable reading matter for women and children (I, 11, p. 53). Cousin's message was that the nineteenth-century philosophy of reconstruction would be largely a philosophy of history. However, it would not be history after the manner of the Idéologues – hence the scorn heaped on Condorcet – but a spiritualist reading of the past as symbol which reinstated the notion of the deity. The historical perspective also allowed for the rehabilitation of religion ahead of its appropriation by philosophy. Cousin was thus quite willing to represent the Middle Ages as the epoch of 'envelopment' out of which the modern world of industry, art, philosophy and politics later developed (I, 2, p. 38).

Cousin was a hero of Restoration liberalism and intellectuals gravitated to his presence. Younger thinkers such as Michelet and Quinet were attracted by his personal charm and his reputation as France's leading philosopher. Cousin's notion that philosophy explained the truths of religion by converting them into its own substance appealed to a generation which had gone beyond the sceptical cast of mind of the Enlightenment. In 1820 his lectures were suspended by the government and he came to embody intellectual resistance to the conservative Restoration, a philosophical equivalent of Guizot. However, the lectures of 1828 and 1829 demonstrated the undercurrent of illiberalism which his historical thought contained. Could the freedom of the subject and notions of representative government be securely founded on a view of history which privileged the role of the great man? Surely Cousin's attempt to comprehend reality in terms of history and metaphysical idealism was leading him to make a fetish out of the Idea, and consequently to value the particular only in so far as it externalised the universal? The extent to which Cousinian history was a discourse of power emerged after the events of July 1830.

HISTORY AND THE 1830 REVOLUTION

We are now in a position to assess attitudes to history in France on the eve of the July Revolution. We have seen the extent to which history was politicised, becoming a terrain fought over by contending ideologies. The Right proposed an idealised picture of medieval society and portrayed the Ancien Régime as the expression of the immutable will of God. Submission to this conservative representation of the past was part of the reactionary forces' demand for a total adherence to order. Liberals responded by denying that the Ancien Régime possessed the consensual character which conservatives ascribed to it. Instead they wrote national histories which described the revenge of the oppressed over their oppressors, the story of the rise of the Third Estate and the vindication of 1789. For the men of the Restoration the events of history always possessed contemporary resonances – we need only think of the treatment of the English Revolution by Abel Villemain, Armand Carrel or, in dramatic form, by Victor Hugo in *Cromwell*. Was it simply chance that in the wake of Waterloo, Augustin Thierry paid such attention to the fate of defeated peoples such as the Saxons and the Celts?

The young men of the 1820s had grown up under the Empire, dazzled by its dreams of glory; for them the Restoration often seemed a constricting, unsatisfying time to be reaching manhood. Part of the enthusiasm for history undoubtedly reflected an escapist desire to discover periods and cultures where life was lived more intensely, where the instant was pregnant with the possibility of fame or death. The members of this younger generation, frustrated by the lack of opportunity in the present, were responsive to the currents of ideas which we term Romantic. While historians such as Thiers and Mignet inclined temperamentally to Classicism,

Augustin Thierry associated political liberalism with Romanticism's imaginative re-creation of past reality, with the spectacle of the masses forcing change and making history. Romantic history did not belittle earlier centuries, but neither was it coldly respectful of the past; it engaged with the contradictory yet meaningful movements of the past, recording them as the gestures of life itself. Liberal Romanticism valorised individuality but inserted it into the drama of collective life. The new history carried the values of individualism and political reconstruction but it also supported social wholeness, even though such a goal might be ill-suited to the emerging market economy. Henceforth it was insufficient to view the past merely as preparatory of the present. History revealed the interconnections between self and world and between self and other. History gave knowledge of the powers which held the nation together as an evolving moral entity (rather than define it as a static unity whose ontological purity rested upon a denial of change as value). Through knowledge of history men became aware of ties and reciprocities, achieved a sense of belonging which related their being to a social entity.

The Romantic consciousness possessed a heightened awareness of freedom but it was also marked by a correspondingly intense desire to belong, to unite with a power beyond itself. The literature of the first half of the nineteenth century was peopled with anguished individuals, dissociated from nature and alienated from culture, cast adrift from their ontological moorings by the revolutioary upheavals and the inception of political modernity. For such men history came to replace religion as a creator of values, as a source for the symbols around which modern life struggled to cohere. Once history was seen as the self-development of reason (or of freedom) or understood as the actualisation of the divine within time its value was transformed. It became a form of revelation. History was more than trial and error, more than the theatre for human reason's struggle against the forces of darkness; history told of the working out of the divine purpose. The Romantic who looked for consolation in communion with nature might also find relief in the contemplation of the past. By the mid-1820s liberalism had integrated much of Romanticism's interest in other times and cultures, its sense of poetry and mystery, its feeling for nature and the infinite. We see this in the pages of *Le Globe*, the most significant journal of the liberal cultural elite of the Restoration. History authenticated the self and assuaged the pain of subjectivity, but it simultaneously rendered the self more complex. Instead of the mastery of the Cartesian subject the Romantic self acquired a collective dimension and an inner depth. As history gained in complexity the self lost its sense of fixity. The dissemination of meaning across time, which on one level authenticated the self, at another level exacerbated the question of personal identity: the recognition of difference and diversity, the emergence of a plurality of vantage points, undermined the notion of stable truth. For the Romantics, however, there could be no true self-knowledge in isolation from historical knowledge.

The 1830 Revolution marked a turning point of major significance in the development of the interpretation of history. With the advent of the July Monarchy liberal intellectuals such as Cousin and Guizot moved from being members of the opposition to being part of the political establishment. Younger men reacted differently. Quinet and Michelet refused to see in the new regime the fulfilment of history. July 1830 demonstrated that the revolutionary spirit was still abroad in the world. Carlyle's response to the general significance of the July days was eloquent:

> The Three Days told all mortals that the old French Revolution, mad as it might look, was not a transitory ebullition of Bedlam, but a genuine product of this Earth where we all live, that it was verily a Fact, and that the world in general would do well every where to regard it as such.[50]

In the 1869 preface to his *Histoire de France* Michelet was to describe history itself as an 'unending July', as permanent revolution. The effect of the July Revolution of 1830 on the collective psychology of the French nation cannot be overstated. Drawing on his knowledge of Vico and his sense of the power of collective life, Michelet made the people the subject of history, the agent of change. In the wake of 1830 the Left absorbed the metaphysical dimension of conservative historiography and used it as a weapon, relating it to the ideas of republican freedom and revolution. The liberal historians of the Restoration had rescued the pre-revolutionary past. What took place after 1830 amounted to a reordering, a recomposition of the national tradition.[51] Michelet went beyond the views of Guizot, Mignet and Thierry and wrote what his contemporaries called symbolic history, an interpretative narrative in which events were related to the unfolding of a more general purpose. He felt he was lending his voice to the people, that he was speaking on behalf of the masses whom previous historians had condemned to silence. National history was related to the patterns of universal history. The Revolution was situated within the vaster continuity of world, even cosmic history.

Of course in a general sense the ideas which I have been discussing were not in themselves particular to France. Nineteenth-century European thought in general was characterised by historicism, by a new sense of process and collective development. The past was reinterpreted as the story of humankind's growth, its moral, intellectual and aesthetic advance. The growing mastery over nature seemed to confirm an optimistic evaluation of human productive capacities as exemplified in the Victorian idea of progress. History was envisaged as a dynamic process which comprised a number of stages and which progressed to a desired goal. In some instances confidence in history joined with the belief in the perfectibility of man to produce the dream of continuous and inevitable progress which served as a substitute for religious faith. Clearly, the nineteenth century looked for more than moral lessons, for more than examples of exemplary conduct, when it turned to the past. At a time of crisis in traditional forms of Christianity, history – like nature – came to function as a ground for belief, a source of value.[52] Spiritual reality existed but was not directly present to consciousness; it was by turning to the collective past that man gained access to a higher reality which was not other-worldly. For the Romantics spirit disclosed itself in both external nature and human history. History at first seemed meaningless, valueless, but by virtue of the historian's labour it was revealed to be rational and intelligible; its purposeful movement testified to the operation of laws akin to the laws of nature.

However, what guaranteed this sense of purpose was less the sifting of historical evidence than the belief that the activity of humankind throughout history could be inscribed within a vast totality of cosmic life. God was active in nature and in history, and his essential nature required the existence of other beings.[53] Ideas moved history. Each period was infused by or was the expression of a governing idea. Each epoch corresponded to a particular way of looking at the world. This meant that whether the historian reanimated national or universal history he discovered difference and otherness as well as identity and continuity. Romantic historicism accommodated this diversity by viewing ages and civilisations as moments in a greater unfolding, as fragments of a larger whole, as stages in the life of humankind valorised as a collective being. History ceased to be viewed in a limited dynastic or chronological perspective. The agents for historical change became impersonal forces, peoples, races, nations, collective entities defined primarily in intellectual as opposed to biological terms. Through the operation of processes of inclusion and exclusion, history offered a unifying, symbolic narrative which created and controlled meaning for the national community. The historian was not a reclusive scholar; he who interpreted the meaning of the past might easily don the mantle of the prophet, guiding the nation, prophesying the future. At the same time his work took on the authority of science. The Romantic age witnessed the emergence of history as an academic discipline. Governments supported archival research and subsidised the publication of materials which they felt substantiated their claims to historical legitimacy. In France the historicist stance permeated all areas of the culture, informing debates about architecture, music and poetic theory. History functioned as the essential point of reference; but this was inevitably a history reconstructed, reconstituted in the light of 1789 and in response to the aftershocks of the revolutionary upheaval. The heyday of the grand overviews of history was the July Monarchy. The failure of the Second Republic caused liberal and republican historians alike to rethink their position. Was the Revolution such a great break with the past after all? As the books and colloquia spawned by the bicentenary of the French Revolution have amply demonstrated, these concerns have lost nothing of their urgency. France has yet to come to terms with the legacy of the Revolution. The relationship between history, revolution and national identity is a difficult one and is subject to revision. In recent times debates within French culture about rights and obligations, about the sanctity of individual conscience, about the role of the intellectual, about the masses as the agent of social and political advance have taken place against the backdrop of the collapse of Marxism in the wake of the events of 1968. Central to this process has been the abandonment of the marxist interpretation of history. However, the fondness of French intellects for such interpretations needs itself to be placed in context, to be viewed within a tradition of historical writing begun during the Restoration by liberals and amplified during the July Monarchy by left-republican and socialist critics. My aim in the present study is to revive interest in this current of historical thought.

2

Augustin Thierry (1795–1856) and the project of national history

'The history of France, such as it has been written by modern authors is not the true history of the country, the national, the popular history' (*DAEH*, 214).[1] It was in this spirit that Augustin Thierry, in 1820, called for a renewal of historical writing in France. He was convinced that earlier historians had transmitted to posterity not only an incomplete but a false representation of events. He argued that the past was not something to be repudiated or disowned; rather, it was to be reclaimed so that the degrees of relation between present and past could be understood in a manner which accelerated positive change. Inaccurate and distorted accounts of past events had acquired the status of truth because they had been relentlessly rehearsed by generations of uncritical historians. Thierry judged that these texts functioned as a source of authority and provided intellectual legitimation for forces which he found uncompromisingly reactionary. He therefore set out to propose a new mapping of the historical field which would render the earlier accounts definitively obsolete. He grasped the supremely political significance of history, that the discourse on the origins and growth of the nation could be enlisted to endorse and justify the political arrangements of those in power. Historical truth in this sense was not something fixed or unchanging. Thierry understood that theories of history were to be related to the social and political conditions which supervened at the time of their elaboration. However, this degree of self-awareness should not be construed as indicating a thoroughgoing relativism. All histories were not contrived fictions. Thierry wrote as a committed member of the liberal opposition, holding that the new type of history which he supported corresponded to the institutional critique that was being developed by his contemporaries. The new

45

historical method was at one and the same time a political strategy which served the causes of liberalism and constitutional reform and an intellectual project understood as a return to fact, to truth. The unmasking of the past amounted to the establishment of a genealogy of liberalism: 'Men of freedom, we too have forebears' (*DAEH*, 183). In order to be effective the political opposition needed to appropriate the historical field and ascribe to it a different set of meanings. The implication of this approach was clear: political freedom did not burst upon France in 1789: it was more accurate to envisage the Revolution itself as the culmination of the general movement of French history. Thierry called for a new understanding of the past which would be liberating in its consequences. What he proposed amounted to a politics – and perhaps by extension a morality – defined by a concept of history.

Thierry achieved prominence as an opposition journalist writing in the *Censeur européen* and the *Courrier français* between 1817 and 1820. Born in Blois he had come to Paris in 1811 to study at the Ecole Normale where Abel Villemain (1790–1870) and Daunou were among his teachers. In May 1814 he became Saint-Simon's secretary and was employed in this capacity for some two and a half years, collaborating on a number of works. The best known of these is *De la réorganisation de la société européenne* (1814) which outlined plans for a peaceful new order based upon a European parliament and federation.[2] The reasons for the ending of the collaboration are not entirely clear. Thierry probably wanted more independence than his eccentric philosophical patron would allow. Perhaps his sense of France's national destiny was not easily reconcilable with Saint-Simon's internationalist humanitarianism. In the view of Frank Manuel Thierry's ideas were too individualist and too Romantic for Saint-Simon's liking.[3] In any case after leaving Saint-Simon Thierry began his association with the *Censeur européen*, the organ of the liberal economists Charles Dunoyer and Charles Comte.[4] However, this move did not indicate a sudden or decisive shift in his intellectual position since in the early years of the Restoration there was much common ground between a social philosopher like Saint-Simon and a thinker concerned with political economy like Dunoyer. Both men shared the desire to reorganise society according to the principles of industrialism.[5] Thierry, for his part, identified wholeheartedly with the liberal cause as articulated by Comte and Dunoyer. Liberals held that the interests of the producers were pre-eminent and deserved to be properly represented in parliament. Indeed, the *Censeur européen* received support from many industrialists, bankers and manufacturers who considered that the political arrangements of the Restoration denied them the power which was commensurate with their actual economic importance.

In Thierry's mind there was no contradiction between increasing freedom and increasing wealth. He frequented the liberal circles of the day, where he met Guizot, Royer-Collard, Daunou, Destutt de Tracy and other leading opposition intellectuals. He appears also to have had links with the Carbonari and to have participated actively in organising anti-government resistance.[6] His main intellectual allegiance lay with the Idéologues. In an article of 1819 he portrayed Daunou as the patriotic defender of those individual rights which alone permitted good government to flourish.[7] In 1818 he published a glowing review of Destutt de Tracy's *Commentaire sur L'Esprit des lois de Montesquieu*.[8] And when Destutt de Tracy died in 1836 Thierry described him as one of the most eminent men, one of the finest minds, he had ever known.[9] Thierry, however, recognised that liberalism needed a sense of history as well as a theory of government and in the writings which he published in the *Censeur européen* and the *Courrier français* he began to provide post-revolutionary liberalism with precisely this historical slant. History and Ideology were to be allies since neither natural law nor utilitarianism was sufficient to ground liberal freedoms. French liberty required its own historiographer (*DAEH*, 215).

What Thierry focused upon, as we shall see, was the phenomenon of conquest and the way in which it moulded behaviour over the centuries. He gave this idea imaginative expression in a celebrated article of 1820, 'Histoire véritable de Jacques Bonhomme, d'après les documents authentiques' (*DAEH*, 201–7). Here the figure of Jacques Bonhomme represented the archetypal French peasant, conquered and oppressed, tricked and deceived by those with power, wanting freedom and property rights but unable definitely to shake off the habits of subjection. Over the centuries the principle of authority always seemed to reassert itself and return the people to their traditional condition of submission. Did a desire for voluntary servitude secretly inhabit the heart of the French people? Thierry's verve and strong-minded crusading style suggested otherwise but he was painfully aware of the pull of the past. Had not Jacques Bonhomme recently been enslaved again as Napoleon appealed to the power of the imperial myth? For Thierry the idea of conquest explained history. Victors and vanquished evolved into social classes whose conflictual relations determined the subsequent development of society. But Thierry also had a strong sense of nations as collective beings, of the masses as movers of change. In his view heroism could be a collective and not just an individual phenomenon. He had been marked by his reading of Walter Scott and Chateaubriand and he lent to collective identities an emotional appeal which was absent from the writings of Dunoyer or Mignet. He stressed the energies of the people and the sense of group identity. Thierry's greatest contribution lay in defining the content of French history for the Romantic generation. He launched a broadside against traditional historiography. His target was the idealised picture of the Ancien Régime promoted by the Catholic counter-revolutionaries. The historians of antiquity were treated with respect but more recent practitioners were disparaged or treated with condescension.

In Thierry's view earlier historians had not half-seen the truth; they had concealed it. Royalist historians stood accused of disfiguring events and hiding the truth from posterity, of imposing upon the past a simplistic interpretative schema which denied diversity, variety and complexity. Historical enquiry was thus by no means a disinterested activity. For Thierry the first step was to represent the past in its otherness, in its difference from the present, shorn of the self-congratulatory and consoling myths that had been woven by royalist historiography. This can be viewed as a process of defamiliarisation which emphasised the distance between present and past: it was necessary to grasp past reality in its otherness before moving on to demonstrate that the sequence of events meant something different, something more. Thierry argued that the task was an urgent one since French history was still being presented to the public in new editions of old works by Paul François Velly (1709–59), and François Eudes de Mézeray (1610–83), old-fashioned textbooks which, he felt, reinforced the appropriation of the past by the conservative ruling order. This influence was generally exercised through the action of received opinion but for that very reason it was judged to be all the more pervasive and pernicious.

In the *Lettres sur l'histoire de France*, which were first collected together in a volume in 1827, Thierry challenged both the implicit value system of traditional historiography and the conventions which governed the production of historical discourse. He argued that it was the historian's task to return to original sources, to weigh the evidence and provide an accurate assessment of historical personages. On this count alone he felt that most histories of France could be dismissed as being full of inexactitudes, inaccuracies and disputable assertions. This was particularly true with regard to the medieval period.[10] Thierry accused historians of committing anachronisms, of failing to appreciate the role played by racial conflicts, of imposing upon events a false logic and an incorrect patterning. For example, instead of describing the reality of medieval kingship historians had seized upon the word *rex*, and read into it a whole set of assumptions concerning leadership and social hierarchy which had only emerged much later and were quite foreign to the Middle Ages. For Thierry the new historical sensibility – whose expression he was quite happy to associate with the fictional creations of Chateaubriand and Walter Scott – signalled a qualitative change in perception, the emergence of a new vision which none the less marked the rediscovery of an authentic past (linguistic diversity, barbarity and violence, local colour). Significantly, he held that the modern historian – precisely because of his post-revolutionary situation – possessed new knowledge unavailable to his predecessors. The historian of the nineteenth century was irrevocably a historically determined individual, not a disembodied consciousness. In the introduction to his celebrated *Histoire de la conquête de l'Angleterre par les Normands* (1825) he observed: 'whatever superiority of mind a man may possess, he cannot go beyond the horizon of his century' (*HCA*, I, 6). In his *Considérations sur l'histoire de France* (1840) Thierry expanded on the consequences of this situation for historians of his generation:

> It is the previously unheard-of events of the past fifty years which have taught us to understand the revolutions of the Middle Ages, to see the reality which lay beneath the letter of the chronicles, to extract from the writings of the Benedictines things which these wise men had not seen, or had only seen in a partial or incomplete manner.
>
> (*R*, I, 211–12)

The men of the nineteenth century possessed what their predecessors lacked, an understanding and awareness of great social transformations.

Thierry's proclaimed intention was to reform the writing of history but he hesitated as to the precise form which the new history would take. He recognised that no historian could pretend to contain all events within the compass of his writing – 'the impossibility of combining all the facts in one narrative' (*HCA*, II, 217) – but at the same time he was aware that writers of historical narratives had as their goal to produce as exhaustive an account of events as was possible. What criteria should preside over the selection and presentation of data? One superficially enticing response involved reducing the intervention of the historian to a bare minimum. This was the view that perhaps the most satisfactory form which a national history could take was simply that of the reproduction of original source material. In these circumstances the historian ceased to fulfil a serious interpretative function. His role was limited to removing unnecessary repetition and providing narrative links where these did not emerge directly from a chronologically ordered sequence of documents. At first sight this approach seemed to promise authenticity and transparency. The historian effaced himself and allowed the voice of history to speak unhindered:

> It seemed to me that from this work in which, so to speak, each century would tell its own story and speak with its own voice, there must result the true history of France, the history which would never be rewritten, would belong to no individual writer, the history which all would consult as the repository of our national archives.
>
> (*DAEH*, 23)

However, in the event, Thierry was not satisfied with history constructed on these terms. He noted that once he and his friend Mignet had carried out the initial research their enthusiasm rapidly waned. The full project was never brought to fruition. Such a compilation, however useful, was not real history. The truth that the historian sought to grasp could not be rendered by just reproducing original sources. His function extended beyond that of mediating between present and past. He contributed to the construction of the object of knowledge which he simultaneously sought to investigate. The historian was charged with endowing the past with a unifying meaning. He could not escape his responsibility to explain how events and individuals had been shaped by forces greater than themselves. In the 1834 preface to *Dix ans d'études historiques* Thierry came closest to defining his ideal:

> In my historical writing I wanted to reproduce neither the manner of the philosophers of the last century, nor that of the medieval chroniclers, nor even that of the narrators of antiquity, however great my admiration for them. My intention was, if I had the strength, to combine, in a sort of mixed work, the broadly epic movement of the Greek and Roman historians with the naïve colours of the creators of legends and with the serious reasoning of modern writers. I aspired, perhaps a trifle ambitiously, to create for myself a grave style without oratorical bombast, a simple style without any affectation of *naïvety* or archaism; my intention was to paint the men of the past with the physiognomy of their time, but speaking myself the language of my own time; finally my intention was to multiply details so as to exhaust the original texts, but without disrupting the narrative and breaking the unity of the whole.
>
> (*DAEH*, 19)

In reality, Thierry redefined the function of the historian as narrator. This point has been fully discussed by Lionel Gossman in an illuminating and penetrating essay. Gossman contrasts Thierry's view of the narrator with that which had been current in the previous century (in the eighteenth century historians addressed their work to an ideal readership of specialists rather than to a more general audience). Gossman finds that a new relation between author and public was obtained in the nineteenth century and he discerns in Thierry's work the emergence of a new narrative convention:

> The narrator no longer carefully preserved the reader's detachment and freedom – the condition of the kind of community the Enlightenment historian proposed to create – by distinguishing narrative from description and commentary, but tried to convey the image of the whole in the account of each part, so that the reader would be enveloped, as it were, in the seamless fabric of the past.[11]

Scholarly research on its own was not enough; erudition had to be infused with imagination in order to bring the past to life. The post-revolutionary historian empathised with the movement of collective life, understood the psychology of nations. He proposed a dramatic reconstruction of the past, a re-creation of lived reality in its difficult complexity. The historical text aspired to scientific rigour and precision but at the same time it aimed to elicit an emotional response; it was an invitation to the reader to use his imagination and collaborate with the author in a project which, in the final analysis, embraced the possibility of transcending time. As Thierry wrote in his study of the Norman Conquest:

> We must reach back across the expanse of time and grasp the men of the past in their lived reality; we must represent them living and acting upon the land, land where today not even the dust of their bones could be found; deliberately many local facts, many unknown names have been placed in this narrative. May the reader's imagination attach itself to these elements: may it repeople ancient England with its conquerers and conquered of the eleventh century. . . . These men have not existed for seven hundred years; but what does this matter to the imagination guided by study? For the imagination, there is no past, and even the future is of the present.
>
> (HCA, I, 312)

Imaginative identification and historical knowledge were thus instruments which combined in this liberal's attempt to wrest the control of the past from the Ultras. History became a repository for the expression of freedoms denied in the present. Moreover, when the historian stripped away the veils of deceit with which in his opinion royalism had concealed the reality of French history he discovered that the past was not in fact a disordered series of events characterised by self-duplication and repetition. History possessed a determinate meaning. Thierry imbued it with a progressivist vision corresponding to the growth of political freedom, a process which began in earnest with the rise of the Communes and which continued until the Third Estate triumphed in 1789. The political implications of this theory were clear. The liberal historian became the spokesman for all who had sought to incarnate freedom in French history; he entered the lists on the side of his protatgonists, selecting, organising and patterning his material in a manner significantly different from his predecessors. Most importantly Thierry offered an interpretation of French history which located the Revolution within a periodisation which attributed legality to 1789 and lent legitimation to the opposition groupings of the Restoration period. The revolutionary past could not be undone but neither could it be avoided. It represented in concentrated form the whole problematic of the meaning of the national past: was French history a struggle for freedom or a tragic sequence of defeats culminating in 1815?

The need to confront recent events, to ascribe meaning to them, was as much the starting point of Thierry's historical reflection as was the overt critique of royalist historiography. Obviously, as a liberal, he was not going to defend a nostalgic theory of organicist order; he recognised that conflict and insurrection had driven the process of historical change. But at the same time he believed that events unfolded in accordance with an underlying purpose which invested them with meaning. Historical laws existed. The disintegration of the old social order was the inevitable result of the movement of French history. Similarly, the triumph of the bourgeoisie after the Revolution of July 1830 seemed to him to be the just culmination of a process which had as its goal constitutional and liberal freedoms. In this manner Thierry exemplified the strategies developed by the liberal historians of the Restoration and analysed by Stanley Mellon in his study of the political uses of history. By inscribing 1789 within the broad sweep of French history he implicitly refuted the royalist charge that the Revolution was an aberration, a deviation from the natural order of things. The assertion that freedom and justice were in fact at work in French history before 1789 meant that supporters and critics of the Revolution alike had to rethink the notion that 1789 marked an absolute break with tradition. Studying national history became a way of avoiding making false judgements in the present. Historical knowledge could be used to foster social life in a manner which eschewed the temptation of utopia. The events of the Revolution had amply demonstrated the unsuitability of models of political organisation drawn from an idealised Graeco-Roman past. Post-Enlightenment liberals realised that it was vital for them to rescue the national past and not abandon it as the exclusive preserve of conservative forces. Thierry's historical effort made 1789 the essential date in French history; he constructed a past which led to the identification of the middle class with the nation. However, if emancipation was understood as an objective in politics, so was order. Freedom remained freedom under the law. For the liberal consciousness man was a citizen who expressed certain freedoms within an administrative and legal framework. Political action was required to inaugurate the kind of order which allowed liberty to flourish – but this was far removed from any idea of order conceived as the restoration, the re-creation of a form of cohesion already realised at an earlier stage in the development of national culture.

Like other liberals of the Restoration Thierry distinguished between the Terror on the one hand and the 'real' Revolution on the other: 1793 undid much of the victory that had been achieved in 1789. The crimes and excesses of the Revolution were admitted and sincerely regretted. The defender of the 1789 revolution felt he could legitimately dissociate himself from the regicides, from the Terror. His ancestors were the more moderate of the revolutionaries, those who themselves often met with a violent end – Bailly, the mayor of Paris, for example.[12] Mellon has described how, during the Restoration, history offered 'the safest terrain upon which to conduct a defense of the Revolution' as well as the best way of educating a new generation in liberal principles.[13] For the liberal of the 1820s the freedoms of the Revolution were not invented in 1789: their roots were to be found in earlier periods of French history and within broader European traditions.

Thierry, as I have already indicated, began by distancing the past from the present, by underscoring difference, not sameness, by emphasising variety and diversity, not unity and cohesion. However, this amounted to a strategy designed to disrupt one particular representation of unity, that promoted by conservative historians. In reality he questioned neither the intelligibility nor the purposefulness of history. French history displayed order, progress and development. The historian's task was to assemble the facts of the past so as to reveal the underlying purpose. Historians might differ in their interests and values but Thierry's new history of France was to be understood as the true history of France. It was not a question of points of disrupted interpretation, a quarrel over the status of documentary evidence; what was at stake was the control of the representation of national time. For Thierry history was constitutive of social life and the dominant qualities of the French people were associated with the concepts of right and good. His fear was less that the past might be forgotten than that it might not be properly known. Like Michelet he believed that authenticity and truth resided in the masses. However, the real history of the masses had yet to be written:

'we lack the history of the citizens, of the subjects, of the people' (*DAEH*, 214–15). In the *Histoire de la conquête de l'Angleterre par les Normands* Thierry expanded on this in a programmatic statement:

> The essential aim of this history is to contemplate the destiny of peoples, and not that of certain famous men, to recount the adventures of social life and not those of individual life. Human sympathy can attach itself to entire populations, as to beings endowed with feeling, whose existence, longer than our own, is filled with the same alternatives of sorrow and joy, hope and dejection. Considered from this standpoint, the history of the past acquires something of the interest which attaches itself to the present time; for the collective beings of which it speaks have not ceased to live and to feel: they are the same beings who still suffer and hope under our eyes.
>
> (*HCA*, II, 289–90)

In Thierry's view previous histories which had centred on court intrigue, on royal power, on diplomacy were less alternatives than obfuscations. The collective dimension was central. Of course this did not mean that Thierry ignored the actions of individuals; it meant that collective life was foregrounded in a manner which showed that, while the masses were often victims, they were also the agents of historical change – even though they were often unaware of their role. It was the function of the historian to make explicit retrospectively the full import of their actions:

> The popular masses, when they are in movement, do not realise the exact nature of the impulse which dominates them; they advance by instinct towards the goal which they do not seek to define precisely. If we consider them only in a superficial manner they appear to be blindly following the particular interests of some leader whose name alone has made an impact in history: however, the very importance of proper names derives from the fact that they have served as rallying cries for the masses who, in shouting them out, knew what they meant and did not for the moment need a more accurate way of expressing themselves.
>
> (*LHF*, 142)

What characterised Thierry's approach was the role he attributed to conquest and invasion. This was most clearly apparent in his analysis of the Norman Conquest. The content of history was made intelligible by introducing a series of oppositions: domination and resistance, 'Conquest and Enslavement. Masters and Subjects' (DAEH, 7). Thierry is remembered for having underscored what he saw as the racial dimension in such conflicts and for trying to establish a causal relation between enduring racial characteristics and social antagonisms emerging at a later date.[14] Racial conflict became a key for understanding not just the Conquest and its aftermath but the course of English history from the eleventh century to the Civil War period. The past lived on in the present, moulding events. At times Thierry extended his argument and suggested that racial differences underlay the class antagonisms of contemporary Europe:

> The upper and lower classes, who today observe each other with distrust or struggle against one another for systems of ideas and of government, are in several countries the conquering and enslaved peoples of an earlier period. . . . The race of the invaders remained a privileged class from the moment it ceased to constitute a separate nation.
>
> (HCA, I, 5).

Clearly it was impossible to divorce historical research from more overtly political concerns. (Thierry's discussion of the Saxon–Norman conflict was itself in part a metaphor for the Gaul–Frank opposition within French culture.) However, it should be said that despite Thierry's reputation as a racial historian he did not advance a theory of biological determinism in a consistent or rigorous manner. Gossman rightly points out that conquest and occupation mattered more to the historian than physiological difference as such. Within a given society fusion did take place between contending groups; the degree of racial difference which opposed them was but one factor among many. England, in Thierry's view, had become one unit by 1450. The really important conflicts had more to do with ideas and power relations, factors which were not ultimately reducible to biology. Conquest and racial antagonisms provided the key but the content of history remained the growth of individual freedoms enshrined in 1789 and finding constitutional expression after 1830. The connection between events established by the historian rested in the final analysis on the saving illusion of the Revolution as the event which, however uncertainly, ushered into being the homogeneous national community which Thierry – at least until the events of 1848 shook his confidence in the permanence of bourgeois rule – believed had lastingly been created by the Revolution of 1830.

From the vantage point of the July Monarchy it seemed as if French history could be presented in terms of the progress of freedom identified with the development of the Third Estate. This was the classic position of the liberal historian. Moments of crisis and violence – the Frankish conquest, the Communes, the Revolution – could be inserted into a new patterning of the events of national history. The history of the Third Estate was a success story, a movement from division and conflict to cohesion and social oneness. As the agent for the production of national unity the Third Estate ceased to exist in 1789, at the moment when Sieyès proclaimed its identity with the nation. The Third Estate, which had brought about the disintegration of the old social order, had no role to play once the new order had been inaugurated. In other words Thierry wished to see the Third Estate subsumed into a unified nation from which social conflict and class antagonisms had been removed. However, it was the Third Estate's role as an agent for transforming France by challenging the established order which lent coherence and purpose to the national past. Emancipation from aristocratic tradition and from royal authority involved, as I have indicated above, the rediscovery of a popular history of revolt, identified with the authentic life of the nation. The continuity and unity of history rested upon a valorisation of difference and conflict whereas the goal of history was conceived as a nation-state which transcended internal divisions. Once royalist historiography had been discarded and replaced by a history of struggle, a way had to be found to prevent the newly defined past from overwhelming the present. Past freedoms supported modern politics but history could not be allowed to dissolve into oppositionist rhetoric.

The central question remained the meaning of the Revolution. How much of the Revolution was acceptable? Thierry welcomed the early constitutional phase. The spirit of 1789 contained the promise of unity and harmony (the peaceful world envisaged by liberal political theorists and economists in which individual freedoms supported commerce and exchange, not war and conquest). The Revolution none the less collapsed in the face of violence and excess. The challenge for Thierry was to show that the self-destructive impulse of the Revolution could be distinguished from the idea of 1789 conceived as the inception of a just order. The argument was complicated by the very insistence on the historical dimension. If indeed the Revolution was less an invention of the eighteenth century than the coming into being of something whose roots could be traced back to the Middle Ages, did this suggest that the past irrevocably controlled the present? The twin goals of national unity and constitutional freedoms had somehow to be reconciled despite the apparent confusion over means and ends. Hence the need to portray the death of the Third Estate as the condition for the emergence of the new France. The historian wrote to prevent the disappearance of freedom, but he also wrote to contain, or more appropriately to define, freedom; he disclosed the truth about French history but by the fact of writing he also pointed to the need for freedom and order to be reconciled within a unified community. Written history enacted on impossible reconciliation between death and desire, revolution and order. Morality was ultimately situated within culture, defined historically.

According to Thierry, it was the collective experience of the Revolution and Empire which made possible the emergence of a new type of history, a history which foregrounded the actions of collective forces, a history which recognised that general ideas influenced – when they did not actually determine – the course of events. The Gaul–Frank opposition, for example, which had been used for centuries as a way of making sense of French history could be looked at anew, reinterpreted in the light of recent events. The period since 1789 marked a shift in sensibility which transcended political boundaries: on all sides the importance of the collective dimension was recognised although, as a governing idea, it was developed and articulated differently. Thierry, for his part, and despite his love of Scott and Chateaubriand, was convinced of the incompatibility between innovative historical writing and political conservatism. The liberal historian, at odds with his society, involved in tussles with the Restoration censorship, was constrained to redefine the relationship between past and present in a manner which sustained his own cause. When the Ultras gained control of the government after 1820 it seemed to Thierry that the displacement of politics into historical research was the only refuge available to conscience. By developing organising concepts and redefining the conventions and the language of history he felt he was helping to effect the transformation of society.

History, in the hands of the Right, had become an agent for
preservation. Hence Thierry's stance: he did not consider that he
was ascribing a political dimension to history out of crudely parti-
san motives; he felt he was setting the record straight, giving
as full an account as possible of previously hidden intellectual,
institutional, social and political continuities. His view was that
no one could be indifferent to history since history contained
lessons, aroused emotions, made claims on our lives. The error of
the Revolution had been the wish to break away completely from
the national past, to disavow the French tradition. But while the
immediate consequences of the Revolution were regrettable, they
did not invalidate the original meaning of an event which was
grounded in the movement of national history. Thierry desired
community with the past but with a past exclusive of those forces
which embodied inequality and privilege. The new history justified
and explained 1789 while at the same time embodying a further
promise of fulfilment. For the men of the Restoration the Revolution remained an imperfect consummation of French history. The
liberal consciousness which encountered disappointment and frustration in the present finally had its expectation of an ending
fulfilled in July 1830.

It would be misleading to exaggerate the unity of Thierry's
thought. The oppositional, at times neo-republican, thrust of the
earlier writings was significantly modified in his later work. To
be sure he retained as his main subject matter the story of an
active Third Estate in conflict with the nobility, defining itself in
terms of individual and collective freedoms; but at the same time,
we see emerging the idea of a Third Estate whose boundaries are
less rigid, an agent operating in conjunction with the monarchy
and eventually producing a politics which could dictate the rules
of conduct for all Frenchmen. (In the final analysis even the
nobility and the clergy were not excluded absolutely.) In sum
Thierry was – and remained – a Restoration liberal who considered
that the July Monarchy fulfilled his expectations: the nation was
reconciled under a constitutional monarchy which endorsed essential freedoms. July 1830 marked the accomplishment of national
history, the reconciliation of the old and the new France, a coming
together which had been arrested and postponed since the replacement of the early constitutionalist phase of the Revolution by the
Jacobin Republic. And since history was inevitably written from
the perspective of the authority of present reality Thierry

59

concluded that the establishment of the constitutional monarchy – marking the achievement of order, freedom and unity – could be taken to signal the completion, the closure of French history. Thierry's most accomplished extended piece of historical writing, the *Essai sur l'histoire de la formation et des progrès du tiers état* (1853), was a product of this mood. Looking back over seven centuries the historian discerned 'a regular series of civil and political progress with at the beginning and at the end of the distance covered, one nation and one monarchy, bound to each other, modified together' (*EHFP*, 1). The emergence after 1830 of a homogeneous nation corresponded to the writing of a history which foregrounded the rise of the middle classes. The Third Estate really had become the nation. As we might expect, Thierry was thrown into utter disarray by what he described as the catastrophe of 1848. February 1848 demonstrated that 1830 was not an ending and that bourgeois history was itself provisional. In a letter of 1850 he confessed the gravity of his position:

> I no longer understand the history of France, the present has turned upside down my ideas about the past and with all the more reason it has overturned my ideas about the future; I have lost my historical faith, and, something which I would never have believed, my political faith is sinking away.[15]

Thierry never anticipated the emergence of a new beginning. He was pained to discover that the liberal retrieval and reconstruction of the past were not definitive. The moment of self-awareness was extreme since it disclosed the vulnerability of the historian, as well as the illusory nature of the closure which his writing seemed to enact. The events of 1848 called into question the stability of self, text and world: 'As much as France herself the history of France seemed to be turned upside down by this new revolution whose spirit and threatening aspect were those of the worst times of the first Revolution' (*EHFP*, 5). The liberal system of French history ceased to be self-evidently true once it lost, in the shape of the July Monarchy, its principle of external validation. Prior to 1848 Thierry had been convinced of the underlying coherence of the past and, despite concerns about the condition of the nation, he envisaged the future essentially as a continuation of the present. There seemed to be no place for substantive change. Personal resentments notwithstanding, he was unable to conceive of the

July Monarchy as a serious obstacle to legitimate demands for self-realisation made by individuals or groups within society. Having related the defining characteristics of this society to general laws of historical development there was no space left to accommodate discontent and dissatisfaction.

After 1848 Thierry was disconcerted. He found himself thrust uncomfortably, and against all anticipation, into an afterwards; he was unable to avoid comparing before and after and found himself experiencing the inner demon of the Counter-Revolution: the sense of loss. In his earlier writing he had not had to face the possibility that the past was superior to the present. Now a new epoch had begun which denied all that earlier had seemed reassuringly permanent and necessary. Suddenly the future became frightening in its unpredictability, enigmatic in its openness. Henceforth, the bond between the Third Estate and the Monarchy which had given order and direction to French history over six centuries was broken. The new historical fracture demonstrated the fragility of schemes of historical interpretation which lost sight of their own provisionality. How would the historian respond? In his preface to the *Essai* he was quite open about the impact which the events of February 1848 had upon him, describing how the Revolution interrupted his writing at the moment when he had reached the beginning of his treatment of the eighteenth century, plunging him into deep discouragement. Nevertheless, the revelation of historical contingency spawned no recantation, no declaration of the insufficiency of his earlier investigations.

Two ideas are prominent in the *Essai*: the rise of the Communes and the collaboration between the bourgeoisie and the monarchy in the construction of modern France. The first point was always of crucial importance for Thierry. In the 1834 preface to *Dix ans d'études historiques* he described the moment when he discovered the true significance of the Communes, previously concealed by conservative historians:

> On simply reading the modern writers on French history, it appeared to me that the enfranchisement of the Communes was a quite different thing from their account of it; that it was a true social revolution, a prelude to all those which have gradually raised the condition of the Third Estate; that there was the cradle of our modern liberty, and that in this

way the common people, as well as the nobility of France, had a history and ancestors.

(*DAEH*, 7)

This view of the communal movement as a revolutionary force lay at the very heart of Thierry's historical enterprise. The historical antecedent and justification for 1789 was to be found in the medieval commune. However, the *Essai* set out to paint an even fuller picture and this involved reaching back beyond the twelfth century to encompass the fate of the Gallo-Roman population after the Frankish invasions. What was significant in Thierry's interpretation was the role he attributed to Roman law and to Roman notions of municipal government. Guizot and Mme de Staël drew attention to Germanic freedoms and to the civilising role played by Christianity. Thierry's sympathies lay more with the urban organisation of the Classical world. He described how after the fall of the Roman Empire the Germanic invaders gave priority to the countryside which they divided up among themselves. Towns fell into decline. Feudalism marked the victory of Germanic over Roman customs. Military virtues were valorised and industrial skills neglected. However, some resistance persisted in the towns where Roman ideas of politics and citizenship survived. This meant that in addition to the aristocratic freedom deriving from the Germanic invasions there also existed a kind of freedom which 'conformed to natural law, was accessible to all, equal to all and which could have been given the name of *Roman freedom* in the light of its origin' (*EHFP*, 23–4). Thierry's thesis was that the twelfth century witnessed a revival of urban culture which asserted itself against feudal and ecclesiastical power by invoking the idea of election and the notion of municipal freedoms. This involved struggle. The emancipation of the Communes resulted from a direct physical challenge to the ruling order:

> The two great types of municipal constitution, the commune as such and the city ruled by consuls, both had insurrection in a more or less violent or contained form as their principle; both had as their objective equality of rights and the rehabilitation of labour.

(*EHFP*, 29)

For Thierry this was the founding origin of modern political freedoms. The value which the medieval commune placed on commerce, industry and exchange provided retrospective justification for 1789. Towns and villages grew in importance but they were unable to transcend their isolation. At this point collaboration between the Third Estate and the monarchy became the crucial factor. An external force was required to constrain the feudal lords, to impose legal and administrative coherence. This was the function of the monarchy. Here again Thierry pointed to a continuity with the Roman inheritance. The Crown acted in accord with the spirit of 'the theory of imperial power, of unitary and absolute public authority, the sole source of justice and law' (*EHFP*, 39). It drew financial resources and soldiery from the towns while promoting the notions of territorial, legal and administrative unity. A new legal system was devised to replace feudal law and with it a class of lawyers emerged. The new jurisconsults and politicians were 'the head and the soul of the bourgeoisie' (*EHFP*, 39); they began the struggle of reason and common law against custom, privilege and irrationality. The bourgeoisie played an essential role in the process which gave legitimation to the Crown as public authority. The new law was subversive of the old law but it marked out the meaning of the French future, 'uniting in one hand divided sovereignty, bringing down to the level of the bourgeois classes the classes which were above them and raising up to the level of the bourgeoisie the classes below them' (*EHFP*, 39–40). This was the spirit which Thierry discerned in the meetings of the Estates General in 1355 and 1356. Clearly Thierry had reassessed his interpretation of the French past. What mattered according to the *Essai* was the anchorage of the commune in the tradition of Roman law. The idea of conquest had ceased to be the central organising concept of historical discourse.

Over subsequent centuries the middle class remained allied with the monarchy. Thanks to the monarchy reforms were introduced which installed a coherent form of public authority and redefined property rights. Progress continued but was not constant. However, the power of the aristocracy declined. Of central importance for Thierry was the role played by Louis XIV in consolidating national unity:

In the midst of the pomp of his court Louis was, in his own way, a leveller; in his view merit had rights superior to those accorded by birth; he opened up broader roads which allowed new men to accede to positions; instead of dividing,

he united. He worked to make complete the political unity
of the country, and, without knowing it, he prepared from
afar the succession of the one great sovereign community of
the nation.

(EHFP, 278)

Louis encouraged industry, reduced the power of the nobles,
developed the moral unity of modern France. In this he was aided
by Colbert who is presented in the *Essai* as a hero of the Third
Estate. And yet the reign of the Sun King marked the end of an
era in French history. Louis was tempted into foreign military
adventures; the hopes raised in the early years of his reign turned
to disillusionment as France fell into economic decline. Political
freedoms were sacrificed in the cause of national unity as the
monarch established a regime based on his own personal power.
In effect, according to Thierry, the reign of Louis XIV brought
to a close the long collaboration between the Third Estate and
the monarchy; it marked the last stage of 'the long social enterprise
accomplished in common by royalty and the non-noble classes of
the nation, the work of fusion and universal subordination [to
law], the work of producing unity of power and administrative
uniformity' *(EHFP, 238)*. History, however, remained purposeful
and Thierry described the task of the eighteenth century as that
of establishing national unity on a different basis, one which
enshrined the legitimate rights of the citizen. The monarchy was
in crisis, divorced from the condition of the people. The nobility
challenged the kind of unity achieved under the monarchy. At the
same time the Third Estate lost much of its legitimacy – the sale
of offices destroyed genuine communal and local freedoms. The
eighteenth century displayed the decadence of urban freedoms;
none of the substance, only the appearance of the original municipal rights remained. Of the institutions inherited from the past
parliament alone retained elements of power and popular support:
'Parliament formed the chain of legality which, by way of the
Estates General whose final convocation it provoked, led to the
new order of things in which it itself disappeared' *(EHFP, 300)*.
This is the concluding sentence of the main body of the *Essai*.
It reveals Thierry's desire to point to some underlying legality,
rationality within history.

Thierry wished therefore to treat French history as a process
of collaboration between the forces of the rising bourgeoisie and

centralising 'imperial' monarchy. History had to be made to contain the contradictory objectives of emancipation and order. The process was at once gradual and susceptible of revolutionary explosions. However, Thierry generally had a confident way with time; he did not show impatience. Sudden and violent change was viewed with suspicion. We are told that Etienne Marcel went too far; he is portrayed as a forerunner of democratic dictatorship and the Terror.[16] However, the overall process is clearly meaningful and the rise of the Third Estate is considered as the guarantee of intelligibility:

> The continuous elevation of the Third Estate is the dominant fact and seems the law of our history. This providential law has operated more than once unbeknown to those who were its agents; those who were to gather its fruits did not know of it or even regretted its operation.
>
> (*EHFP*, 167)

French history was not chance; it moved in accordance with a providential design. The historian revealed the rationality of the historical process. The bourgeoisie was the bearer of truth, of universal values; it was the agent for the embodiment within history of the 'eternal principles of reason, justice and humanity' (*EHFP*, 237). History told of the realisation of these eternal ideals within time. Thierry offered what was essentially a hopeful account. However, he had to confront the Revolution.

The French Revolution was understood philosophically as the implementation of ideals defined as being in accord with reason; historically it was the outcome of the process begun by the Communes. Thierry's position was that the claims of reason needed to be tempered by the realities of the historical situation. The theory of natural law needed to be balanced by reference to historical rights. Within Thierry's construction of France and Frenchness this implied that individualism and claims made for the autonomy of the subject similarly needed to be balanced by societal considerations and institutional arrangements. In other words the progressive lesson to be drawn from French history before the eighteenth century was that in order for liberal freedoms to flourish royal power was called upon to offer a unified administrative and legal framework in which individual initiative could develop productively. For Thierry the legitimate Revolution was that of the period 1789–91 whose spirit was embodied in the legislation enacted by the Constituent Assembly, notably the abolition of feudal rights and privileges and the introduction of guarantees to protect the liberty of the subject.

Thierry believed in the capacity of human reason to devise a better, freer world. However, he recognised that the eighteenth century had turned reason against itself by endeavouring to establish a regime of abstract virtue. The only analogy available for democratic politics was that provided by Sparta and the Roman Republic. French history seemed to lack useful precedents. According to the *Considérations sur l'histoire de France* (1840) the disavowal of the national past was on one level a necessary spur to revolution: 'it was necessary for [French] history to be disdained or distorted in order for public opinion to surge forward in the direction of reforms whose ultimate aim was inscribed in the secrets of Providence' (*R*, I, 110). Up to a point the repudiation of the past was successful: in the Constituent Assembly 'everything took its point of departure in pure reason, in absolute right and in eternal justice; for according to the conviction of the century, man's natural and imprescriptible rights were the principle and the end, the departure point and the goal of every legitimate society' (*R*, I, 153).

However, Thierry qualified his position by adding that the historical (i.e. collective) dimension was not after all absent from the new legislation since the latter, while taking account of the conditions of modern life, 'only restored on our territory . . . the old type of civil order, bequeathed by the Roman Empire' (*R*, I, 154). And yet, the Roman law tradition within French culture did not ultimately determine the course of events. The dominant model became that of the Spartan and Roman Republics as articulated by Rousseau and Gabriel Bonnot de Mably (1709–85), ideals founded on what Thierry held to be misconceptions about the ancient world and developed against the French national tradition. Instead of renewing French society, they precipitated violence and division, facilitated the transfer of power to the populace. The error of the Revolution was to concede too much to the claims of abstract political theory. In the *Essai* Thierry described the tensions within the nation and suggested that it was the social context which led to the dangerous dominance of natural rights theory. In France reform could not be portrayed as restoration:

The inauguration of a society founded on the principles of

rational law only took place when the national masses had fully experienced the nothingness which a restoration of historical rights signified for them. Pure reason and history were like two diverse well-springs at which regenerative opinion drew [sustenance] from the very beginning; but, whether by necessity or by imprudence, it drew more and more from the former and less and less from the latter. On one side the current was weak and inert; on the other it grew ever greater, driven by the twin forces of logic and hope, managing to control everything and sweep it along.

(*EHFP*, 272)

In the wake of the Terror such theorising inspired aversion and repugnance. There was no doubt, however, that society needed to be stabilised. Thierry considered that given the grave circumstances in which the nation found itself Napoleon fulfilled a necessary role. He was charged with pacifying, reuniting and finally 'fixing' the nation. Thierry noted that Napoleon understood correctly that in order to achieve this objective he needed to turn to the institutions of the past; however, Napoleon's error was that he denied the legitimate claims which were made in the name of political freedom. The Restoration equally failed to resolve the conflicts in French society. Instead of returning to the spirit of 1791 and reasserting the role of the monarchy as unifier, the Bourbons exacerbated the divisions between the old and the new France and highlighted the tensions between reason and history. According to the Charter the monarchy was the sole legitimate constitutive authority in French history, a perspective which failed to recognise the historic role played by the people in the construction of civil society. Hence, for Thierry, the supreme importance of the July Monarchy: the Revolution of 1830 restored the link with the spirit of 1789 but, by retaining the monarchy, it also advanced the cause of national unity. Once again the monarchy was acting in alliance with the Third Estate (now the nation) and in accord with the designs of Providence. Order was restored but the liberties of the people had to be respected: 'The constitutional monarchy will undoubtedly endure but on the express condition that it remain bound to the guarantees of our political freedoms' (*R*, I, 229).

It is easy now to envisage the scale of the problem put to Thierry by the Revolution of 1848. His theory of history posited rationality and an underlying community of interest between people and king. The Third Estate had defined itself against the nobility and the clergy but at the moment when it seemed that the twin authorities of the people and the monarchy were at last acting in concert the stability of the nation was again catastrophically disrupted. Thierry's sadness and disillusionment were apparent in a letter of April 1848 in which he explained that 1830 had marked the fulfilment of his political dreams; he just could not understand why intelligent and patriotic citizens had opposed Louis-Philippe, 'the most sensible and patriotic king that France had ever had'.[17] February 1848 destroyed national unity. The events of June 1848 further aggravated the condition of the nation – Thierry placed responsibility for the June days squarely on the socialists and communists in whose doctrines he saw a threat to reason, morality and private property. Drawing on his knowledge of revolutionary history he predicted that what he considered the anarchy of the Second Republic would eventually be ended by the necessary but regrettable reimposition of order. In later years Thierry, like Guizot, stayed loyal to his liberal convictions and remained faithful to his belief in representative institutions. He was no friend of the illiberal and dictatorial regime born of the *coup d'état* of December 1851. Nevertheless nothing could alter the central fact that in 1848 the forces of history revealed themselves to be irrational and irresponsible. Thierry's history was political, ideological and moral but after 1848 it could no longer make an implicit claim to foreknowledge.

Thierry's response to the Revolution of February 1848, a combination of frustration, anger and stoical gloom, illustrates the distance which separated him from historians and intellectuals of the republican Left such as Michelet and Quinet who welcomed the explosion of 1848 in which they saw the revival of France and of democracy. After 1830 Thierry viewed the task of history as the consolidation of present reality. Michelet, on the other hand, envisaged France as a collective personality charged with a redemptive mission; the nation was identical in essence with an idea yet to be realised. Michelet admired Thierry. Indeed, at times Thierry's language had the ring of Michelet's, for example when he spoke of the 'war of rational law against existing law, of ideas against facts, which erupts at intervals within human societies' (*EHFP*, 40). However, the older Thierry was troubled by violence, distrustful of the people, and in the end wary of the consequences of the actions of the masses whose existence he brought back to life. His thought was anchored in the intellectual universe of the Idéologues. Like Daunou he was suspicious of philosophical forms of history. He disliked Michelet's tendency to generalise, to interpret, to concern himself with meanings as much as with facts.

In the *Considérations sur l'histoire de France* he spoke out against the influence of Vico and of German philosophy on the writing of history in France. He was unhappy with the German approach which discovered 'in every fact the sign of an idea' and which turned the course of human events into a continuous conflict of ideas (*R*, I, 232). Thierry also quoted with approval a statement by Cousin to the effect that history should remain within the limits of its discipline. The goal of history was analysis and not transcendental synthesis. Thierry observed that 'every national history which takes ideal form and moves into abstractions and formulas leaves behind the conditions of its being; it is denatured and perishes' (*R*, I, 233). We have seen how Ideology examined the past with the presupposition that analysis, not imagination or sympathetic projection, was the means for establishing the greatest certainty. At most such history might bring a substantial increase in knowledge but it could never offer the simulacrum of redemption promised by Romantic history in the grand manner. Thierry's writing reflected the liberalism of the Idéologues, their sense of individual freedom and their awareness of the importance of industry. Freedom was his rallying point, his standard, the central truth of his message, but in his work freedom was embodied in history, in the movement of collective life. Thierry went beyond Ideology by making history an involving form of writing; the historian drew on both his documentation and on his own inner resources, he established a relationship of identification with his subject matter, and this process of exchange was echoed, re-enacted within the reader. Here the historian was more than a detached observer; he became a sympathetic re-creator whose task was to articulate the unformed desires and to utter the unspoken thoughts of previous generations.

Thierry's practice of history taught how identity was tied to a sense of time and it spoke directly to the condition of the young men of the 1820s and 1830s. He succeeded in making the remote at once recognisable and seductive, present and yet dismayingly different (in his *Récits des temps mérovingiens*, for example). History written in this spirit rested upon the idea that the fullness of the past could be opened up to contemporary readers if they were willing to engage with kinds of difference and diversity which could not be contained within the norms of a neo-Classical aesthetic (even though neo-Classicism with its Enlightenment pedigree appeared at first sight to connote liberty). Thierry's writing endorsed the perception that what set the present apart from the past was the fact of the Revolution. His history bore an assurance of superiority which depended upon the liberating distance which the Revolution had seemingly introduced into the perception of past reality. The challenge he set himself was to make the heroic insubordination of the French people a source of order and not of discord. He claimed to demystify the role played by kings and generals. In this he felt he was arguing for something which was beyond argument – the need to be suspicious of the tendency of the powerful to use the representation of the past as a means of ensuring that things remain the same from generation to generation. The post-revolutionary climate was invoked as the enabling agent which had allowed history to reinvent itself as a serious discipline. Thierry dismissed the dubious manipulations of royalist historians in a manner which recalled the revolutionaries' own violent denial of the past. But Thierry's revolutionary vandalism was presented as liberating. It was not an unthinking rejection of the past but a metaphorical bludgeoning of those who had connived at the concealment of the truth about the past. Thierry used the ideas of racial conflict and conquest as keys to unlock the meaning of the past. The rise of the Third Estate was revealed to be the organising force in French history, the inscription of Reason, the plan of Providence. In 1789 the conquered had finally humiliated their conquerors. Thierry's own historical writing could be viewed as marking a further stage in this process of emancipation. Thierry's control of the past enabled the Third Estate to conquer the discourse within which collective identity was formed and articulated; the Third Estate was reborn, remythologised as the unified nation, the product of the newly uncovered history of freedom.

3

François Guizot (1787–1874) and liberal history: the concept of civilisation

The authority and legitimacy of the state born of the Revolution was the central issue for French political culture in the nineteenth century. The case of Augustin Thierry has already demonstrated how the writing of history could be used to forge a sense of social integration, with the middle classes emerging as the agents of progress, as the bearers of meaning. François Guizot developed an idea of history which had marked similarities with that proposed by Thierry. First, he enlisted the past in the cause of liberalism. Second, he recognised the importance of the Revolution as the event which ushered in political modernity. For Guizot the Revolution lay at the origin of a social order which embodied moral self-consciousness in the Kantian sense. He described freedom of conscience as the 'religious idea of our time' (*DMG*, 156). In his view, freedom of conscience, the right to own property and the right to protection against the unjust actions of individuals or governments were essential human rights – 'rights which each man possesses simply because he is a man' (*DGF*, xxxvi). At the same time Guizot deeply regretted the excesses of the Revolution (his father had been a victim of the Terror) and he held the social disorganisation wrought by revolutionary violence to be responsible for precipitating the curtailment of precious freedoms during the Empire.

Like Thierry, Guizot used the writing of history as an instrument for change and a tool for reconstruction. The strength of liberalism as a political doctrine lay in its appropriation of the past, in its laying claim to a different tradition. This new history included more than events. It distinguished between significant and non-significant facts and had pretensions to a higher form of knowledge. Understanding the past was part of a broader quest

71

for meaning and rationality, a quest which in Guizot's case was informed by his commitment to Protestantism. At the same time Guizot's concern lay with the distribution of political power in the present. He wished to restore social cohesion by generating new values and reforming institutions in such a manner as to simultaneously disarm the pretensions of radical politicians and disable the project of the ultra-conservatives. He envisaged new political arrangements which reflected his conviction that social cohesion was more important than increased equality. In his view liberalism did not imply democracy and its limits were defined less in relation to political theory than in relation to an idea of history. His aims were to control the past and tame the Revolution while keeping the forces of reaction at bay. It was by enhancing public awareness of the processes which transformed the past into the present that Guizot hoped to unify society. At the same time he drew attention to the forces which undermined the social bond.

His thought resembled Thierry's in many ways – the understanding of history in terms of class antagonisms, the interest in the English Revolution, the commitment to liberalism, an increasing conservatism after 1830; however, the breadth of Guizot's work and his use of the idea of civilisation as a guiding concept make his writing more impressive.[1] And his direct involvement in the formulation of government policy, particularly after the July Revolution, lends an extra dimension to his thought.[2] His achievement exemplified the interrelation between historical consciousness and statecraft in nineteenth-century France: the leading historian of the 1820s became Minister of Education, Foreign Minister and Prime Minister under the July Monarchy.

What compels our attention in Guizot's political writing of the 1820s is the emphasis he placed on the radically new nature of the social relations engendered by the Revolution. He demonstrated not so much the falseness as the irrelevance of the claims made by supporters of the Ancien Régime and Revolution alike to possess a workable model for the future organisation of French society. Guizot saw himself as the spokesman for what he called the 'new France' (*DMG*, 41). By this he meant the society produced by the Revolution, a society which accepted essential freedoms and equality before the law. His point of departure was the Charter of 1814 which effected a reconciliation of sorts between the old France and the new. In his mind there was no doubt that the future lay in the consolidation of the idea of representative government. He argued that society and government coexisted in the sense that a system of rules was integral to both social relations and government. He repudiated Rousseau and rejected the revolutionary attempt to use the state to regenerate citizens. Popular sovereignty was held to be a dangerous doctrine, not simply because the majority could well be wrong, but because sovereignty in the real sense was absolute and could never fully be embodied in either the person of the king or the collective will of the people. In fact, the true allegiance of human beings was to a power which transcended this earth. Men had an innate awareness of the moral law, a sense of obligation to a higher, divine order: 'man recognises something which is not his will but which must regulate his will' (*HOGR*, I, 90). Conscience revealed the existence of a transcendent power: Guizot referred to 'the consciousness of justice and right, that is of a rule independent of human will' (*HOGR*, I, 90). Man possessed an inner sense of what was right and this awareness expressed itself in the form of resistance to tyranny. Of course human beings were fallible creatures and there could be no certainty that they would act in accordance with the higher rationality. None the less, Guizot's conclusion was that the present situation warranted optimism. He viewed the task of politics as a noble one, that of unifying society in the name of justice and reason. In an important sense the social was prior to the political. Political power did not institute society; it had to work with existing social dispositions and aspirations. Government was powerless unless its actions were supported by social forces (*DMG*, 105–6). But when seen from the vantage point of the higher plane of reason, government and society were together involved in realising a more rational and just order:

> All the combinations of the political machine must . . . tend, on the one hand, to extract from society whatever reason, justice and truth it possesses in order to apply it to its government; on the other hand, political arrangements should stimulate within society the progress of reason, justice and truth and constantly transmit this social progress into the activity of government.
>
> (*HOGR*, I, 98)

Guizot's defence of individual freedoms was balanced by an emphasis on general societal concerns. It was not enough for the state to endorse private relations between individuals for, in

Guizot's view, government drew its strength, energy and legitimacy from the population at large: 'Dealing with the masses is the great mainspring of power' (*DMG*, 108). Societies were stirred by collective passions and these were not to be ignored. Guizot's thought thus marked a departure from the liberalism of a Benjamin Constant which lent priority to the private realm over the public and whose object had been to reduce as far as possible the role of the state. Guizot, by contrast, viewed government as the necessary embodiment of the dominant elements in social life. He departed from classic liberal theory by being generally in favour of centralisation and the effective use of state power: 'societies and states are only created by the centralisation of interests and forces' (*HOGR*, I, 150). A critical point of his argument was that in order for individual freedoms to flourish they needed to be rooted in law and be protected by central authority: 'The progress of civilisation places the guarantee of individual freedoms in the hands of public authority' (*EHF*, 158). Freedom had to be enshrined in law.

There was no need to turn to theocratic prescriptions and the myth of organic order. Instead the general interest would be protected by involving in government the most knowledgeable and enlightened members of society, by relying on intelligence and reason rather than birth and privilege. In this way it was hoped that any tendency on behalf of either the crown or parliament to exercise arbitrary power would be avoided. Guizot believed that a form of representative government reduced the risk of despotism. Such constitutional arrangements as prevailed during the Restoration – the division of power between the King, the House of Peers and the Chamber of Deputies – were considered to be appropriate for they allowed for a process of reasoned deliberation to be carried out before action was taken. However, Guizot was no egalitarian. Privilege, in the form of the hereditary peerage, was not called into question. More importantly Guizot repeatedly stressed the extent of natural inequalities and concluded that only the best minds should be associated with the activity of governance (his theory of the 'capacités'). He did not envisage that political rights should be equally distributed. As Douglas Johnson has observed, what Guizot proposed was a theory of government and not a theory of representation.[3] Political rights were special and did not belong among the more fundamental human rights. The aim of politics was to represent reason, not the will of the people. Each society, declared Guizot, marked a certain stage in the growth of human knowledge; by the same token it signalled the achievement of a certain awareness of truth and justice. Unfortunately historical accident and man's fallen condition meant that the ideas of truth and justice were widely dispersed and unequally distributed among the members of society. None the less, it was possible to gather together the scattered fragments of legitimate power and organise them as government, to constitute a rightful public authority which commanded respect and obedience – in so far as it approximated to the will of God. The activity of politics and the theory of representative government corresponded to a unifying, generalising force. Government actualised the legitimate essence of social life, the latent legitimate power: 'it is a question of . . . concentrating, of realising public reason and public morality and summoning them to occupy power' (*HOGR*, II, 150).

This way of relating the citizen to society was Guizot's answer to revolutionary individualism. It was also his way of demonstrating that social cohesion could be reconstructed without restoring traditional hierarchies. However, the practical consequence of his political theory was to endow the middle classes with a new legitimacy since commerce, wealth and property seemed necessary prerequisites for the advent of enlightenment.[4] However, could a middle-class elite – however rational – continue indefinitely to function as the organ for the expression of the general interest and thereby guarantee social stability? Guizot admitted that the organisation of the new France entailed a recognition that irreversible changes in the structure of society had taken place. The difficulty lay in the fact that the Guizot of the 1820s, the oppositional intellectual, espoused the cause of change and employed a rhetoric of movement. In his view the function of government was not just to control and administer; it was to articulate aspirations and respond to needs. Beliefs and social practices were constantly intertwined and the government of the 'new France' needed to be in harmony with the evolving beliefs and passions of society at large. What then was the relation between contemporary politics and the fact of the Revolution?

Guizot – who devoted many volumes to the English Revolution – was never impelled to write a fully developed history of the French Revolution in the manner of Thiers or Mignet. None the less, the events of the revolutionary period remained a persistent preoccupation, inescapable as fact and unavoidable as idea, informing his writing through the medium of history, implicitly redefining the shifting meanings of before and after, underpinning his key structuring concept of civilisation. Guizot portrayed the Revolution as having in reality two meanings. First, it was the consequence of the social conflicts which made up French history. Second, it marked an attempt to implement the rule of law and justice. The Revolution was legitimate in intellectual, political and moral terms. It was much more than a conflict between haves and have-nots: 'The Revolution was right . . . in its principle and in its direction . . . it sought to introduce justice, the empire of the moral law, into relations between citizens and into those between government and citizens. It is this which makes the Revolution invincible' (DGF, 139). However, despite this endorsement, Guizot was at pains to remind his readers that the idealistic spirit of 1789 descended into a maelstrom of barbarity, cruelty and repression.

Like Thierry, Guizot was in a difficult position; he had to rescue what he viewed as the positive contribution made by the Revolution while distancing himself from the indefensible. He asked his readers to accord general significance to an event which, whatever its imperfections, inaugurated the political culture of modernity. He made the point that in the Revolution the will to a new order became a will to violence, but he did not focus his attention too much on the discontinuity between idea and action since to do so would have lent support to his political opponents in their complete condemnation of the Revolution. Guizot considered the counter-revolutionaries of his time to be destructive of social stability and dishonest in their use of the past. In emphatic utterances he urged the public to regard the Revolution as a complex, contradictory but none the less intelligible phenomenon. It possessed unity and direction. It was both a concrete fact and an idea, an interlocking of thought and action. If care were taken it was possible to assess the Revolution in moral terms without giving undue weight to the gap between intention and achievement. Above all the Revolution needed to be placed in a proper historical perspective. Violence had not occurred because all restrictions on freedom had been removed; the Revolution was the culmination of the process of class struggle which constituted French history: 'For more than thirteen centuries the defeated people struggled to shake off the yoke of the victors. Our history is the story of this struggle. In our time a decisive battle has been fought. It is called the Revolution' (*DGF*, 1–2).

This did not mean that Guizot believed that the French still formed two warring factions descended respectively from the Franks and the Gauls. In fact he held that the French existed as one people since the Middle Ages. What mattered was that the conflicts between the Third Estate, the king and the nobility were part of a social process – the progressive elimination of privilege, the removal of those inequalities not rooted in any natural superiority. In the manner of Thierry, Guizot described the Third Estate as a new nation creating its own identity by opposing and defeating its former masters and oppressors (*DGF*, xi). This social advance, the progressive dispossession of the nobility of its rights, was the truth of French history. The Revolution promised the final resolution of the tensions of national history in identity and unity, but its destructive energies prevented the realisation of the new order, thrusting into the future the attainment of the desired resting point.

The collision of the defiantly assertive ideologies of Left and Right rendered Restoration France difficult to govern. Guizot's problem was how to reconcile the authority of the state with the exercise of liberal freedoms. An orderly distribution of power in the present could not be achieved by ignoring the past or by dissimulating the irreversible consequences of the revolutionary period. By 1820 the time had come to consider the Revolution 'from an elevated point of view, and to refine it while preserving it' (*DGF*, xviii). Many conservatives found this attempt to discriminate between good and bad aspects of the Revolution objectionable. Guizot thought otherwise and argued that by adopting the Charter the king accepted and legitimised the Revolution in its positive aspects:

> the Revolution, brought about by the necessary development of a society in progress, founded on moral principles, undertaken in service of the general good, was the *terrible, but legitimate* struggle of right against privilege, of legal freedom against arbitrary power . . . it is the business of the Revolution alone to consummate the good which it has begun and repair the evil it has done by regulating itself, purging itself and founding the constitutional monarchy.
>
> (*DGF*, xxviii)

In Guizot's eyes the arrangements embodied in the Charter provided the only way forward. An alliance between monarchy and a form of parliamentary government alone offered France both a legitimate authority and a framework within which interactions between citizens could take place peacefully and productively. However, the balance was fragile. In *Du gouvernement représentatif en France* (1816) Guizot contrasted the French and American revolutions and observed that whereas a revolution undertaken in order to achieve a people's freedom was a revolution which could be easily ended, a revolution which identified the fight for freedom with a struggle for power between rival social groups admitted no simple resolution (*MPH*, 1–2). Peace and security would remain fragile in France. None the less, unity could not be achieved by repudiating the Revolution. Of this Guizot was certain. To do so would be to deny the historical forces at work in earlier centuries and to cast doubt on the moral superiority of the idea of the autonomous individual. The reference back to 1789 explained the present predicament and provided the framework within which political thought moved. More important than brooding on the errors of the Revolution was an awareness of the irreversibility of the new moral, psychological and intellectual climate. The Restoration needed to consolidate the rule of law and implement legal equality. Future stability rested upon the emergence of a society of rights, obligations and duties. Without reciprocity of rights individuals would not be bound together and society would again fragment.

Guizot elaborated quite a complex and subtle argument when he addressed questions of political theory. However, by implication he faced a problem encountered by earlier liberal thinkers, by Benjamin Constant in particular, that of re-establishing the legitimacy of theory.[5] In the wake of the Revolution Constant had attempted to rescue the project of political theory from the blanket condemnations proposed by those who alleged that theory and abstract thought led inexorably to violence and terror. Constant grappled with the conflicts between reason and passion which had been underestimated by the optimism of the Enlightenment and catastrophically disclosed by the Revolution. He turned to history but he did not locate his moral individualism within a fully articulated historical narrative of collective purpose. His thought was fragmentary, paradoxical, painfully self-aware, conscious of the provisionality of its own conclusions. Could subjective freedom and collective truth be united?

Guizot shared Constant's suspicion of abstract speculation concerning the ideal society of the future; he also shared his perception of the fragility of constitutional arrangements. Guizot considered that to analyse the structure and distribution of power within a given political system was an interesting but not necessarily fruitful activity. He admitted that theorising could be carried too far, that it might become disabling, even destructive. He recalled that the eighteenth century – which had excelled in this field – had also exposed its limitations. The example of the Enlightenment demonstrated that knowledge of the way in which power was organised in the past was far from forming a sure method of protecting rights and freedoms in the present. Guizot spoke for the rising Romantic generation when, in contrast with what he considered the dry, analytical approach of the Enlightenment, he emphasised the creative dimension of politics, the complex interplay of forces set in motion in order to build society. Analytical knowledge was one thing; lived reality was different, 'something very complex requiring the participation, the amalgamation of a multitude of diverse elements, each modified and sustained by the others' (*HOGR*, II, 219). It followed from this that political reality was more likely to be grasped by way of a historical explanation which took account of a variety of factors: 'The institutions of a people cannot properly be understood without knowledge of its history' (*HOGR*, I, 127–8). Furthermore, the history of each European nation was seen as part of a greater whole, a drama in which each people played a role. The past could no longer be disregarded in favour of abstract political theory. Quite the reverse: historical knowledge was declared to be essential for any citizen contemplating participation in public life. Like Thierry, Guizot envisaged the turning to history as a movement of recomposition, of national reassessment and reconstruction:

> we feel the necessity to unite our feelings with our habits, to connect our institutions with our memories, to *join together* at last the links in the *chain of time* which never allows itself to be completely broken, however violent the attacks upon it may be.
>
> (*HOGR*, I, 5)[6]

In this way, despite his philosophical turn of mind, Guizot's concern lay with political practice and its insertion into history rather than with the more abstract questions of theory. Whereas Constant elaborated a historical underpinning to his argument which amounted neither to a fully developed theory of progress on the nineteenth-century model nor to a straightforward extension of eighteenth-century views, Guizot made history a principle of mediation. And for Guizot, as we shall see, history carried the values of western liberalism, values whose claim to universality could be invoked to explain and justify the advance of the middle classes.

Guizot rejected the idea that there was something fixed or immutable about the past. The present which rediscovered the past brought to it its own particular preoccupations and perspective. In his eyes there was nothing remotely contentious about this assertion; the transformations wrought by social and political crises inevitably enhanced the capacity for understanding by moulding new ways of looking at earlier centuries. Guizot, like Thierry, underlined the extent to which the impact of recent events had transformed the past: 'It is not to us alone that political life has been restored; it has also returned into history' (HOGR, II, 10). However, this did not mean that Guizot questioned the status of historical facts. He claimed that whereas the viewpoint of the historian changed, the object of his gaze did not. It was legitimate to see something new in the past, to envisage new interpretations; however, he felt that in order to be admissible new readings had to be faithful to what we might term the potential contained within historical events:

> The facts with which history deals neither acquire nor lose anything as they are transmitted from age to age; whatever has been seen in the facts, whatever will be seen in the facts, was contained in them from the day on which they were accomplished.
>
> (HOGR, I, 2)

This suggested that a deeper, essential reality underlay the successive phenomenal perceptions of events. How then was one to distinguish between truth and error? How was one to know if an interpretation was correct? Guizot certainly left his readers in no doubt that the past had often been misused. He accused historians of bias, of sloppy and superficial research, of erecting theories on insufficient evidence, of seeing in the past what was never there.

His own view was that the historian should dispense justice and truth, eschewing cold neutrality in favour of what he termed 'that energetic and fertile impartiality which is inspired by the love of truth and the sight of truth' (HOGR, I, 13). But what guarantee could there be that Guizot's truth was anything other than bias, a further expression of the complicity between history and ideology? His answer was his exploration of European history, illuminated by the concept of civilisation. This provided an explanation of the totality of events by disclosing a patterning, a developmental process which Guizot related to a higher purpose. From this vantage point distortions and falsifications could be identified. We should remember that the new political organisation which Guizot wanted to see emerge drew its legitimacy, not from the sovereignty of the people, but from the ideas of justice, reason and right. These were less abstract formulations than ideas produced by the onward, progressive movement of history.

Guizot held that each period in history possessed an intellectual cohesion. Each epoch had its dominant idea which it held to be true and which provided the ground of governmental action (DMG, 155). I have already described the role played by reason in Guizot's conception of sovereignty and his understanding of the individual's relation to the moral law. Reason was also present in history. History produced rationality, truth and justice. Guizot presented a vision of history animated by ideal forces which were embodied in the civilisations of the past. His entire approach stressed the relationship between ideas and social realities and posited a vital connection between thought and value. Activity of mind was generally viewed as an ameliorating power. At the same time he described the way in which intellectual advance meshed with material reality, for example in his extended treatment of the way in which shifting property relations allowed particular ideas of freedom and right to emerge. The historian ordered his material by relating the course of events to a deeper causality, to the ideas which they embodied. The progress of civilisation, opined Guizot, consisted in extending the authority of reason over individuals while at the same time restricting the arbitrary exercise of an individual's will over other individuals. Civilisation implied the rule of law and the triumph of right over force.

Like Thierry, Guizot felt that he was writing a new type of history, a history which reassessed received opinion and reconstituted past events in a new patterning. He warned his listeners that to appreciate his approach they needed to come to his lectures already armed with a knowledge of the chronological sequence of events. Guizot wanted to disclose some general laws. However, unlike Cousin, Michelet or Quinet, he did not propose a grand scheme of universal history in the Romantic manner. He did not dispute that a comprehensive history of humankind was feasible and worthwhile but he chose instead to focus his attention on a more limited subject area, the history of Europe. His aim was to describe the evolution of social forms, to trace the emergence of rights and freedoms, to follow the changing role of institutions. However, this process of making sense of history entailed much more than simply laying before the reader a coherent pattern of events. Guizot considered that his account was true because he attended to the relations between events and ideas. He disclaimed the grander Romantic ambitions but his approach none the less involved a broad metaphysical underpinning: Providence was invoked and historical change was declared meaningful when judged in relation to the development of reason, truth and justice. Guizot's key concept for understanding history was civilisation. However, civilisation was itself a totalising concept which concili- ated seemingly opposing forces and energies within a higher syn- thesis or unity. Guizot's approach was rooted in his belief in universal reason. Historical reason revealed that reason was the essence of temporal reality.

In practice Guizot traced the roots of European civilisation to three elements: the Germanic idea of independence, the Christian sense of spiritual life and inwardness, and the Roman ideas of empire and municipal freedoms. The task of the historian was to describe how these discrete elements combined to produce modern Europe. Guizot never questioned European superiority or doubted the value of civilisation – we are a long way from Rousseau's critique. In large measure the fact of civilisation corresponded to the emergence of individual autonomy within a rational state. France is presented as lying at the heart of modern European values and culture. We learn that ideas originating in other countries usually underwent a second preparation within France before proceeding to fertilise European civilisation as a whole.[7] But what did Guizot mean by civilisation? He begins by stating bluntly that civilisation is a fact, complex but nevertheless amenable to investigation. However, it soon becomes apparent that civilisation differs from events, that it possesses an invisible reality. To study civilisation is to examine the underlying ideas which lend coherence to all aspects of social life. The historian of civilisation does not therefore narrate events; he looks for what he terms the general and hidden fact; what matters is the ideal content which is the truth of history: 'facts only have value in so far as they express truth, and tend to assimilate themselves more and more to the truth . . . all true greatness derives from thought . . . all fruitfulness belongs to it' (HCE, 114). The events of history form the outside, the envelope which surrounds the spirit of civilisation which constitutes the inside, the essential core. History is held to be rational and therefore amenable to rational interpretation. Specific events take on meaning when related to the leading ideas of each period. Civilisation inheres in the relationships, the interconnections which are uncovered by the historian.

Guizot once described the task of the historian as threefold. First, he resembled an anatomist dissecting the body of history, accumulating materials, isolating facts and events. Second, he acted like a physiologist describing how the organs of the body were related and what functions they fulfilled. Third, the historian aimed to represent the past as living reality, in a sense to restore and revitalise its physiognomy. In the last two elements we can see the Romantic spirit at work, transcending the more analytical ambitions of eighteenth-century scientific method. The analogy clearly had its limitations as far as the practice of history was concerned but it did at least suggest ways of conceiving the different dimensions of historical explanation. Guizot himself was concerned to understand events and processes by relating them to greater wholes but he also gave great attention to factual detail, to sources and documentary evidence. He was in his terms an anatomist and a physiologist. The historian might envy the formal order of abstract thought but could not escape the fact that historical truth was revealed successively and that his work had to reflect this temporal sequence. The historian could not simply align abstractions or describe ideal essences. His object of study was a process unfolding in time. The labour of the anatomist – an intervening subject operating on a lifeless object of study – could not be dispensed with. Indeed at this early stage of his investigation the historian could fairly be represented as doing violence to the body of history, depriving it of its vital being by dividing it up into its constitutent parts. At a later stage he would restore unity and life to the past but first he deprived it of the network of interconnections which constituted its being. We see this clearly in some remarks which Guizot made when treating the evolution of feudalism:

> I would like to follow in their totality the destinies of feudal-ism during these three centuries [tenth, eleventh and thir-teenth centuries]. I would not wish to divide it up, but keep it constantly under your eyes, and make you thus see its successive transformations at a single glance. This would be its true history, the only truthful image of the reality. Unfortunately, this cannot be. In order to study, the human mind is obliged to divide, to analyse; it only acquires knowl-edge successively and in pieces. It is then the work of imagin-ation and reason to reconstruct the demolished edifice, to resuscitate the being destroyed by the scientific scalpel. But it is absolutely necessary to pass through this process of dissection: such are the demands made by the weakness of the human mind.
>
> (*HCF*, IV, 142)

Guizot's work impresses as much by its rigour as by its sweep. The historian not only connects and analyses phenomena, he places a value upon them. There is in fact an Arnoldian ring to many of Guizot's pronouncements for, like the author of *Culture and Anarchy*, he understands civilisation in the broad sense as a moral force, as a humanising power which brings the inward moral and spiritual development of the individual into harmony with the forms of social and collective life. Guizot holds that the history of civilisation can be studied from two distinct but closely related perspectives. The first gives priority to the individual and to the development of the intellect and the inner life. The second privileges human interaction and social life. Guizot considers that his own histories adopt the second, socially oriented approach. At the same time he recognises that the two processes are in fact closely entwined. He observes that Christianity, which began with a concern for the inner, spiritual life, led over time to a transform-ation of man's social condition. In reality 'the inward is reformed by the outward, as the outward by the inward' (*HCE*, 67–8); in other words Guizot stresses the interdependence of individual and social reality and views the twin tracks of development as strug-gling through time to effect reconciliation and harmony: 'the two

elements of civilisation are closely bound one to the other...
sooner or later they will rejoin each other; that is the law of their
nature, the general fact of history, the instinctive belief of the
human race' (HCE, 68). Most important is the primacy which
Guizot consistently ascribes to mind which is the force which
ultimately constructs social reality:

> whatever the external events, it is man himself who makes
> the world; it is in proportion to the ideas, the feelings, and
> the moral and intellectual dispositions of man, that the world
> becomes regulated and advances; it is upon the inner con-
> dition of man that the visible condition of society depends.
>
> (HCE, 104)

Civilisation includes religion, art and philosophy but it also
encompasses commerce, industry and material well-being. The
historian of civilisation has ambitions which extend beyond those
of a Bossuet or a Montesquieu, since, rather than focus exclusively
on either the religious or the political dimension of history, his
intention is to include the full range of human activities.[8] For
Guizot this breadth is necessary if we want to grasp the general
truths which underlie social existence. Instead of composing separate political, literary, legal or religious histories the student of
civilisation aspires to synthesis, to a perspective which unifies
these different fields, seizing them 'at one glance, in their intimate
and fertile union' (HCF, III, 137). The new history reveals unity
in variety, identity in difference: '[the history of civilisation] is
the summary of all histories; it needs all of them as materials, for
the fact that it relates is the summary of all the facts' (HCF, III,
137). At first sight the history of civilisation strikes us as an
impossible task since its achievement would involve the amassing
of an endless amount of data. However, the historian's task is in
fact more manageable than this suggests because his concern lies
with the modes of expression of the central idea of civilisation
rather than with the totality of its manifestations across the full
range of individual and social practices.

The diverse elements which make up civilisation are presented
as constituting a positive richness, a richness which Guizot sees
mirrored in the different European national traditions. He considers that Europe's contrasting forms of social and religious
organisation should not be taken as signs of an absence of unity;
on the contrary, this very diversity and complexity form

distinguishing features, marking Europe off from earlier civilisations. He claims for example that in ancient Egypt a single governing principle had informed all aspects of individual and collective life and that social unity had been enforced by coercion; in Europe, on the other hand, diversity signalled not a disruptive disunity but a healthy variety of social experiences which allowed freedom to develop. In fact Guizot defines civilisation as intrinsically progressive in nature: 'The idea of progress, of development, appears to me to be the fundamental idea contained in the word, *civilisation*' (*HCE*, 62). The historian of civilisation studies the progressive actualisation of principles. Since civilisation designates a process and not a state and since Europe alone displays real progress we should perhaps conclude that, in this sense, only Europe is truly civilised. One consequence of this valorisation of change is that while in theory civilisation is held to thrive in times of peace, in practice conflict and division are viewed as agents of improvement. Hence Guizot's view of class conflict:

> Modern Europe was born from the struggle of the various classes of society. . . . Neither of the classes has been able to conquer or subdue the others; the struggle, instead of becoming a principle of immobility, has been a cause of progress; the relations of the various classes among themselves, the necessity in which they found themselves of fighting and yielding by turns, the variety of their interests and their passions, the desire to defeat one another without managing to do so; from all this arose perhaps the most energetic and fertile principle of the development of European civilisation.
>
> (*HCE*, 182)

In his *Histoire de la civilisation en Europe* and in the five volumes of his *Histoire de la civilisation en France* Guizot traced the development of the processes by which tensions and oppositions resolved themselves into both national consciousness and European civilisation. European civilisation corresponded to the working out over the centuries of the consequences of political ideas, the actualisation of the principles of aristocracy, monarchy and democracy. History was progressive but its movement was impelled by crises such as the Reformation or the Revolution. The history of the nations which make up Europe was divided into three main stages. First, the condition of confusion consequent upon the fall of the Roman Empire; second, feudalism and the conflicts between church and state, between municipal and royal authority; third, the modern challenge to absolutism in religion and politics, from the Reformation to the French Revolution. Justice and reason are not necessarily overtly formulated as the goals of human conduct; they may be the unintended consequences of individual actions or social processes. The philosophical historian, however, holds the key to meaning for he can recognise which changes are meaningful. He knows that while man is intelligent and free he is simultaneously involved in the execution of a providential design. This knowledge is deemed necessary if we want to arrive at a true account of past events. In fact the historian seems to want to occupy the perspective of God in order to disclose the hidden continuities which lie behind events, thus rendering them intelligible and meaningful.

It was axiomatic for Guizot that progress exists and is a good. History leads in effect to the triumph of the principles of Enlightenment liberalism. Indeed it was in this spirit that Guizot addressed his listeners: 'Let us attach ourselves firmly, faithfully, to the principles of our civilisation – justice, legality, publicity, liberty' (HCE, 72). To trace the development of European civilisation was to describe the advance of mind, rationality, unity, justice and order. Unhesitatingly Guizot ascribed divine legitimacy to this process: 'European civilisation has entered, if I may so express myself, into the eternal truth, into the plan of Providence; it advances according to the ways of God. This is the rational principle of its superiority' (HCE, 78). Guizot's approach was that of the philosophical historian who recognised that knowing the past in anything other than a superficial manner required the exploration of a deeper level of causation; simply to trace events to their immediate and direct causes was to be unfaithful to the idea of the development of reason. The internal relations which make up the life of a civilisation could only be grasped once the ideal content of history had been privileged. On the other hand the historical reason which invested change with meaning itself occupied a vantage point whose legitimacy rested upon the truth of the process which it was investigating. The element of circularity could not be disguised. Moreover, Guizot did at times lend an air of inevitability to his analysis as when, like Saint-Simon, he alluded to the general course of events or suggested that despotism, like anarchy, in the end served the cause of progress. The movement of history was progressive and purposive. The great men who imposed their authority on events were those, such as Charlemagne or Napoleon, who understood the general needs of their society and directed collective energies towards their actualisation. Such figures fell from grace when private and arbitrary goals replaced their concern for collective destiny (*HCF*, II, 199–201). Here Guizot was close to the Hegelian or Cousinian notion of the world–historical individual which Quinet too found deeply attractive. However, he did not give the impression that historical facts should be seen merely as contingent manifestations of the life of Spirit.

Guizot's lectures of the late 1820s recovered the meaning of the past. They also – and much more than is usually recognised – looked forward to the future, at times adopting the rhetoric of renewal and transformation.[9] The study of civilisation does not emerge as an entirely disinterested, scholarly activity. It had more immediate consequences: 'intellectual development today cannot, must not remain an isolated fact; we are required to derive from it, for our country, new means of civilisation, for ourselves, a moral regeneration' (*HCF*, 1, 27). Truth needed to be actualised as virtue and embodied in concrete reality. Increasing knowledge needed to be distributed throughout society 'in the form of beliefs capable of inspiring us with disinterestedness and moral energy' (*HCF*, I, 27). This is, however, all rather vague. What Guizot seemed to be doing was looking forward to a society which would fully realise the mobile and complex unity which was the defining characteristic of modernity but which would equally exhibit a principle of organisation promoting both individual freedom and association. In other words Guizot offered a variation on the Romantic aspiration to intellectual synthesis and social unity.

In the first instance Guizot presented human freedom as unconditioned, as independent of external and internal determinations. He distinguished between the mental processes, the deliberations which precede a free act, and the act itself:

When the deliberation has taken place, when man has taken full cognisance of the motives which present themselves to him, and of their value, at that moment there arises a completely new fact, quite different, the fact of liberty; man makes a resolution, that is to say he begins a series of facts which take their origin in him and of which he considers himself to be the author, these facts arise because he wishes it, and would not arise unless he willed them, and would be different if he wished to produce them differently.

(*HCF*, I, 134)

The free act thus emerged as ontologically pure. The individual was responsible for his actions. The ego perceived itself as a cause. However, when exercising his free will the individual remained subject to the moral law. Religious sentiment, according to Guizot, was the power which made men aware of their weakness and insufficiency. In practice freedom was not unlimited because men inhabited a moral world of intersubjectivity. If the twin perils of tyranny and anarchy were to be successfully avoided, then a general truth was required. Common assent to this general truth constituted the social bond: 'If there is a right of enquiry for individual reason, it nevertheless remains subordinate to that general reason which serves as a measure, as a touchstone for all minds' (*HCF*, I, 329). For Guizot it was axiomatic that the meaning of history lay in the growth of individual freedom, moral autonomy and self-consciousness. What was the history of civilisation if not the story of the emergence of a world modelled by reason? According to Guizot the purpose of social progress was the creation of the conditions in which individual freedom would develop and flourish: 'The progress of society consists above all in changing man himself, in rendering him capable of being free, of governing himself according to reason' (*HCF*, I, 266). The problem was how to co-ordinate the world of self-aware subjective freedom with the social domain. On the one hand Guizot rejected the traditionalist view that the individual only had genuine reality when conceived as an element in a social group. On the other he needed to escape from a self-enclosed individualism. He does this by ascribing priority to the growth of rationality which he relates to willed human activity. Man is more than the product of external sensations. He is charged with what Guizot himself called a mission:

we feel ourselves called upon to reform, perfect, regulate that which is: we feel ourselves capable of acting upon the world, of extending within the world the glorious empire of reason. This is the mission of man: as spectator, he is subject to facts; as actor, he takes possession of them, and impresses upon them a more regular, purer form.

(*HCF*, I, 23)

Mind is as an active force intended to transform reality. However, the success of the process could not be assured since human beings had the power to misuse their freedom. The problem for modern philosophy was that its espousal of individual freedom excluded the traditional notion of a religious authority whose function was to ensure conformity to social norms. As a believer Guizot could rely upon the promptings of conscience and the resources of his Christian faith. However, he did not rule out the possibility that a more general reorganisation of attitudes and beliefs might be required. He envisaged further developments of civilisation which would reconcile the development of subjective freedom with the need for order in social relations:

> Henceforward the development of civilisation must be accomplished under the influence of a two-fold faith, a two-fold respect; universal reason will be sought as the supreme law and final goal; individual reason will be free and incited to develop, as the best means of attaining to universal reason.
>
> (*HCF*, I, 330)

Guizot's exploration of the European past amounted to an attempt to describe the slow emergence of stable and unified states. He covered much of the same ground in a number of works, concentrating most of his attention on the cases of France and England. His prime aim was to explain why France had not produced representative institutions on the English model. By implication, his historical argument also provided a yardstick by which to measure the usefulness of the English analogy for French politics. Considerable space was devoted to a reappraisal of the period from the fall of the Roman Empire to the tenth century. Ever alive to the manner in which a theory of national origins could be used to legitimate political doctrine, Guizot was unhappy with the manner in which earlier theorists had turned to pre-feudal France when seeking a historical justification for their views. Guizot discounted the three main currents of historical explanation loosely inherited from the eighteenth century: Henri de Boulainvilliers (1658–1722) had produced a history which sought to legitimate aristocratic rights and privileges by reference back to the Frankish conquest; Jean-Baptiste Dubos (1670–1742) had composed a royalist version of the past according to which the power of the monarchy derived from the Roman Empire;

Mably had discovered in the Dark Ages the embryo of free institutions.[10]

Guizot dismissed all three theories as intellectually unsophisticated and politically motivated.[11] In his view the evidence led to a different conclusion. He denied that there had existed an enduring form of organised society prior to the emergence of the feudal system. The period from the fifth to the tenth centuries could best be envisaged as a time of transition, as a form of non-society out of whose conflicting elements feudalism eventually emerged. Guizot emphasised the otherness of this pre-feudal world, characterised by instability and the absence of community. In his view the barbarian invasions ushered in five centuries of disorder and anarchy (the only real exception being Charlemagne's attempt to consolidate authority). Guizot consistently presented his readers with the picture of a scattered population, dispersed across the land, no longer united by proximity and tribal ties. This was a world of antagonistic individualism. France was then a collection of local despotisms and different jurisdictions. Might was right and individual interest excluded collective interest. General social cohesion had been lost. Neither church nor monarchy was sufficiently powerful to act as a unifying factor. Guizot accepted the general idea of Germanic freedoms – often employed to depict the Franks as a body of free individuals, meeting in assemblies and choosing their chiefs – but he contended that this form of social organisation disintegrated once the invaders ceased to form marauding bands and colonised the territory which was to become France. The energy of the earlier barbarian freedom was rapidly lost, or more accurately it came to be used to promote individual and family interests alone. Guizot's position was thus at odds with that adopted by Montesquieu who, in *L'Esprit des lois*, had tried to locate the origin of representative institutions in Germanic freedoms. But neither did Guizot – at least in his early essays – advance strong arguments in favour of the survival of the Roman tradition of law and municipal government. (His view in his *Essais sur l'histoire de France* (1823) was that among the Gallo-Roman population the middle classes had lost effective power by becoming mere agents for the despotic central authority of Rome.) Furthermore, Guizot played down the importance of racial factors, arguing that by the tenth century the Franks and Gauls could no longer be distinguished and that French territory was occupied by contending aristocratic despotisms. Guizot recognised that barbarian freedom was essential to the western tradition of liberty, but he refused to view it as a unique, definable origin. It formed an element within the spirit of European civilisation. In his view the barbarians appreciated neither the true value of freedom nor the need for individual wills to act in concert and according to a principle of rationality. Prior to the tenth century the inhabitants of France lacked any shared institutional framework. Feudalism imposed itself precisely because it did provide such an institutional structure, a pattern of rights and obligations which gave to isolated individuals the sense of belonging to a common entity. Feudalism unified, organised and stabilised the population. However – and this was the crux of the matter for Guizot – the establishment of feudal society was less an achievement of equilibrium than the mechanism which enabled other struggles to begin. Feudalism, we are told, was endured but not accepted: from the outset it was contested by the Crown's desire for supremacy and by the people's struggle to extend their rights. Guizot described feudalism as vitiated by the absence of a collective, public dimension. Instead of growing into a broader association, members of the feudal hierarchy pursued their own interests, each oppressing his own population. Feudalism merely consolidated local power. What was lacking was 'a superior force' which would transcend local interests and put an end to the 'division of society and of power' (*EHF*, 433). In the end the Crown became the unifying force, advancing the cause of equality but at the expense of political freedoms.

It is at this point that the English example became of vital importance as a point of comparison. Why was it that in England the turbulent transition from feudalism to representative institutions had been successfully achieved whereas in France the Third Estate created modern society but was unable to enforce social order or establish social cohesion? Guizot's response was to describe at length how English institutions grew out of a substantially different historical matrix and reflected a different collective psychology. The key date was of course 1066. However, Guizot was reticent about making too much of the Saxon–Norman conflict in so far as in his judgement it was the unfolding interplay of historical forces rather than the power of inherited characteristics which moulded national character. He took care, for example, to distance himself from the enabling myths about the Norman yoke which had currency in nineteenth-century England. He accepted that the germs of later English institutions were present in Anglo-Saxon society before the Conquest (for example in the form of the Witenagemot) but he was hesitant about lending too much importance to such prefigurations. He began by contrasting eleventh-century England with fifth-century France. He reminded us that the Normans were not primitive barbarian tribesmen overcoming by force an alien culture. They invaded and occupied a country which already contained proto-feudal elements and they brought with them to England a sense of social organisation and central authority. Initially the mutual hostility felt by Normans and Saxons served to reinforce their opposing cultural identities. The Saxons made their indigenous traditions a rallying point; the Normans on their side used feudalism as a unifying doctrine. However, a sense of national unity slowly developed. English history, in any meaningful sense, began after the Conquest.

Guizot observed that the English nobles were less divided than their counterparts in France and were thus better equipped to resist the extension of the authority of the Crown. And among the English nobility he detected a growing awareness of the collective interest, a development of national settlement which found expression in the Magna Carta (*EHF*, 351). In France the feudal ethos persisted more strongly and the centralisation of power followed a different path. Guizot pointed to another area of significant difference when he examined the development of municipal freedoms. He contended that whereas in France the period from the tenth to the fourteenth centuries was characterised by inconclusive struggles between municipalities and feudal lords, in England institutions evolved which gave protection to rights and encouraged a growing participation of the middle class in the affairs of state. This process was well advanced by the early fourteenth century. Diverse interests were represented in parliament and participated with the king in the activity of government. Parliament acted in the name of the common interest and its authority, so Guizot claimed, emanated from the country at large (*EHF*, 376). The picture which Guizot was painting was clear enough: by the fourteenth century England, unlike France, was becoming a more homogeneous, inclusive culture with a sense of national identity and common purpose.[12]

In Guizot's view the meaning of European history lay in the development of national unity, individual rights and legal equality. Moral and intellectual progress accompanied this movement. Class conflict also served this end and was not to be viewed merely in restricted terms as the expression of sectional interest. However, the interlocking tensions between nobility, middle class and Crown operated differently within individual national cultures (although the presumed end of the process – the replacement of feudal privilege by equality before the law – was held to be a unifying, common goal). Political arrangements needed to be understood in relation to the broader perspective of cultural history. We have noted the attention which Guizot paid to English medieval history. He devoted even more time and effort to exploring the Civil War period. In 1823–5 he opened up this area for serious academic enquiry in France by publishing twenty-five volumes of documents, the *Collection des mémoires relatifs à la Révolution d'Angleterre*. This was followed in later years by a series of volumes of narrative history devoted to the Civil War and its causes.

However, the question underlying this vast enterprise was made explicit in an essay which Guizot published in the wake of the events of 1848: *Pourquoi la Révolution d'Angleterre a-t-elle réussi?* (1850). What could be learnt from the English experience which might explain why the French Revolution had not led to an equally satisfactory outcome? The points of similarity between the two events were plain to see. In both countries transgressive acts of collective violence were undertaken in order to rid society of absolutism and install a regime grounded in justice and right. In both countries – according to Guizot – the process of change was initiated at a historical moment when the forces traditionally at work in the organisation of national life (the monarchy, the nobility and the clergy) were weakened. In both cases the initial impulse to increase individual freedoms gave way to authoritarian rule and the curtailment of rights. The major difference was that whereas the French Revolution was a political revolution arising within the secular culture of the Enlightenment, the English Revolution was a religious as well as political movement. In England the assertion of individual rights was accompanied by claims for spiritual autonomy which made political gains more secure. Of equal significance was the fact that the English Revolution occurred within the wider cultural formation and political structure which I have been describing above. In England parliament was a national institution, sensitive to collective needs and desires, and when it resisted the absolutist tendencies of royal authority in 1640 this resistance took the form of a reference back to ancient rights. Unlike France in 1789, England did not deny the past in order to invent a new pattern of social relations. The English were protected by their sense of history which put a brake on extremist political parties. The Glorious Revolution inaugurated a return to peace, stability and social cohesion – Guizot had no time for the argument that beneath the surface the settlement of 1688 amounted to a reassertion of traditional, aristocratic influence. To his mind 1688 marked the realisation of the constitutional monarchy towards which England had been moving since 1640.

England survived its Revolution and prospered under a constitutional monarchy which represented an outgrowth of national history. The French Revolution, on the other hand, repudiated the national past in order to overcome feudalism and absolutism. Guizot's argument followed the line taken by Thierry: in the absence of a historical point of anchorage the revolutionaries took refuge in abstractions and in due course the despotic and absolutist character of the Ancien Régime returned in the guise of the revolutionary republic. England could rely on collective traditions, on patterns of conduct, on the reference to historical rights. In France the passions of social and civil conflict were such that the torn fabric of society could not be mended. The individual was left standing alone in the face of revolutionary despotism. The society which invented the modern idea of revolution lacked the English awareness of the need for power to be limited by checks and balances as it was deficient in the American sense of national unity and purpose. But in Guizot's eyes these handicaps were part of the nature of things, the inheritance of preceding centuries. Clearly the French could not simply emulate the English example. On the other hand, Guizot was far from indicating that the French Revolution was inferior to the English Revolution. Whereas in his studies of England he drew attention to the increasing homogeneity of medieval society and contrasted this with the greater disunity present in France, when he shifted the focus to his own nation he adopted a new stance. Instead of lamenting the lack of stability he praised the unique contribution made by the Third Estate in challenging and eventually overturning the established order.

France in 1789 is represented as carrying further than any other nation the European-wide movement towards legal equality and individual rights. We are told that in France alone did the Third Estate reach its fullest development. Indeed at one moment Guizot comments that only in France was there truly a Third Estate. To substantiate his argument he adopted and refined Thierry's theories on the importance of the communal movement, arguing that the decline of the Communes did not hinder the rise of the Third Estate since its members went on to serve in the administration of the centralised monarchy. (Unlike some liberals – the historian Prosper de Barante, for example – Guizot was no defender of localism and never hankered after lost provincial authority.) He showed how the Third Estate and its values came to dominate national life and proclaimed that nowhere else in the world was there an equivalent example of a social class rising and finally becoming so dominant that it became identified with the country itself. In political terms the Third Estate of 1789 was declared to be 'the descendant and heir of the Communes of the twelfth century' (*HCE*, 173). In this way Guizot, like Thierry, established the historical legitimacy of 1789 and political liberalism. The present was securely bound to a newly rediscovered and reordered past. But Guizot still had to deal with the consequences of 1789. After all, the identification of the Third Estate with the nation did not inaugurate a homogeneous, peaceful community. The national self remained divided.

The Revolution of 1830 and the accession to the throne of Louis-Philippe appeared to confirm Guizot's theory of history. Surely here was a re-enactment of 1688. The House of Orleans replaced the Bourbons as the House of Orange had replaced the Stuarts. Guizot endorsed the new regime and was not overly concerned by the fact that the transition was brought about by insurrection and violence. In 1830, he later observed, the middle classes were 'called upon to found a new monarchy' (*DF*, 94). For Guizot, as for Thierry, the new regime seemed to mark the culmination of history. The king embodied the authority of tradition but effective power passed to the middle classes and was exercised through representative institutions. Of course Guizot did not consider that everything was perfect once the new government was in place. The Lyon rising, popular disturbances and social antagonisms demonstrated that the implementation of the new order had not stabilised French society. Nevertheless, Guizot was clearly fortified by his knowledge that France's destiny was now in the hands of the middle class, an enlightened elite which understood the inscription of reason in history. He remained confident that constitutional monarchy joined with limited suffrage provided France with the best form of organisation. As time showed, he underestimated the class divisions consequent upon increasing industrialism and failed to appreciate either the persistence of the revolutionary tradition or the weight of support behind electoral reform.

The events of 1848 finally demonstrated that Guizot's attempt to portray the middle class as an essentially open social formation progressively extending its influence and creating a national culture of moderation did not correspond to French reality. The Revolution of February 1848 forced Guizot, like his king, to seek refuge in England. In exile he wrote an angry and bitter pamphlet, *De la démocratie en France*, in which he denounced democracy as the destructive passion of modern societies, inimical to all forms of social order. Democracy was weak government, it had a dangerous taste for experiment and social engineering. Its spurious slogans disguised an absence of thought, a reluctance to determine the conditions within which real freedoms were possible. At times Guizot struck a more Tocquevillian note emphasising the need to guide and direct the democratic temper of modern states. However, his aversion to popular sovereignty was usually uppermost. In the communism and socialism of the 1840s he detected an 'idolatrous enthusiasm for humanity' (*DF*, 134) which confined human beings within a this-worldy future and left them without any access to the divine. He charged the promoters of the new social theories with reviving the catastrophic enthusiasm for humankind which had characterised the radical leaders of the French Revolution. Guizot was no longer interested in purifying the inheritance of the Revolution in order to preserve what was worthwhile. His main priority was the defence of private property and the bourgeois family against Proudhonian socialism which he accused of destroying communality and eroding the ties which bound individuals to a collective past. Like Thierry he had discovered to his cost that the historian's mastery of the past did not provide him with the gift of foresight. Guizot had been at his most productive during the Restoration, at the period when, while wishing to stabilise the conflicting traditions within French society, he located this resolution in the future. Although 1830 seemed to confirm his understanding of history, it led to an impoverishment of his thought which, as Pierre Rosanvallon has noted, became increasingly moralising in tone, especially after 1840. Instead of articulating an imaginative response to France's condition, he propounded a conservatism which amounted to an immobilism. *De la démocratie en France* was a poor piece of writing, ill-tempered and replete with the clichés of a resentful conservatism. Instead of developing historical analyses Guizot turned to explanations of human conduct in terms of moral evil, explanations which were validated by a view of man's fallen nature.

Theological concerns predominated in his writings after 1851. He brought out a series of dry, austere works which included three volumes of *Méditations* on the Christian religion and a biography of Calvin. Rather than pick up the threads of his study of European civilisation he revised and expanded the more theologically oriented of his earlier writings, devoting his still impressive intellectual energies to matters of Christian doctrine and Protestant theology. It was an age marked by important religious controversies. One only has to think of the impact of Ernest Renan in France or of Matthew Arnold in Britain. Guizot, however, was not following fashion. He had arrived at a conservatism which could only adequately be expressed in theological terms. But if the emphasis on theology seemed to have displaced the focus on history we should not conclude that Guizot had abandoned his general interpretation of the historical process. He retained his belief in progress, moral and material; he stood by his commitment to representative government. What appalled the older Guizot was the realisation that his contemporaries had not learned from the mistakes of 1789. Socialists still held to the view that man was sufficient unto himself, and that evil arose out of the imperfections of society (*MEM*, 5–7). In belligerent mood Guizot described the revolutionary spirit as Satan in human form, at once sceptical and fanatical (*MEM*, xvi). Only Christianity – Protestant or Catholic – offered a bulwark against the rising revolutionary tide. In his view the very idea of Christian democratic socialism was absurd, a contradiction in terms. Revolutions, opined Guizot in 1864, were profoundly imperfect and impure even when they were ultimately salutary (*TG*, 52). However, Guizot did not side with the Counter-Revolution. In his eyes the Reformation remained a just insurrection of the human spirit against absolute authority and the English and French Revolutions continued to be viewed as attempts to actualise freedom. What worried Guizot were unreasonable hopes and expectations, utopias which inflamed the passions of the masses with an excessive desire for change. Rights and freedoms had to be protected from the unprincipled passions of revolutionaries. Guizot held firmly to the idea of immortality, to the conviction that the destiny of the human individual was not completed on this earth (*MEM*, 90–131). He had an instinctive faith in the existence of a supernatural order. However, his commitment to the centrality of the idea of personal salvation was never at odds with his belief in the social and moral dimensions of religious experience. Religion, he observed, offered humankind 'a powerful and fertile principle of association' (*HCE*, 134). But if religion defined the social world this was as an organising power, a unifying force which placed necessary restraints upon the exercise of human freedom:

> [Religion] aspires to govern the human passions, the human will. All religion is a restraint, a power, a government. It comes, in the name of divine law, in order to tame human nature. It is human freedom, then, with which it chiefly concerns itself; it is human freedom which resists religion, and which religion wishes to overcome.
>
> (*HCE*, 161)

In the 1850s and 1860s Guizot reaffirmed this view that the task of religion lay in the controlling of human passions. He had never been naïvely overconfident in human goodness but he had hoped that 1830 would produce an enduring stability, a redistribution of political and institutional power in such a way as to banish any possibility of further revolution. His view of history linked progress with order, with the emergence of new forms of social organisation. By turning increasingly to theology and condemning socialism Guizot was trying to halt a movement which to his mind represented not progress but a repetition of the errors of the French Revolution. Theology was not an alternative to history since, as we have seen, Guizot's underlying religious views always conditioned the perspective from which he judged the collective European advance to greater intellectual and moral freedom. What was lacking from his later writing was a perspective on the future. Theology did not deny history but it seemed only able to offer the prospect of immortality joined with arguments which resisted change. Guizot held to his political beliefs – only an enduring liberal government was capable of reconciling opposing forces, encouraging moderation and avoiding renewed revolutionary dislocation – but the reader of his works notes that this ideal future had already been actualised, between 1830 and 1848, and found wanting.

Guizot envisaged history in terms of the cumulative realisation of individual rights and freedoms. European history was, in political terms, a movement away from arbitrary power to a form of representative government. Civilisation was the mediating concept which allowed Guizot to pass from liberal individualism to a recognition of collective value. Guizot's approach recognised the insufficiency of the model of human conduct proposed by strict utilitarianism. He opposed antagonistic, self-interested individualism. He considered instead that in order to be creative, freedom needed to operate within a shared world of ideas and values. The individual was impoverished if he was regarded as an isolated self, inhabiting a self-enclosed point in time and space. Guizot brought individual and society together in such a way as to suggest that in order to be truly himself, to experience the fullness of his being, the individual needed to transcend present reality and participate in a process of exchange involving self and world, self and other.[13] Human beings lived individual and social existences but the two were, as we have seen, intimately related. Participation in social life extended beyond normal daily interaction to include a process of sympathetic understanding and imaginative identification:

> the social life of each man is not concentrated in the material space which is its theatre or in the fleeting moment; it extends to all the relations that he has contracted upon different points of the country; and not only to those relations that he can contract or merely might conceive of contracting; it embraces not only the present, but the future; man lives on a thousand spots which he does not inhabit, in a thousand moments which do not yet exist; and if this development of his life is removed from him, if he is forced to confine himself within the narrow limits of his present material existence, to isolate himself in space and time, social life is mutilated and society is no more.
>
> (HCF, I, 228)

As these lines show, Guizot shared the Romantics' sense of the self as part of a greater whole, as implicated within a set of relations extending beyond other selves and the external world to include potential, possible realities. The lectures delivered during the Restoration reveal an orientation towards an idea of the future conceived as an extension of the authentic spirit of civilisation. The future world would entrench the legitimate claims of the critical intelligence but at the same time promote a belief system which fostered the spirit of association. Guizot, however, offered no blueprint for a perfect society. He always recognised that freedom of choice meant that men could choose wrongly. Hence the need for collaboration and discussion. Constitutional monarchy was Guizot's favoured form of political organisation because, by encouraging compromise and negotiation, it offered an opportunity to bring together individual needs and collective purpose. Guizot eschewed the idea of indefinite, necessary progress. The dream of absolute equality held no more attraction for him than did the utopia of the rehabilitation of the flesh. His interpretation of history certainly lent particular significance to France's contribution, but his overarching conception of European civilisation distanced his formulations from the prophetic utterances and messianic pronouncements of those such as Quinet, who made bold, uncompromising assertions of national destiny. His prose contained a large measure of austerity and he felt a distinct distaste for Michelet's expansive, lyrical identification of the movement of history with the mission of revolutionary France. At the same time Guizot had a strong sense of national identity and a firm belief in France as the agent for the actualisation of essential freedoms – after all, the rise of the Third Estate coincided with the general project of human emancipation. However, while republican history possessed a clear, nationalistic conception of the good, Guizot insisted on the need for a framework of legality.

Although he viewed the Revolution as an essential fact it did not become for him a grand sustaining myth. The lesson of history was a different one: a workable compromise had to be established between the new France and the old. The revolutionaries' attempt to suppress the Ancien Régime by eliminating collective memory had failed. Guizot showed that it was wrong to belittle the past. He was open to different values and he demonstrated how the meaning of the past could be recovered and used in support of the idea of freedom. His understanding of the development of the Third Estate can be viewed as a history of fulfilment since the suffering of the oppressed was ultimately justified by the conclusion of the process. However, in his reordering of the flux of human affairs Guizot generally avoided the language of religion and the sacrilisation of history. Human beings inhabited history, made history, but Guizot held to his belief that salvation and redemption were essentially matters of personal rather than collective destiny. In his mind history and nature both displayed a divinely instituted order but he did not seek to present nature as the objectivisation of Spirit or history as God's journey to self-knowledge.

Whereas Victor Cousin's Hegelian view of history led to an amoral optimism, Guizot urged the claims of morality. He would certainly have repudiated any idea of the future in which the conflicts between individual and society would be resolved by suppressing individuality and by attributing authority to a metaphysical general will. There would be no philosophical dismantling of the concept of selfhood, no assertion of the illusory nature of individuality. As we have seen, Guizot's hope was that tensions would be reduced in a France equipped with a constitutional monarch and proper representative institutions. Such a society would depend upon restraint and co-operation but the expectation was that a balance of interests would emerge. Such was the position of the theorist of the *juste milieu*.[14] Guizot wanted change – but not too much; political rights – but not for all; respect for the past – but not an uncritical admiration for tradition; acceptance of the centrality of religion – but not reverence for an unchanging theocratic ideal.

Guizot doubtless considered his vision of the future – essentially one of unity without uniformity – as an advance of civilisation, as an increase in the power of mind and freedom. On one level civilisation emerges as the other of passion, of instinct, of violence; it involves negotiation and peaceful transactions. But on another level we are obliged to recognise that the goals of disinterestedness and moderation are to be pursued with passion and commitment. Civilisation was reason but it was also desire; the energy of the barbarians was a necessary component of the idea of freedom – but such force needed to be controlled and directed, for in certain circumstances freedom could become destructive of the public good. What Guizot feared most was the febrile, unpredictable nature of revolutions. Avoidance of revolution was the prerequisite for the building of civilisation. Guizot aspired to a unified but complex society, a society which embodied the rationality disclosed by history. In his writing we do not see the unhappy consciousness hankering after a nostalgic return to oneness with nature and the circulation of universal life. Guizot did not seek to ground his concept of culture in nature, in geography, as did Quinet and Cousin. Neither did he explain the phenomenon of civilisation in economic or racial terms. Civilisation had to do with the transformative power of mind, with human reason imposing order and regularity upon the external world. The self as reason recognised that its nature was embodied in civilised forms of society as it recognised that the same activity of reason was at work in the shapes and patterns of historical change. Civilisation was at once the moving force behind events and the goal of history.

The recovery of the national past by the liberal historians was also the recovery of the idea of the Revolution as the outcome, albeit unfortunate in its final execution, of the concealed designs of Providence. The problem for Guizot – as for Thierry – was that while it was possible to describe the movement of European history as an unfolding process, 1789 inaugurated not fulfilment but a perverted, corrupt consummation. Neither 1793 nor Napoleon corresponded to the realisation of reason.[15] Reason and reality had yet to be fully united in the form of representative institutions and legal equality. The constitutional government which came into being after 1789 died in the Terror. The balance of forces governing France after 1815 was unstable. Hence Guizot's desire to purify the Revolution, to restore the promise of its original impulse. But did this mean that history was reversible, that the desired consummation could be retrieved? Did this imply that the act of writing history might somehow alter the status of the revolutionary event and reactualise it, redeploy it as an ambiguous new beginning? The historian demonstrated that within his discourse order and progress, rights and obligations could be reconciled. Guizot's argument suggested that the civilisation of the future would contain within itself, would hold within the confines of a united but complex social formation, the contradictory forces which move history – but would hold them in equilibrium. The task of nineteenth-century politicians was to purify the revolutionary inheritance and implement a balanced compromise. The task of historians was likewise one of refining and purifying, of revealing the ideal meaning which unified events and bound people together. Historical reason was an organising, idealising power whose activity mirrored processes at work within social reality. The Revolution failed in its attempt to transform society by denying tradition; the liberal historian who restored historicity and community to culture at the same time revealed the particular challenges which faced France. Guizot's career exemplified the liberal historians' conviction that reconstructing the past was an inevitable part of rebuilding society.

4

The historical vision of Saint-Simon (1760–1825) and the Saint-Simonians (1825–1832)

The liberal historians produced an account of national history which made France both a moral agent and an instrument for the establishment of enlightened, representative government. History possessed meaning since the unfolding process was related to the inscription of reason. At the same time conflict between social groups or classes seemed to provide an operative model for understanding the mechanism of change. However, not everyone shared the liberals' optimistic evaluation of the future. Surveying the post-Napoleonic world, many became painfully aware of the loss of community and the atomisation of society. The impact of industrialism was of course central to this process, producing urbanisation and a breakdown in traditional structures. Economic liberalism – as articulated by Dunoyer and Say – claimed that unrestricted competition led to individual fulfilment. By the 1820s, however, it was becoming apparent that relentless competition and a night-watchman state did not ensure widespread happiness or social order. England already offered examples enough of the ravages caused by industrialism. In France Catholics of a traditional disposition perceived moral disarray, intellectual anarchy and the dissolution of the bonds which unconsciously united the members of society. They placed the blame squarely on the spirit of individualism and free enquiry inherited from the Reformation and embodied in eighteenth-century liberalism. In their mind political and economic liberalism were manifestations of the same spirit. Freedom of thought and of the press went hand in hand with the pursuit of self-interest in a new world dominated by market acquisitiveness. Liberalism, they felt, promoted an arrogant self-interest which threatened the traditional family and encouraged a social mobility which overturned power relations and hierarchies. Industry and the revolutionary idea seemed to them to go hand in hand. However, as we have seen in the Introduction, the Catholic recipe for reunifying society was essentially back-ward-looking, involving a reassertion of the values of an imagined past. The return to stability seemingly required a complete resto-ration of the principle of authority embodied in throne and altar. Catholicism felt that it alone could reforge the social bond and it stood for a paternalistic, anti-industrial, anti-technological society, rooted in the traditions of rural France.

This diagnosis of the problems of France struck a chord with a number of men of the 1820s who, although they did not share the faith of the Catholics or their prescriptions, recognised as a fallacy the idea that competition between individuals could pro-duce a harmonious society. The difficulty which they faced lay in reconciling the collective interest with individual freedom. Were traditionalists correct in asserting that the re-establishment of social cohesion necessarily required that the claims of freedom and selfhood be abandoned? Were progressivist and class-driven interpretations of history suddenly redundant? Was there no alter-native to relinquishing the modernising power of technological reason? The most significant non-Catholic intellectual response to the social crisis produced by industrialism and liberal individual-ism was made by the Saint-Simonians who gained a European audience for their ideas between 1825, when they came together in earnest to promote Saint-Simon's theories, and 1832 when the school, which by then had become a religious movement with a communal organisation, broke up in the wake of the successful prosecution of three of its leading figures – Prosper Enfantin, Charles Duveyrier and Michel Chevalier – on charges of offending against public morals.

The movement took as its slogan: 'To each according to his ability, to each ability according to its works.' The Saint-Simonians were shocked by the misery of the labouring classes. They repudiated liberalism's assertion that social harmony would result from contending individual interests. Their aim was to trans-fer power to a technological elite which would be charged with organising society and transforming nature in order to achieve communitarian goals. In their view political and economic liberal-ism alike produced social disintegration. They followed the tra-ditionalists in giving priority to society over the individual, and inveighed against the egoism of modern times, considering rights as abstract fictions and constitutions as a sham. However, their response to the crisis inaugurated by the introduction of industrial modes of production went far beyond the solutions proposed by Catholic philanthropy. They envisaged a new form of social relations, a new community whose members were joined together not so much as a political group but as workers and producers. The economic forces of modernity – banking and technology – were not to be rejected. On the contrary they were to be put to serve the collective good.

The followers of Saint-Simon considered that industrial develop-ment, correctly planned, would co-ordinate and not disrupt social relations, that industrial activity would promote an ideal of brotherhood as far removed from the heartless competition of liberalism as from the outdated claims of inherited privilege. The Saint-Simonians identified the problems faced by the atomised individual in modern society but instead of urging a return to the habits of the past they set about challenging traditional morality, particularly in the sphere of human sexuality (the theory of the rehabilitation of the flesh). They rejected the prohibitions inherited from the old religion and urged the development of industry. But – and here they demonstrated a disorienting leap of the imagin-ation – they simultaneously asserted the need for society's new guiding idea to be constituted as a principle of authority, as a fully-fledged religious doctrine. Moreover, the new faith required the full trappings of organised religion – ritual, liturgy and a priestly hierarchy. Hardly surprisingly, such attitudes profoundly offended many liberals.

History was an idea which stirred the emotions of the gener-ation of the 1820s.[1] Saint-Simonians and liberal historians possessed a similar generational mind-set: Augustin Thierry and Prosper Enfantin were both born in 1796. The mental horizons of the younger generation had been formed by the aftermath of the Revolution as opposed to the events themselves. As our discussion of Thierry has demonstrated, they struggled to deal not only with the political consequences of the Revolution but with its broader intellectual and cultural legacy: the nation-state as source of value and site of belonging, the importance of eighteenth-century critical thought for the post-1815 world. By turning to historical modes of explanation the men of the 1820s indicated their independence from their elders; they also signalled a generational solidarity which transcended many ideological boundaries. The Saint-Simonians came together as a group after Henri de Saint-Simon's death and their first joint manifestation was the publication of the journal *Le Producteur* (1825–6).[2] The original six main editors were P. Enfantin, Ph. Buchez, St.-A. Bazard, M. Rouen, P. M. Laurent and Olinde Rodrigues. At first they were somewhat reticent about declaring their allegiance to Saint-Simon's views and the journal set out to appeal to a broad section of the liberal opposition. When they did make clear where they stood a number of erstwhile supporters including Armand Carrel, Adolphe Blanqui and Félix Bodin withdrew. In its latter period the journal took up Saint-Simon's concern for the welfare of the masses and his call for a reawakening of the spirit of human brotherhood. Liberalism was subjected to critical evaluations. The Saint-Simonians were persuaded that liberalism encouraged a divided society made up of self-imprisoned individuals, consumed with egoism and unrelated to the collective. The restoration of community became a major concern. To the horror of conventional liberals – Benjamin Constant was alarmed by the journal's authoritarian streak – the *Producteur* argued that society needed order and a governing principle. Enfantin and Rouen took issue with Dunoyer and Charles Comte. The temper of the times was changing. Two years later the theories of the Saint-Simonians received their classic form in a series of lectures subsequently published under the title *Doctrine de Saint-Simon. Exposition. Première année. 1828–1829* (1830). This is a landmark text of nineteenth-century thought and most of my analysis will be based upon it. The lectures were delivered by Bazard but prepared by a group of major Saint-Simonian intellectuals which included Enfantin, Buchez, Hippolyte Carnot, Laurent, Margerin and the brothers Eugène and Olinde Rodrigues.[3]

An interpretation of history lay at the core of the new doctrine. By challenging the value of unlimited freedom of conscience the Saint-Simonians were also challenging the historical analysis which underpinned the liberals' claim to possess political legitimacy. Since the master–slave relationship was clearly not withering away in modern industrial society in the manner that Dunoyer had predicted, then perhaps the way in which liberals interpreted the dynamism of class conflict warranted revision. Were individual liberty and freedom of conscience after all the ends of history? The Saint-Simonians were not Idéologues engaged in a last-ditch battle against clerical reaction. It would be more accurate to say that many of their number had traversed scientific materialism but now wanted to unite their knowledge with a more spiritual, progressive view of history (without, however, collaborating with Cousinian rationalist idealism which they perceived as the intellectual underpinning of political liberalism). Saint-Simonianism grounded both its critique of traditional morality and its vision of the future in a reading of history. It articulated a vision of the historical process which took into account the impact of the French Revolution but which came to conclusions considerably at variance with those arrived at by liberals. History was called upon to endorse the conclusion that politics, as ordinarily conceived, was no longer able to order and unify social existence. The Saint-Simonians used the past to illuminate the future. Their priority – unlike republicans but in accord on this issue with liberals – was the avoidance of further instances of violent social change. However, in their case, the aim was not so much the stabilising of industrial capitalism as its replacement by a new and different set of communal values. In the eyes of the Saint-Simonians the study of the past both justified the critique of the old order and taught the form that the future organisation of society would take. History supported the idea of association, the offering up of negative selfhood to the collective in a spirit of love. History did more than authorise the Saint-Simonians' feeling that they were standing on the edge of a new era of renewal. It seemed to confirm their view that their new values needed to be expressed in the form of a religious idea and be embodied in a principle of authority.

The Saint-Simonians accorded their master the status of a modern messiah. For this reason, before directing our attention to the writings of the Saint-Simonians themselves, we need to take a preliminary look at the main aspects of Saint-Simon's own thought and establish how he viewed the nature of historical change. However, it should be said from the outset that the relationship between the Saint-Simonians and Saint-Simon is not without its problems – in fact it has become something of a scholarly minefield. Frank Manuel, the foremost authority on Saint-Simon, put the matter bluntly when he observed that Saint-Simon 'surely was not a Saint-Simonian'.[4] A fundamental difference of approach distinguished Saint-Simon's rationalist view of society from his disciples' desire to create a new religion in which feminism and pacifism combined with economic progress. Scholars

whose sympathies lie with Saint-Simon the revolutionary and athe-
ist have presented his disciples as religious eccentrics, political
reactionaries and dirigiste technocrats. However, a close reading
of Saint-Simon's works suggests that it is rather facile to presume
that he would have repudiated the views of his followers who in
effect gave substance to his guiding ideas of association and
terrestrial morality. This case has been cogently argued by the
best recent historian of the movement, Robert Carlisle.

At this point a further matter needs to be raised. This is the
charge of totalitarianism which has been levelled against both
Saint-Simon and the Saint-Simonian movement since the end of
the second World War. The Saint-Simonians have been denounced
as dangerous precursors of fascism and communism. They have
been accused of sacrificing the individual to the collectivity, of
denying freedom of thought, expression and enquiry, of transforming art into a channel for state propaganda, of curbing individual initiative in the name of central planning and state control.
These views were articulated with differing degrees of virulence
in the 1940s and 1950s by Friedrich A. Hayek and Georg Iggers.
Carlisle, however, argues that these judgements are too extreme,
that it is unfair to evaluate the contribution of Saint-Simon and
his disciples without giving proper weight to the social evils which
they were seeking to remedy. Also, the character of Saint-Simon's
writings needs to be borne in mind. While no one can deny that
there is a strong dash of authoritarianism in his output, any fair
assessment must recognise that consistency was not his strong
point. He often tailored his ambitious plans for social reform to
the nature of the regime currently in power. He was a prolific
writer whose ideas underwent a significant evolution and who
responded swiftly to the conditions created by a changing political
climate. Quotations can be found in his writings which support
quite contrasting views. The texts themselves are open to many
and varied interpretations. In fact, as Keith Taylor has observed,
Saint-Simon's thought was authoritarian rather than totalitarian in
the twentieth-century meaning of the term.[5] The illiberalism of
both master and disciples was a response to the lack of attention
which political liberalism paid to the sufferings occasioned by the
impact of industrialism. We should also perhaps recall that after
the break-up of the organised Saint-Simonian religion its leading
members found no difficulty in pursuing successful careers within
the France of the July Monarchy and the Second Empire as bank-

ers, administrators, organisers of public works projects, builders of canals and railways. A false picture of the Saint-Simonians is produced if they are demonised as forerunners of the command economy, centralised planning and state control. Their ideas need to be placed in context.

SAINT-SIMON

Saint-Simon's thought evolved but its roots remained firmly in the intellectual and political culture of the Enlightenment. He believed ardently in the power of human reason to improve the living conditions of all citizens provided that its operations were no longer impeded by religious prohibitions or metaphysical constraints. As a young man he served with Lafayette's forces in North America. He welcomed the French Revolution and had no regrets about the overthrow of the old order to which he belonged by birth. In his view it was a good thing that the privileges of what he considered the theological and feudal age had been destroyed. He played an active role in revolutionary politics, indulged without restraint in financial speculation and was imprisoned – probably by mistake – during the Terror. This last experience left him sceptical as to whether violent mass movements could produce much beyond social dislocation. He concluded that the revolutionary crisis could only successfully be brought to an end if society were reorganised around a new governing principle. In an outpouring of publications which continued despite periods of poverty and depression until his death in 1825 he advanced a variety of solutions. However, he was consistent in his underlying conviction that modern scientific method, free of any restraining religious sanctions, should be applied to the study of man in society. In the light of the results obtained, action was to be taken to improve the general welfare and happiness of the population. However, Saint-Simon departed from mainstream Enlightenment liberalism by believing in natural inequality. He followed Bichat's view that human beings could be classified by science into three main types, the brain type, those with the motor capacity and the men of sentiment. For Saint-Simon these types corresponded to divisions in society: a) scientists; b) workers; c) artists and men of religion.[6] Egalitarianism was an unsound idea which when put into practice compromised social cohesion. In his *Lettres d'un habitant de Genève à ses contemporains* (1802) he argued that

111

spiritual power in the modern world should rest with the scientists and temporal power with the property-owners. He proposed that a 'Council of Newton' be established, supported by subscription, a form of world government which would foster the development of science and oversee the implementation of new ideas. Social unity required a new synthesis of useful, positive knowledge, a new encyclopedia.

Saint-Simon's reverential attitude towards Newton is interesting since we might expect a thinker so influential for the development of nineteenth-century historicism to favour organicist theories over the mechanistic vision of the universe derived from Newtonian physics. In fact what appealed to Saint-Simon in Newton was the desire for unitary modes of explanation. Saint-Simon believed that the law of gravitation accounted for the movement of social as well as natural phenomena (a similar view was held by Charles Fourier who explained movement and desire in terms of 'passionate attraction'). In writings such as *Introduction aux travaux scientifiques au XIXe siècle* (1807-8) and *Mémoire sur la science de l'homme* (1813) Saint-Simon manifested a wish to explain mental and physical phenomena in the light of one law, one governing principle.

Despite a lack of formal training in science he was not overburdened by modesty. In a host of publications he argued his case, proposed new projects, asked for sponsors. Sometimes he relied upon the determining role of science; on other occasions he foregrounded the role of the productive forces in society. He retained the Enlightenment's positive evaluation of humankind's potential. However, for Saint-Simon, the main model for the understanding of social processes was provided by the biological sciences – rather than by mathematics, as had been the case with Condorcet.[7] Under the Directory and in the early years of the Empire he drew on the writings of philosophers and scientists such as Cabanis, Bichat and Vicq-d'Azyr in order to formulate a general theory of social physiology. Society was envisaged as an organism and the task of the philosopher–scientist was to observe social change and identify the laws which governed movement. The manner in which a healthy society functioned could be understood; likewise, collective dysfunctions – such as the Revolution – could be accounted for. A great mood of confidence accompanied this espousal of physiology. In future, according to the *Mémoire sur la science de l'homme*, politics would become a positive science with decisions being taken on the basis of observable facts alone. In a similar fashion morality would become an entirely this-worldly affair, the province of the scientist:

> The physiologist is the only scientist who is in a position to demonstrate that in all cases the path of virtue is at the same time the path of happiness; the moralist who is not a physiologist can only show the recompense of virtue in another life, because he cannot treat questions of morality with sufficient precision.
>
> $(O, V, 29)$[8]

In the course of his researches Saint-Simon found that he had much in common with the liberal economists. Like the liberals he welcomed industrialism and appreciated the power of technological reason to transform the world. He shared their view of the rise of the Communes and the progressive advance of the industrial classes from the Middle Ages to the French Revolution. In *Du système industriel* (1821) he commented: 'If one absolutely wants to assign an origin to the French Revolution it must be dated from the day when the enfranchisement of the Communes began and the cultivation of the sciences of observation commenced in Western Europe' (*O*, III, 78). In *L'Industrie* he observed that 'the *communes* and *industry* are one and the same thing' (*O*, II, 143). Saint-Simon valued work and despised idleness. He considered that all who were involved in productive work of some kind – bankers, artisans, workers, manufacturers – formed a single class, that of the 'industriels' against whom were pitted the idle members of society, the nobility, the sluggardly *rentiers* who obtained profit without effort.

For Saint-Simon, economics rather than politics lay at the heart of social reality and he constructed a project for the future according to which the administration of objects would replace the government of men. The transformation of the natural world would replace the struggle between classes. After 1817, however, he began to distance himself from liberal economics, ascribing primacy to social organisation rather than to the satisfaction of individual desires and choices. In his view society should be made responsible for the well-being of all its members. Saint-Simon perceived that unfettered liberalism on the English model produced misery, deprivation, alienation and class conflict and was incapable of improving the general lot of the working population.

The third volume of his periodical *L'Industrie* (1817) displeased his liberal friends on account of its critical views of religion and its support for 'terrestrial morality'. Christian morality, as traditionally understood, was deemed inadequate when it came to organising relations in modern society. Saint-Simon had no reservations about rejecting the notions of original sin, the immortality of the soul and the whole question of rewards and punishments after death. He admitted that Christian morality had been a good thing in the past – it had put an end to slavery – but he argued that over the centuries it had allied itself with authority and had preached submission and obedience. However, since in Saint-Simon's view the human spirit had moved on since the foundation of the Christian church, it was folly to continue to base morality upon ridiculous prejudices inherited from the past. In *L'Industrie* Saint-Simon renewed his claim that in the modern world morality could become a positive science:

> The era of positive ideas is beginning: we can no longer ascribe to morality purposes which do not correspond to palpable, certain and present interests. Such is the spirit of the century and such will be the spirit of future generations, for ever, and increasingly more so. That is the great step which civilisation is going to take; it will consist in the establishment of positive, terrestrial morality.
>
> (*O*, II, 38)

After the political crisis of 1820 a deeper gulf opened up between Saint-Simon and his erstwhile associates among the manufacturers and industrialists. In 1819, in another of his journals, *L'Organisateur*, he had published his famous 'parable' which described the irrelevance to the nation of the idle upper classes. In the wake of the assassination of the Duc de Berry in January 1820 Saint-Simon's remarks seemed subversive, provocative, treasonable. He was brought to trial and found guilty. The verdict was reversed on appeal but it damaged his reputation and he found he could no longer rely upon the support of moderate industrialists who were worried by the prospect of renewed political and social upheaval. Henceforth he struck out on his own and gave his social philosophy the well-defined aim of improving the condition of the poor. In the works of his last years (*Du système industriel* (1821–2) and *Catéchisme des industriels* (1823–4)) the critique of economic liberalism and representative institutions was unambiguous. In

1825 he published *Le Nouveau Christianisme* which gave his system religious trappings, if not respectability.

Saint-Simon was not a professional historian. What he did, however, was bequeath to his disciples the awareness that historical knowledge was becoming central to any project of social reform. He did not offer detailed analyses of past events; he proposed instead a broad philosophical overview of historical change informed by a moral imperative. The historical work of Volney, Daunou and the Idéologues was held to be too limited in scope.[9] Saint-Simon wanted a larger canvas. In an admittedly schematic and often poorly documented way, he represented history as a grand development of cultures which in totality constituted the development of the human spirit. Religion and politics, economics and philosophy were all intimately related. Saint-Simon did not pretend that his type of historical enquiry was motivated by a disinterested love of scholarship. History had value because it was useful. It taught lessons – not lessons concerning matters of personal conduct but with regard to the nature of the society of the future. In *L'Industrie* Saint-Simon tells us that he began his study of the past when, as a young soldier in North America, he turned away from a military career and decided instead to devote his energies to serving civilisation:

> My vocation was not that of a soldier: I was inclined to a very different and, I may say, contrary type of activity. The goal I proposed for myself was to study the forward movement of the human spirit, in order to work subsequently for the perfecting of civilisation.
>
> (O, I, 148)

History was more than a sub-branch of literature. It contained the secrets of the future. In the *Mémoire sur la science de l'homme* Saint-Simon imagined Francis Bacon travelling to the present to give Napoleon the benefit of his wise counsel regarding the organisation of intellectual life. And he took the opportunity to place in Bacon's mouth his own complaint that genuine history, in the sense of the scientific investigation of humankind's general purposeful advance, still remained to be written:

> History is said to be the breviary of kings. Given the way in which kings govern we can clearly see that their breviary is worthless; in fact history in its scientific dimension has

not yet emerged from its swaddling clothes. This important branch of our knowledge only has existence in the form of a collection of more or less well-established facts. These facts are not bound together by any theory. They are not linked in the order of consequences; in this way, history remains an insufficient guide for kings as well as for subjects; it provides neither kings nor subjects with the means to establish *what will happen on the basis of what has happened*. There exist as yet only national histories whose authors have proposed as their principal aim to show off to advantage the qualities of their compatriots, and to depreciate those of their rivals. No historian has yet taken up the general viewpoint; none has yet written the history of the Species; none, finally, has said to the kings: this is what will result from what has happened, this is the order of things which will result from [increased] enlightenment, here is the goal to which you must direct the use of the immense power which lies in your hands.

(O, V, 245–6)

Sentiments such as these were clearly in tune with the broad spirit of reform – if not with the overtly populist and nationalist orientation – which characterised Augustin Thierry's project of historical reconstruction. The fundamental reliance upon history was enough to distinguish Saint-Simon from the Idéologues. History yielded a stable meaning. It taught that humankind progressed from conjecture to verifiable truth, from religion and metaphysics to science, a view that Auguste Comte, despite his later hostility towards Saint-Simon, shared with his mentor.[10] Whereas the Enlightenment notion of progress as a growth in knowledge used reason as a universally valid yardstick with which to judge cultures, Saint-Simon was more inclined to consider history in terms of the fulfilment of a process which involved all humankind.[11] The direction of progress was in effect governed by necessity. History had its own momentum. Its direction could be followed and perhaps – within limits – be hastened; but it could not be diverted or halted. The question of the relationship between thought and action, theory and practice was a moot one, as the Saint-Simonians would discover. Ideas for Saint-Simon were not simply the result of material and economic progress. They were the manifestation of a force immanent within time. The goal of history was the establishment of the industrial system for the benefit of all, but it was ideas which drove the historical process. Saint-Simon's overriding aim was to persuade his readers of the inevitability of the future. With this objective in view he put forward a periodisation of the past which appeared to lead inexorably in the direction of what he estimated was best for humanity. Change was progressive and irreversible. Hence Saint-Simon's oft-quoted remark that the Golden Age lay in the future and not in the past. The argument was circular. The meaning of past events was understood in relation to a desired future, the supposed inevitability of which rested upon the notion that the past was intelligible and disclosed the operation of historical laws. The study of the past was a predictive device. Saint-Simon did not simply evaluate the past with regard to an ideal of reason. His historicist approach emphasised the totality of the process. This inclusiveness justified the past as necessary, a view which extended to the Middle Ages which rationalists usually condemned as a time of ignorance and superstition.

Saint-Simon saw things differently. The Middle Ages constituted an orderly, unified European culture which organised the division of temporal and spiritual power. The intellectual achievements of the clergy were substantive and needed to be taken seriously. This, however, did not mean that Saint-Simon admired the medieval system in the sense that he recommended it as a model to be imitated in the nineteenth century. Saint-Simon was not a de Bonald. What he was drawing attention to was the fact that the Middle Ages corresponded to a necessary and worthwhile stage in human development, not to a regrettable moment of regression and ignorance. However, the operation of the general law of progress – related to the development of scientific knowledge – meant that the medieval system could not be permanent. The enfranchisement of the Communes bore witness to the gradual replacement of military power by industrial power; at the same time science was beginning to challenge the truths of religion. Finally the Renaissance and the Reformation inaugurated a new period of critical thought which extended until the French Revolution. According to Saint-Simon 1789 accomplished the destruction of the theologico-feudal order.

Saint-Simon's approach to history was therefore highly deterministic. The spirit of the age could neither be eluded nor transcended. Progress took different forms but appeared inevitable.

In *Le Nouveau Christianisme* he declared categorically and with characteristic emphasis: 'The human species has never ceased to make progress' (*O*, III, 181–2). He was happy to make frequent use of expressions such as 'the natural march of things' which lent to his theories the air of historical fatalism which we have seen associated with Thiers, Mignet and Cousin. It followed from this reading of the past that revolutions too were necessary. History became a secular theodicy; suffering was the unavoidable price which had to be paid for the advance of the human spirit. In his *Introduction aux travaux scientifiques du XIXe siècle* (1808) Saint-Simon observed: 'Revolutions are terrible evils, and at the same time inevitable evils. The great advances made by the human spirit are the result of great crises' (*O*, VI, 166). This meant that the violence of the French Revolution itself was in the end justifiable. In an unpublished manuscript note probably dating from the early years of the Restoration Saint-Simon, with remarkable understatement, likened revolutionary disorder to teething troubles:

> He who is saddened at the sight of a child's gum opening to make room for his growing teeth is not using his emotions correctly; he who regrets the popular excesses committed in France during the course of the Revolution is employing his feelings equally badly, for these excesses were indispensable experiences in making the French people aware of the limits within which it was necessary to remain in order to enjoy a calm and enduring freedom.
>
> If anarchy, whose terrible consequences are happily still present in our memory, had not ravaged France, had not caused famine in the midst of abundance, it would sooner or later have established its empire. Let us take delight then, in this connection, in the misfortunes which have befallen us because they protect us from similar evils which would [otherwise] befall us.[12]

Revolutionary excess therefore amounted to a necessary and salutary warning. While Guizot and Thierry struggled to keep 1789 separate from 1793 Saint-Simon was willing to countenance violence in the past because, being protected by the certainties afforded by his interpretation of history, he knew that revolutionary ideas were no longer the way forward. The destruction of the old order had been accomplished. It was time revolution gave way to intellectual and social reconstruction.

In addition to determinism there is a strong element of relativism in Saint-Simon's thought. In the *Introduction aux travaux scientifiques du XIXe siècle* he reminds us that 'Each age has its character, each institution its duration' (*O*, VI, 169). The usefulness of a form of social organisation is not judged in its own terms or by absolute standards but in relation to the supposed final outcome of the process of historical development. There can be no return to the past. In the *Nouveau Christianisme*, for example, Luther is criticised for endeavouring to recreate the spirit of primitive Christianity in the sixteenth century. No institution could remain indifferent to the forces of change and by this Saint-Simon usually meant intellectual, scientific and technological advance. Religions – which Saint-Simon tended to assimilate to their institutional expression – did not stand outside time. Saint-Simon capitalises for emphasis: 'RELIGION AGES AS OTHER INSTITUTIONS AGE. IN THE MANNER OF OTHER INSTITUTIONS RELIGIONS NEED TO BE RENEWED AFTER THE LAPSE OF A CERTAIN TIME' (*O*, VI, 169). As humankind advanced, so paganism gave way to Christianity and in due course traditional forms of the religion would surely give way to Saint-Simon's own brand of 'new' Christianity, the religion of brotherly love.

However, by making religion central to the periodisation of history Saint-Simon was not abandoning the critical vantage point of the Enlightenment in favour of a surrender to the irrational. He expressed approval for Dupuis's influential *Origine de tous les cultes* (1795) with its explanation of all religious phenomena in terms of planetary worship. In practice this meant that while Saint-Simon did not usually dismiss all religion straightforwardly as superstition he redefined its significance by presenting moments in religious history as concrete manifestations of scientific world views. Revealed ideas were described as 'scientific ideas produced by mankind in its infancy' and quite insufficient for modern needs (*O*, VI, 329). Religion began when men perceived the relationship between cause and effect, and the subsequent rise and decline of religions corresponded to the progressive development of scientific modes of understanding. The Egyptians worshipped nature, Homeric Greece regarded the human faculties as divine, Socrates 'invented God' by unifying the faculties. Jesus transformed speculative ideas into theism. (When Saint-Simon talks of the divinity of Jesus he appears to mean that it was the Christian morality of brotherly love which defined the social bond in its most general terms – Jesus's function was clearly to establish philanthropy rather than to convey any promise of salvation.) Christian doctrine was subsequently systematised by Saint Paul. During the medieval period the clergy was the strength of European civilisation. However, by the fifteenth century scientific advance was taking place outside the church and the introverted clergy lost influence and compromised itself by siding with the idle nobility. The Revolution ensued.

Did this mean that in the nineteenth century religion would finally give way to science? Saint-Simon's views altered on this question. In 1808 he noted that while the enlightened and educated could be expected to accept the truths of science (what at this stage he called 'physicism'), none the less a form of Christian theism remained appropriate for the majority and necessary for the general maintenance of social order. In the longer term he considered that physicism would itself become a religion, although the nature of the new faith was left unclear – it would probably take a form not unlike Saint-Simon's cult of Newton with scientists forming the new clergy. And yet all of this did not really alter the view that religion was in essence a popularisation of science suited to the needs of the masses and employed as an instrument of government. In his later work, however, Saint-Simon gave more prominence to passion and desire and relatively less importance to knowledge and science. The spirit of the workers needed to be fired with a collective enthusiasm for building the new industrial and moral world. In this context Saint-Simon paid more attention to art and to religion. In *Le Nouveau Christianisme* he expressed a missionary zeal as he reinstated religion as the legitimate horizon of collective experience. However, what appealed to Saint-Simon was Christianity's belief in brotherly love and compassion for humankind, aspects which he identified with his own plans to organise society for the benefit of all, especially the poorest members. Love of God did not figure in the programme. Morality remained absolutely terrestrial. The reader can easily be misled by Saint-Simon's willingness to employ traditional religious language, to talk of impiety and heresy. Whereas Guizot wanted to purify the revolutionary inheritance, Saint-Simon wanted to purify Christianity whose true spirit had been betrayed by Catholicism and Protestantism alike. His 'new' Christianity emerged as marking simultaneously the rejuvenation, the retrieval and the completion of the spirit of the Gospels. Saint-

Simon claimed that God was speaking through him, that he had a mission to fulfil. What he offered was a vision of a this-worldly future supported by a historicist reading of the past.

THE SAINT-SIMONIANS

Between 1825 and 1832 the disciples of Saint-Simon set about articulating, consolidating and propagating what they called the idea of universal association.[13] This idea was their response to the sense of disconnectedness and alienation which characterised liberal industrial society. They dwelt upon the notion that the present was a time of crisis and transition but they remained confident in their hope that the future would be transformed by the full implementation of their theories. They also drew on the comforting and ennobling analogy which compared the travail of their own times with the sufferings and persecutions endured by the early Christians. The Saint-Simonian community of men and women felt itself charged with what amounted to a redemptive mission. Believers engaged the totality of their being in the propagation of the new faith; they underwent a conversion experience, a self-change which corresponded to the casting off of outworn religious and political orthodoxies. Drawing most upon *Le Nouveau Christianisme* they argued that a form of religious organisation was the best way of capturing the allegiance of the population. Their new church would have a body of doctrine, a hierarchy and a firm direction (in 1829 Bazard and Enfantin were made the twin 'Supreme Fathers').

In this way the Saint-Simonians rapidly went beyond the ideal of positive science which Saint-Simon had shared with the liberal economists. They stressed instead the interrelatedness of things: in their view the truth of the social order of the future lay in the network of relationships which constituted its being. Their objective was the restoration of community but in a manner which avoided both Catholicism's hostility towards modern science and the cold-hearted calculations of economic liberalism. Their new social hierarchy would be based upon capacity and merit and not upon birth and privilege. The moral subject would be firmly embedded in the forms of social existence. The proponents of the doctrine reserved their harshest criticisms for those who asserted the self-sufficiency of the individual. In their view the ideology of liberal individualism was responsible for the division of society into haves and have-nots.

However, this critique of individualism extended far beyond a denunciation of the evils of wage exploitation. The Saint-Simonians proposed a social morality according to which vice and virtue were defined in relation to the collective good and not in terms of individual value. In their eyes any appeal to conscience or reason (described with sarcasm as the 'mystical divinities of modern ontology' (*DSS*, 12)) smacked of withdrawal from the public into the private sphere. Virtuous actions were those which hastened 'the march of society in the direction of the goal which it has decided to attain'; evil actions were those which placed obstacles in the way of this process (*DSS*, 305). Social truth was what mattered and this truth was embodied in a power which was to be loved, venerated and obeyed. If the Saint-Simonians spoke warmly of liberty and individuality, then they intended something very different from what apologists of liberal freedoms meant by the words. In effect they redefined the meaning of the terms to fit in with their own ideological preconceptions. An article by Laurent which appeared in the *Organisateur* in 1829 demonstrated this approach:

> The individual, according to us, becomes increasingly free as social action masters him progressively in order to help him to develop his special aptitudes, to exercise his faculties fully, and to overcome his evil propensities which would expose him to the vindictiveness of the laws and of infamy.[14]

The Saint-Simonians dreamt of a restored community, unquestioningly united in a shared purpose, cleansed of the sin of individualism. Under the rule of universal association moral and social antagonisms would dissolve, together with the internal contradictions of the self. Duty and inclination, theory and practice, systems and facts, general good and particular interest were dichotomies characteristic of critical epochs. Such incompatibilities ceased to structure experience within organic periods (*DSS*, 186–7).

There is a strong air of self-righteousness and authoritarianism in many of the pronouncements made by the Saint-Simonians. Had they been conventional believers Louis de Bonald would surely have found much to commend in their approach to religion. He would undoubtedly have found congenial the notion that the health of society would be improved if the critical disposition of mind could be discarded. Saint-Simonianism shared conservative

Catholicism's alarm at the Protestant inheritance of independent criticism. (By way of contrast we should keep in mind that positive valorisations of the spirit of Protestantism informed the interpretations of history proposed by Guizot and Quinet.) Dogmatic assertions of truth were to be preferred to the sceptical temper of Constantian liberalism. This lack of caution went hand in hand with the rejection of most parliamentary institutions – Guizot, we recall, had argued that the advantage of representative government lay precisely in the fact that it allowed for argument and discussion to take place. We would be ill-advised to look to the Saint-Simonians for pious statements in support of a system of judicious checks and balances. At the top of their agenda was the re-establishment of authority, not the limitation of power. Their approach to the public domain indicated that little room would be left for dissidence. In statements which chilled the blood of crusading liberals the Saint-Simonians celebrated their anticipated release from the chains of critical individualism: 'we shall return with love to OBEDIENCE' (*DSS*, 330). Authority was a good and its power was not to be limited. Private property, that foundation of liberalism, would no longer determine social relations. The transmission of property by way of inheritance would cease and property would instead be distributed in accordance with the needs of society (*DSS*, 193). Children would become the responsibility of the state; parents did not need to know their offspring. Work was of course perceived to be central to social life but in the new organisation the circulation of goods and capital would produce not competition and rivalry but a peaceful world order. Art would galvanise citizens into behaving in a socially beneficial manner (*DSS*, 272).

In Saint-Simonian terms the new society would be intrinsically religious. Religion was understood as the power which bound human beings to one another and to nature. The unified society based on the principle of association would embody both the legality and the dynamism of the cosmos. The idea of association carried with it not just a sense of human fellowship but also more metaphysical notions of oneness and wholeness. In the society of the future religion would enter the practices of daily life and the distinction between spiritual and temporal power would cease to have meaning:

Not only will [the religion of the future] dominate the political

123

order . . . the political order will, in its totality, be a religious institution; for no fact must any longer be conceived *outside* GOD, or develop *outside his law*; finally let us add that [the religion of the future] will embrace the entire world, because the law of GOD is universal.

(*DSS*, 334)

The Saint-Simonians did not try to set up firm boundaries between the religious, moral and political dimensions. They preferred to subordinate all areas of life to an overarching notion of religion viewed as the manifestation of collective truth. What held society together was religion, and religion alone could positively direct the restless movement of modern society. Saint-Simonianism proclaimed itself to be innovatory but it also sought to inscribe itself within the processes of historical evolution. Collective self-realisation involved controlling time as well as organising production. The new faith was self-reflectively assertive regarding the extent to which it signalled separation from the values of the Christian past, but at the same time it laid claim to be the culmination of religious history: *Le Nouveau Christianisme* broadcast to the nineteenth century the good news of brotherly love, originally announced by Moses and later expressed in the teachings of Jesus. In fact – and this suited the apocalyptic millenarianism abroad in France in the wake of the July Revolution – this signified that God's Kingdom was being realised upon earth thanks to the efforts of the Saint-Simonians who proclaimed the rehabilitation of the flesh and the sanctity of industry (*DSS*, 70).

The central notion of social unity involved more than voluntary co-operation; it meant a coming together in love – the Saint-Simonians under the leadership of Enfantin valorised sexual as well as industrial energies. Their religion was driven by the rejection of original sin and by the belief in a this-worldly future – although more esoteric notions of reincarnation and the transmigration of souls were entertained by some, notably Enfantin. Traditional ways of conceiving the oppositions between male and female, east and west, spirit and matter were challenged. A new pantheistic credo emerged which suggested that an androgynous deity might replace the god of monotheism. God was the unified totality of all things and was directly present in experience. God took the form of the universal force of love and desire and was identified with the cosmic movement to unity and oneness. The male and female principles were embodied in the authority figures who, in theory at least, would rule over the hierarchy of the church-society, the 'Père' and the decidedly more elusive 'Mère' whom those Saint-Simonians calling themselves 'The Companions of Woman' tried to find in the Middle East. Indeed, Saint-Simonianism, which set about revalorising woman and improving her position in society, expectantly awaited the coming of a new female messiah. The religion of the future embodied the general idea, the grand theory, the unitary doctrine. To experience the reality of religion was to engage with the divine life which was active in nature and in history.

The defining characteristic of this religion lay precisely in the fact that it did not situate the core of its being within the inner life of an individual engaged in a living relation to a personal deity. Saint-Simonian religion was expansionist, it conquered social space, manifesting itself as 'the explosion of the collective thought of mankind, as the synthesis of all its conceptions, of all its modes of being' (*DSS*, 333). Instead of a dualistic view of the world and of human experience Saint-Simonianism sought to grasp thought and action within a totalising synthesis. Instead of trying to cure the spiritual condition of the 'old man' ('le vieil homme' (*DSS*, 300)) after the manner of Christianity, the new faith wanted to revitalise, re-energise humankind in order to create and animate something truly different, 'l'homme nouveau', the new man, understood as an active, productive force. Religion would speak to the condition of the new man, facilitating his embedding within a network of social relations which was the manifestation of the divine in time. The advent of the new order was at hand. Catholic attempts to revive traditional forms of faith were treated with condescension: they were doomed to fail because they denied industry, matter and the lessons of history. Such attempts at religious restoration recalled Julian the Apostate's impotent efforts to revive the pagan gods. Time had moved on. History had spoken.

Saint-Simonianism disconcerts the modern reader most of all by its willing identification of knowledge with power and its undisguised and seemingly obsessional desire to control individual lives. What is of prime importance for our present discussion, however, is the fact that Saint-Simonianism was a secular religion whose claim to truth rested upon a theory of history. History provided a retrospective justification for the imminent advent of the ideal society. History furnished a yardstick with which to judge the rightness or wrongness of actions. Crimes, for example, were not just antisocial acts. They were unacceptable because they were intrinsically regressive and retrograde; the guilty person had in effect reproduced a form of behaviour which was appropriate in the past but inappropriate in the present (*DSS*, 316). History disclosed essential social truths. The Saint-Simonians' claim was that, thanks to their master's researches, history had now fully become a science, a science whose conclusions allowed the future to be predicted with certainty. In their writings the indeterminacy of the future largely disappeared. It was clearly understood that historical knowledge was the seat of power and that those who could grasp the relationship between past, present and future were empowered to effect political transformations:

> the power to *constitute a society* is only accorded to those men who can find the *bond* between the past and the future of the human race, and are thus able to co-ordinate its *memories* with its *hopes*, in other words to attach *tradition* to *predictions*, and satisfy equally the *regrets* and *desires* of all people.
>
> (*DSS*, 13)

The point of departure for the Saint-Simonians was that humankind should be envisaged as a single entity, as a collective being developing over the centuries, the stages of whose growth could be explained in terms of the operation of the law of progress. History's claims to authority and scientific respectability were frequently supported by biological metaphors. Saint-Simon, keen on the idea of applying physiology to the study of society, had described the history of civilisation as the development of an organism which created new organs. His followers likewise made much of physiology and organicist explicatory language. Buchez described humankind as a 'function of the universe'.[15] History was the science of collective growth. Facts on their own were of little interest: 'What use to us are all these facts, unless we can discern in them, in distinct characters, a *will*, a *desire*, a sought-after *goal*?' (*DSS*, 136). Saint-Simon's major contribution, in the eyes of his followers, was to have completed the inadequate notions of history and human perfectibility proposed by Vico, Lessing, Turgot, Kant, Herder and Condorcet (*DSS*, 106). The error of earlier historians had been to suppose that events had their origin in abstract human individuals; in reality events needed to be related to culture and context and made to disclose an overpowering sense of teleology. The Saint-Simonian view was that events were neither fortuitous nor explicable in terms of the choices of contingent individuals. History was essentially progressive, collective and logical:

> For a long time philosophers have made mankind the object of their investigations; they have studied its history in diverse ages, and meditated upon the revolutions which it has undergone. But instead of envisaging mankind as an organised body, growing progressively according to invariable laws, they have only considered it in relation to the *individuals* who compose it; they have thought that at each period of its existence it had reached its full development. They have likewise, without hesitation, accepted that the same facts could always be reproduced identically, in all periods. From this point of view, history only appeared to them as a vast collection of facts and observations; and if they have studied the causes of human revolutions, it has been with the sole aim of extracting from them precepts for conduct in similar occasions.
>
> (*DSS*, 113)

For the Saint-Simonians therefore, history was intrinsically progressive. Instead of constituting a collection of dramatic episodes which appealed to the imagination history took on the mantle of science. It offered 'a successive table of the physiological states of the human race, considered in its collective existence' (*DSS*, 117). The rigour of history was, we are told, as great as that of the exact sciences. (We have clearly moved on from the sceptical cast of mind of the Idéologues – history now gives reassurance and ontological confidence and its content is held to be thoroughly reliable.) If, however, we enquire what this rigorous method actually entails we find that it largely adds up to the Saint-Simonian view of cultural change, to the dynamic of organic and critical periods. Within the general exposition of the doctrine this process is investigated in respect of European, not world history. In broad terms it is argued that an organic period existed in Greece until the time of Socrates (and subsequently in Rome until the time of Augustus). This was followed by a critical period out of which Christianity emerged. The Catholic Middle Ages represent the next organic period. Disintegration set in with the Reformation. This critical age culminated in the French Revolution.

The Saint-Simonians often observed that organic periods were characterised by harmony and faith, and were governed by a general idea or belief system whose authority was accepted without question. Organic periods were by nature religious and were stamped with the figure of order and unity. However, in the course of time the harmony which sustains an organic epoch begins to break down; Saint-Simon had shown how scientific advance legitimately questioned received wisdom. Eventually the cohesion of the organic age gives way to a critical period characterised by doubt, disharmony and disorder; analytical reason flourishes and religious certitudes are undermined. In an organic period the passions are generous and are mobilised to serve the collective good. In a critical period atheism, religious indifference, egoistic calculation and individual interest prevail. However, from the vantage point of world history the movement from organic to critical periods describes not a vicious circle but progress. We must remember that – in addition to scientific and technological advance – the criterion by which progress is assessed is that of the development of universal association. Taken as a whole, the historical movement of civilisations testifies to 'the uninterrupted PROGRESS of association' (*DSS*, 146). The developmental sequence slavery–serfdom–proletariat is held to describe a definite positive movement towards greater association. A similar view is taken of the sequence family–city–nation–federation (the latter stage is for example embodied in the Catholic Middle Ages). The Saint-Simonians held fast to their conviction that in the future peaceful and industrial state of universal association the master–slave relationship would finally disappear. The central point was that history as science seemed to provide the Saint-Simonians with a secure foundation of meaning. To their satisfaction progress had been established as a historical law. In the light of historical knowledge the future could be predicted with confidence. Humankind was not conceivable in terms other than historical and progressive:

> The law of perfectibility is so absolute, it is such a fundamental condition for the existence of our species, that upon every occasion that a people placed at the head of mankind has become static, the seeds of progress, which were compressed within its breast, have been immediately transported else-

where, to a terrain where they could develop.... The tradition of progress has never been lost, and perfectibility has never been refuted; we have simply seen civilisation migrate, like those birds which journey and seek in distant lands a favourable climate and an atmosphere which their homeland can soon no longer provide them with.

(*DSS*, 112–13)

The Saint-Simonians rejected the dualism of mind and matter, spirit and nature which characterised the Christian world view. In their judgement Christianity was exhausted, incapable of responding to new needs. But at the same time they found the scientific materialism of the Enlightenment and the Idéologues inadequate as well. Instead they made man a desiring subject, implicated in the world and embedded in social relations. In the new age whose coming they foretold, science and faith, individual and society, spontaneity and reflection would once again be brought into harmony. The false gods of the critical period (individual freedom, absolute equality, private property, parliamentary government, natural rights) would be rejected and replaced by new forms of knowledge and ways of feeling.[16] Moreover, the new organic age was not presented as a further provisional embodiment of the urge to order and social wholeness. It was described as the *definitive* epoch whose unifying doctrine synthesised all which had gone before. Does this mean that the Saint-Simonians considered that the end of history was near, that the replacement of wage exploitation by the transformation of nature signalled the transcendence of all forms of struggle? It is only fair to say that the Saint-Simonians point out that progress will not cease once the definitive condition has been realised, that knowledge will continue to grow. However, they also postulate that the social organisation itself will not develop further (*DSS*, 159). To this extent therefore the 'definitive state' seems to mark the coincidence of self with its collective essence and its actualisation within the flowing currents of social energy. The definitive state marks the union of intellectual life and collective passion, the fusion of mind and matter.

By the late 1820s the Saint-Simonians felt secure in their conviction that their founder had defined the content of the future – a peaceful, productive, industrial society in which terrestrial morality would replace celestial morality and where egoism and class antagonisms would give way to universal association. The Saint-

Simonians were Romantics in their adhesion to the truths of feeling. They rehabilitated the imagination as prophetic and anticipatory; but at the same time they wished to reconcile it with reason. In practice this tended to mean one of two things: either the imagination served science in a propagandist mode (representing the ideal society of the future) or the imagination had a more prophetic function (announcing that which science would confirm in due course). When dealing with the future, Saint-Simonian doctrine endeavoured to combine reason (the supposedly scientific conclusions drawn from the laws of history) and the imagining of the future (more in tune with sympathy, passion and love).[17] This meant that reason would be rehabilitated along with the imagination and shorn of its associations with revolutionary individualism. History became a principle of mediation legitimating reason and imagination alike. But history was also the discourse of truth and this implied that the only future considered legitimate was that forecast and authorised by the doctrine. Good art was defined as that which promoted the proper historical lessons in terms of human perfectibility. The uniqueness of the present resided in its mastery of the meaning of the past.

The attempt to conjoin reason and imagination represented an effort to effect regeneration without violence, to pass from disorder and division to the new harmonious social order of unified humanity. Thanks to their control of the meaning of the past the Saint-Simonians felt empowered by history to describe a future which seemed imminent and knowable. This future appeared: a) desirable; b) attainable; c) inevitable. The sense of certitude was such that the use of the term 'utopia' could be dismissed as inappropriate. Members of the movement adopted supremely confident tones: 'We know the future of mankind and will unveil it before your eyes.'[18] The future was not an impossible dream; it was guaranteed by the laws of history, although the intervention of human agency was still required: 'from a providential point of view, there are no more utopias: all that which is good is realised: it is sufficient to will [the new society] and WE WILL [it]'.[19] The precise nature of the transition from present to ideal future, to the definitive state was, however, left vague – although at first sight political violence in the revolutionary tradition was unlikely to be the approved method for inaugurating the peaceful internationalist future.

The events of July 1830 gave the Saint-Simonians serious pause.

On 28 July 1830 Bazard and Enfantin issued a proclamation instructing their followers not to participate in violent struggle. The movement wanted a moral transformation, a religious renewal, not a further episode in a history of insurrection. The 'fathers' judiciously counselled calm while not going so far as to recommend inaction. However, it was not easy for the younger generation to stand aside as events unfolded. Hippolyte Carnot and others made use of their firearms. Rapidly the leadership changed tack and in a new proclamation which appeared on 30 July the two 'fathers' praised the achievements of the 'children of the future' who had conquered the forces of the past. These diverse reactions say much about the different desires for change which contributed to the dynamics of Saint-Simonianism. In one sense Saint-Simonianism was a phenomenon of the opposition of the late 1820s which bore witness to a movement away from the usual forms of insurrectionist activity in the direction of broader intellectual and moral reform. We should remember that a number of leading Saint-Simonians, Bazard and Buchez for example, had previously been active Carbonari and members of secret societies. It is not really a surprise therefore if, under the pressure of dramatic events, the movement responded in a somewhat ambiguous way to renewed revolutionary upheaval. The temptation to participate actively in the events of 1830 must have been irresistible for some. Did Saint-Simonianism necessarily encourage passivity? Surely there remained some work for individual agency to accomplish? However, in the wake of the *Trois Glorieuses* the Saint-Simonians soon reaffirmed their non-violent line with its accompanying longer-term strategy:

> The great and final evolutionary step which Saint-Simon will make mankind take will be brought about only after a long time by imperceptible assimilation to the association already formed by us. Doubtless our political role will begin only after our doctrine has penetrated the upper classes and through its cult has been presented to the lower classes so that the assumption of power can take place simultaneously *from above* and *from below*.[20]

The movement benefited from the initial feeling that in the wake of 1830 all manner of grand enterprises of religious and intellectual reconstruction were possible. However, the fundamental Saint-Simonian stance remained one of distrust of violent mass action, joined with the belief that real change could only be achieved gradually and under the impetus of an elite. In 1831 for example, at the time of the Lyon uprising, they urged the workers not to resort to violence but to turn instead to the idea of association. Despite their visionary excesses and religious ambitions the Saint-Simonians were in fact clearsighted when it came to assessing the current condition of France. They perceived that victory had been snatched away from the forces which had brought about the 1830 Revolution. They were under no illusions concerning the real nature of the new constitutional monarchy: political realignments were superficial and nothing of substance was going to alter as far as the population at large was concerned. In August 1831 Emile Barrault declared that it was now the bourgeoisie which was living in idle luxury, exploiting and oppressing the masses. He warned that a new Spartacus was likely to emerge as long as the new regime left economic relations unchanged. Only the idea of association could heal the social body. After 1830 liberals such as Thierry and Guizot believed that history confirmed the structure of society. The Saint-Simonian interpretation of history subverted this view. In their opinion 1830 did not signal the actualisation of the frustrated promise of 1789 which had been delayed by 1793, 1799, 1815 and then postponed by the inflexibilities of the Bourbon Restoration. Certainly 1830 completed the destructive work begun in 1789 by definitively eliminating the religious and political order of the Ancien Régime, but it did not inaugurate a new, different order. In fact, far from resolving class antagonisms it redefined them and exacerbated them. The real message of history was that all good men should redouble their efforts to convert the population to the cause of peaceful transformation. The critical period, the transitional age, was not over yet.

However, the relationship between Saint-Simonianism and liberalism was never simple or clear-cut. I have alluded above (p. 131) to the irresistible temptation which some Saint-Simonians experienced in July 1830 at the prospect of transforming thought into reality by way of action on the barricades. Could the new church remain on the sidelines, immured in its historical optimism, disdaining the path of intervention? In 1831 the question was again posed but on this occasion in collective rather than individual terms. The Saint-Simonians were in theory internationalist and suspicious of liberal and revolutionary nationalism. According to the *Exposition de la doctrine*, national egoism and love of one's country were supposed to give way to a general love of humankind (*DSS*, 98, 104). However, as was the case in July 1830, a certain drift in the direction of the ideas of the revolutionary age could occur under the pressure of events. So it was that in 1831 we find the *Globe*, by then a mouthpiece of Saint-Simonianism, using its columns to support the demand for French military intervention in Poland and Belgium, a cause more readily associated with those well to the Left who conceived of France as the revolutionary nation-state *par excellence*. By aligning themselves, however temporarily, with an interventionist nationalism the Saint-Simonians revealed the way in which a theory predicated upon general humanitarian progress could shade into different valuations of collective identity and extend rather than resolve the intellectual disorder of the critical age.

The difficult relationship which Saint-Simonianism entertained with the revolutionary idea – and with the liberal and republican theories of history which relied upon the notion of the Revolution as founding moment – is nicely caught in the debate in Saint-Simonian circles after 1830 concerning the appropriateness of the 'Marseillaise'. The 'Marseillaise' was popular with the masses but in the mind of Saint-Simonians its warlike tones did not correspond to the needs of society in a post-revolutionary world. The music which paid tribute to collective action resonated through the culture but it only served to reinforce divisions within society. What was required was a new piece of popular music which extolled peace, work and association. An intermediate step proposed by the Saint-Simonians involved adding new words to revolutionary songs such as the 'Marseillaise' and the 'Ça ira'. Ralph Locke refers to at least three new texts written for the 'Marseillaise' in which the themes of work, industry and woman replaced the warlike spirit.[21] The most elaborate, by Vidal and Bertu, began: 'Allons, enfants de l'industrie, /Voici venir des temps nouveaux'. However, was altering the words enough to change the meaning of a song with such strong associations? When the Saint-Simonian missionary Vinçard performed a suitably rewritten version of the revolutionary 'Ça ira' in Charenton in 1832 he encountered divergent but equally hostile responses from his audience. Locke suggests that some might well have thought he was betraying the revolutionary cause by changing the words while others probably feared that the melody alone was sufficient to incite insurrection.

To my mind this anecdote about revolutionary music encapsulates many of the difficulties which the Saint-Simonians faced when dealing with national myth, the revolutionary idea and the discourse on history which supported these notions. Could social conditions and human relations be transformed without revolution, without marshalling society's malcontents, without urging the proletariat to seize the power of the state, without locating the agency for regenerative change within the national will? Was it sufficient to adapt and remodel the symbolic languages available within the culture, be they Catholic or revolutionary in origin? Like Guizot and Thierry, the Saint-Simonians in effect dealt with 1789 and its aftermath by historicising the sense of fracture, by viewing the Revolution against the general backdrop of western history. But the Saint-Simonians were not encumbered with the qualifications, distinctions and second thoughts which beset liberal historians as they did their best to incorporate a positive valorisation of the Revolution into a political programme which claimed for itself the virtues of moderation and compromise. Neither were they tempted to mythologise the Revolution after the manner of republican historians. For the Saint-Simonians, the Revolution, necessary in its time and context, marked the end of a historical cycle; it did not function as the unique founding origin of the new order – but neither was it an unacceptable aberration. The structure and pattern which they placed upon history meant that the Revolution, however sterile its immediate consequences, was part of a process which carried meaning. History had its sharp edges and the Revolution was one of them.

Whereas those who sought to reforge a republican identity needed to revive the mobilising revolutionary myths of 'la patrie en danger' and 'la levée en masse', the Saint-Simonians, by contrast, could make seductive promises which relegated transgressive violence to the past. The substance of the past was repudiated as irrelevant to contemporary reality but its forms could seemingly be reinvigorated and reappropriated, modified in order to carry new meanings and hasten the advent of the collectivist social order. The 'Marseillaise' would signal peace and the priesthood would embody a form of sexual equality. By controlling the meaning of history the movement demonstrated the inevitability of 1793 and justified the bloody fall of divine-right monarchy. However, by revering the person and memory of Saint-Simon his followers also effected a restoration of paternal authority; the word of Saint-Simon recapitulated that of Christ and revealed to the faithful the true meaning of the past.

We have seen how the ideal Saint-Simonian society, one in which all groups and classes would magically work in unison and in the service of the collective good, drew its legitimacy from the general movement of history. Events were no longer puzzling in their randomness once they were related to the growth of association and the increase in scientific progress. The form of periodisation adopted by the movement recognised the importance of 1789 but relativised its significance. Neither an idealised consti-tutionalist 1789 nor an egalitarian 1793 were to the liking of the Saint-Simonians – although they annoyed liberals by praising the Convention (and sometimes the Empire) for trying to overcome disorder. Liberalism used history to validate a definition of national identity which justified 1789 as the apotheosis of the Third Estate and the prelude to the secure establishment of consti-tutional politics. The Saint-Simonians retold history in the service of new desires and apprehensions and had no time for the arrested development of the liberal state. In 1830, despite the real pull of national sentiment, they wanted neither a refurbished consti-tutional monarchy nor a return to the revolutionary republic. They used history to deny republicanism its historical legitimacy and to refuse liberal capitalism its claims to represent an ending – both were outworn, exhausted, obsolete doctrines.

The Saint-Simonians disrupted the confident liberal–national construction of history by offering an alternative – but an alterna-tive which they held was the only true account of the past. Uni-versal Association was justified by history as the only legitimate post-liberal, post-revolutionary, post-Christian ideology. The Saint-Simonians' historical determinism meant that they, like their founder, believed that they owned the true meaning of the past. Whereas liberalism implied pluralism – and this meant that differ-ent readings of the past were at least in theory possible – authori-tarian Saint-Simonianism denied pluralism: there was one correct form of social organisation and its advent was announced by the sole correct interpretation of history. This implied that Saint-Simonianism effectively denied value, even usefulness to other interpretations. Alternative readings and ways of relating to the past were effectively excluded. One populariser of the doctrine explained to his readers that the purpose of history was 'to inspire in men a passion for an ever more attractive social future'; beyond that, he continued, the study of the past was a quite superfluous activity.[22] What was of importance to the Saint-Simonians was the general schematic interpretation of history as scientific progress moving towards ever greater association. Their thought was so oriented towards the future that they devoted little time to the Romantic nostalgia for origins and community. True community was yet to be established. They showed little interest in the detail of past events and little inclination to rewrite national history in the manner of Thierry or reconstruct the life of the masses in the manner of Michelet. Liberal history needed an idea of the people as collective subject but had to take care that popular energies somehow conformed to the parliamentary outcome. Republican history made *le peuple* the real agent of change and endowed the masses with right and virtue. Saint-Simonianism was not much taken with the sentimental and reverential attitude towards the masses which characterised the republican Left. The movement believed in growth, not revolution, and eschewed the volcanic and atomic metaphors beloved of some democrats and left-republicans. Could the people as collective agent be relied upon to implement the new principles of universal order?

The entire Saint-Simonian ideal rested upon the conviction that the new science of history guaranteed the desired future. History became a discourse of truth, an infallible guide. Belief in the future was the real driving force although it presented itself in the form of a theory of scientific progress. The will to historical knowledge was a surrogate manifestation of the will to power. We have seen how the Saint-Simonians hankered after the authority principle and were drawn to the notion of a population united around an uncontested truth. From the outset their overwhelming certainty that history possessed a unitary and determinate meaning was potentially oppressive and intolerant. It is, however, stretching a point to portray either Saint-Simon or his followers as fathers of the totalitarianism experienced in the twentieth century, if by that we mean the unambiguous and overarching exercise of state power and the use of institutionalised violence to crush dissent. Frank Manuel put the whole matter in its proper perspective when, having remarked that the Saint-Simonians never spilled a drop of blood, he commented: 'Remembrance of [the unique German experience under the Third Reich] should not be diluted by the discovery of antecedents that are of a qualitatively different character.'[23] On the other hand it is perfectly clear that the Saint-Simonians wanted to control urges which they viewed as destructive of the collective. They never concealed their aversion for liberal freedoms or their preference for community over individuality. They managed to combine a notion of obedience which they inherited from the religion they rejected with an espousal of modern industrial processes which validated a globalising project based upon the expansion of western energies and technological reason.

Their objective was the welfare of all citizens and with this end in view they accepted that it was legitimate for society to place constraints upon the individual's right to express his nature freely. Instead of personal fulfilment defined in terms of the maximisation of private wishes, they proposed the goals of association, sympathy and love, in other words the primacy of collective oneness over individual difference. In their view this amounted to a higher freedom than the personal fulfilment advocated by utilitarians and bourgeois theorists. The Saint-Simonians sought to obstruct self-directed egoism, a fraudulent form of freedom. They had different priorities. They wanted to raise the status of woman and rescue the material world from Christian dualism. In their view civilisation was not the counterweight to desire which it became for Guizot or Matthew Arnold. Saint-Simonian society would have room for energy and movement, and not simply embody an order born of reason and the established moral law. They invoked the power of the imagination in the service of the new era of union and synthesis.

Their harmonious resolution of history was envisaged as a liberation of energies, a release from traditional constraints, the triumph of their master's this-worldly, terrestrial morality. They remained confident that the pitfalls of anarchy and disorder could be avoided. The reconciliation of man with himself was not to be achieved by personal striving or by channelling disaffection into direct action but by rediscovering the justness and the beauty of hierarchy, the joy of obedience. Belonging implied activity, not quietude, participation, not contemplation, but it required acceptance that the doctrine embodied definitive truth – a view which was anathema to libertarians of all persuasions. Saint-Simonianism offered a cure for the Romantic sickness whose symptoms were the divorce between thought and action, between reason and sensibility. However, the remedy could only become truly effective when the critical period had given way to the organic age. Hence the reliance upon history since, as we have seen, it was the structure of history which assured the Saint-Simonians of the inevitable triumph of their ideas and explained the nature and duration of

137

the current transitional period. The inception of the definitive organic epoch of the future would effectively mark the closure of bourgeois history; but might it not also mean the end of history in a wider sense, the inauguration of a post-historical age no longer driven by the collective aspiration to change social relations but by the desire to transform nature? Might not the society of the future prefer to celebrate the victory of unified mankind over the physical universe rather than devote its energies to the potentially contentious subject of the past? The Saint-Simonians' ideal world rested upon historical justifications but, once actualised, would the new society have much need of memory?

5

Edgar Quinet (1803–1875): history, nature and religion

With Edgar Quinet we encounter a thinker fully engaged with the reality of his time, a writer who consistently drew upon an understanding of the past in support of his political values. Liberal in the 1820s, republican under the July Monarchy, deputy in 1848, exiled after the *coup d'état* of 1851, Quinet is representative of the French Left's anchorage in the founding moment of the Revolution. He is usually best remembered for two things: first, the lectures he delivered at the Collège de France between 1842 and 1845 which challenged government policy and the dominance of the clerical party; second, the publication in 1865 of a controversial history of the French Revolution in which he argued that, in the light of the sad condition of France under the Second Empire, the time had come to reconsider what the Revolution had actually achieved, to learn from past mistakes and develop policy accordingly. *La Révolution* has been exhumed in the 1980s by French historians and philosophers such as François Furet and Claude Lefort, and has been elevated to the status of a central text of the revisionist canon.[1] This concentration on *La Révolution* has unfortunately tended to obscure the importance and value of Quinet's other and varied writings. Unlike his great friend Michelet, almost all of whose work was either strongly historical or broadly philosophical in character, Quinet tried his hand at epic poetry, travel writing, literary criticism, political polemics and aesthetic theory, as well as religious, cultural and intellectual history. All of this work was informed by a particular sense of the nineteenth century's relation to the past. Like Thierry and Guizot, Quinet placed the foundation of truth in a developmental theory of history. However, in his work the Romantic themes of regeneration and renewal are more prominent. Quinet identified the national will with the energies of history and the Revolution with a moment in the self-revelation of the Absolute. In Quinet we are dealing with a Romantic author with a religious sensibility who turned to history in search of something more than a foundation for political authority. Like other literary figures of his generation he suffered from the *mal du siècle*; he felt isolated, disconnected, alienated from nature and from society. The Romantic consciousness countered this sense of dispersal and discontinuity by seeking within nature a divinely instituted pattern of meaning which mysteriously underpinned human reality; the Romantic consciousness likewise united with the past in such a way as to allow history to confirm the status of the self and underwrite its moral integrity.

In Quinet's writing we see how history fills the inward depths of self, how the act of knowing the past is also an act of self-knowledge. By re-establishing community with the past the self united with the active principle which was manifesting itself in time. In the wake of the discrediting of traditional forms of belief Romantic religious thought rescued man from meaninglessness by displacing value onto nature and purpose onto history. In Quinet's writing we also see how forces beyond the rational could be integrated into history. He rediscovered within history the creative forces of life, the powers which animated and shaped the cosmos, Eros and Thanatos, not simply the ordering principle which guaranteed the regularity of the universe. Contact with the energies of the past restored to the isolated self a sense of belonging to the cosmos. But could the legality and intelligibility of history rest upon an undetermined cosmic will? Were moments of passion and violence, moments of collective disorder such as the French Revolution, fully explicable in terms of the desire for political freedom and social justice? Or were they to be related to currents of vital energy, at once creative and destructive? Quinet's historical thought raises these questions. It places any reflection on the revolutionary process within a broader consideration of man's relation to the cosmos, a context which, despite Quinet's at times strongly felt anticlericalism, it would be churlish not to call religious.

The young Quinet's political and intellectual allegiance lay with the liberal opposition of the 1820s. He came from a well-to-do family in the Bresse.[2] His father had served as a war commissionary in the army of the Republic and his mother – to whom Edgar was devoted – came from Protestant origins. She fostered in her son an admiration for Mme de Staël. Much later, reviewing the events of his early years in *Histoire de mes idées* (1858), Quinet drew attention to the effect which the invasions of 1814 and 1815 had had upon him. An impressionable youth, he had seen France invaded and occupied. His residence was searched when his family was suspected of harbouring a friend and former member of the Convention, Baudot. In 1858 Quinet claimed that the experience of the new barbarians sweeping through France inspired in him his feeling for history (*OC*, X, 233–4). In 1820 he came to Paris to study law. He was not overly committed to his studies but thanks to family connections he moved in the wealthy salon society which remained hostile to the conservative values of the Restoration. His reading at this time included Rousseau, Grotius, Adam Smith, Robertson and Hume. Like Victor Cousin he had a strong sense that after the necessary negations of the Enlightenment the nineteenth century was destined to be the great age of reconstruction. His correspondence with his mother reveals a firm desire to contribute towards the perfection and moral development of humankind.

Like other liberals Quinet was drawn to history and he drafted a number of essays which remained in manuscript form: *Essai sur l'histoire moderne dans ses rapports avec l'imagination*, *Histoire de la personnalité*, *Etudes sur le moyen âge*.[3] His first actual publication was *Les Tablettes du Juif errant* (1823), a satirical piece very much in the Voltairian manner and in tune with the anticlerical spirit of the liberal opposition. Quinet sent a copy to Benjamin Constant and was delighted when his hero acknowledged receipt. The *Tablettes* – which made no impression on the wider reading public – used as its central organising device the figure of the Wandering Jew which Quinet would employ to much greater effect a decade later in his epic poem *Ahasvérus* (1833). The immense distance which separates these two works involves more than the abandonment of Enlightenment literary conventions; it corresponds to Quinet's discovery of the notion of history as collective process. The new attitude to history was crucial to his intellectual development and can be traced to 1824 when he was lent by a friend an English translation of Herder's *Ideen zur Philosophie der Geschichte der Menschheit*. Quinet was overwhelmed by the power and range of Herder's achievement. Soon afterwards he began working on a French translation and rapidly cast himself in the role of cultural intermediary between France and Germany. In 1825 he met Michelet for the first time. He was also introduced to Cousin and initially fell completely under the spell of eclecticism. At the close of 1826 he left for Heidelberg where he was to study for two years under Karl Daub and Friedrich Creuzer. The translation of the *Ideen* came out in 1827 and 1828 and was well received.

The two essays on Herder which accompany the translation show Quinet to be deeply interested in the process by which meaning is assigned to historical change.[4] The essays demonstrate that self-knowledge is inseparable from historical knowledge. Quinet begins with the anxious condition of the isolated, disconnected modern self searching for a stable meaning. What is immediately apparent in his approach is the extent to which the relationship to the past fulfils a deep, emotional need. In Quinet's case, much more than in that of Thierry, Guizot or Cousin, we witness an insecure personality transforming the mind's relation to history into a mode of self-exploration, self-revelation. Faced with the seeming nullity of things the self seeks reassurance from an ordering principle which is active in the unfolding of events. At times the confessional tone may seem misplaced, too personal, posturing even – for example when Quinet declares how much he would have wished to have known Herder as a friend.

However, we need to be on our guard against misreading these signs. In the first place Quinet was using the language of his times, the language of the *mal du siècle* which Chateaubriand largely forged and which was amplified and reworked by later generations as they struggled to cope with personal and social crises. Second, while keen to defend the idea of history as science, Quinet sought to incorporate into his approach the Romantic quest for truths of feeling. To identify deeply with events and personalities, to project oneself into the past were ways of appropriating difficult truths, of grasping the complex unity of cultural life. The imagination was a legitimate instrument of knowledge. The unfolding of events itself possessed a genuine poetry, quite different from the deceits of fiction. Quinet wanted to use history in order to seize hold of another world, an invisible world of ideas. This was history as understood by Cousin, not by Daunou. In the post-revolutionary social world the disintegration of traditional ties and structures left the individual isolated, self-enclosed. Quinet suggested that by turning to history the individual might regain his sense of belonging to a community, that the meaning of the particular depended on the general. Awareness of history offered a form of unconscious association. The individual recognised that he was tied to humankind by bonds of sympathy. The Romantic self discovered that its own meaning was implicated in the past.

According to Quinet it was consciousness of time which separated man from the rest of creation which lived in an eternal present. This historical sense was coexistent with human freedom. Man alone struggled to understand the past, to create a future in accordance with his highest aspirations and to impart an element of duration to the spectacle of flux and transience. Quinet's point of departure was the apparent pointlessness of all existence, the triumph of death over life, the spectacle of the rise and fall of empires. In his view the philosophy of history marked a noble attempt to bring order to historical phenomena by introducing into the representation of events what are termed elements of fixity. This means that the events of the past can only properly be understood in relation to a transcendent purpose. When seen in this perspective history loses its apparent unpredictability and can be interpreted as a process of unfolding, as an orderly and meaningful movement which progresses in accordance with certain laws.

The particular character of Quinet's philosophy of history becomes evident from the criticisms he makes of Herder whom he considers too much of a determinist. Despite his enthusiasm for the German philosopher, Quinet explains that he went too far in viewing man as part of the natural universe; in order to explain the act of emancipation by which man separated himself from nature and attained self-consciousness and consciousness of time, Herder had allowed for a direct divine intervention. Quinet, in contrast, declares that this act of separation was neither unique nor mysterious. At all times and regardless of the dangers involved, men have chosen to modify, change or overthrow prevailing conditions in order to create for themselves a new destiny. Freedom is the content, the very stuff of history:

> History, from beginning to end, is the spectacle of liberty, the protestation of the human race against the world which enchains it, the triumph of the infinite over the finite, the freeing of the spirit, the reign of the soul. If one day liberty

were to be absent from the earth, history would cease to
exist.

(I, 34)

This growth of freedom is moreover inseparable from an
accompanying development of selfhood. History in its totality can
be viewed as 'a vast and eternal deduction from the general to the
particular; it is the labour of the *self* which gradually becomes
visible, disengages itself little by little from what is foreign to it
and aspires to express itself in its freest form' (*E*, 500).

It is axiomatic for Quinet that men are constituted to actualise
freedom. At the core of our personal being lies resistance to those
external impediments which hinder our activity as free individuals.
The realisation of freedom takes the form of a growth in individual
liberty and self-consciousness. Men have progressively freed themselves of external determinations. Consequently Quinet divides up
universal history into a number of periods – for the most part
identified with moments in religious history – which correspond
to the progressive emancipation of the personality and the growth
of individual freedom. He begins with oriental pantheism, associated with India. Here man did not clearly differentiate between
past, present and future, and the personality did not possess an
independent existence since the individual was absorbed into
divinised nature. The next period comprised the empires of the
Medes, the Persians, the Assyrians and the Egyptians. Here the
individual remained unfree, essentially dependent upon the society
to which he belonged. A much greater degree of liberty was
achieved in Greece and Rome but the self was still not free since
it identified its life with the existence of the city. The coming of
Christianity signalled the beginning of true individuality. Christianity corresponded to the birth of interiority, to the emergence
of subjective spirit. The process was carried further by the Reformation and by Cartesian philosophy.

Quinet's patterning recalls similar schemes put forward by
philosophers of history in the early nineteenth century, the most
celebrated being that proposed by Hegel: humankind progressively freed itself from the impediments of nature and the constraints of oppressive forms of social organisation. Consciousness
and freedom defined human nature but the content of consciousness altered and the degree of freedom increased over the centuries. It was possible therefore for history to be constituted as a

form of authority and be invoked in the cause of political freedom. Quinet, however, suggested that the development of individuality had been carried too far in modern times and that the self had become estranged from nature and from community. The dominance of critical and analytical modes of thought since Descartes had heightened the dualism of mind and world, subject and object. Reason and observation gave men a growing mastery over the external world but deprived them of the powerful sense of purposeful belonging which characterised the traditional religious world view. Scientific method understood the universe as fact not as value. It was liberating and positive in its consequences but it also engendered an erroneous over-evaluation of individual self-sufficiency. Quinet's position can be summed up as follows: he recognised that personal independence, the product of both secular rationalism and the Christian idea, was the guiding idea of modernity but at the same time he noted the deficiencies of subjective freedom. What were men to do with their liberty? If freedom constituted the essence of the self what limitations were to be placed upon the exercise of the will? Quinet stressed the inner emptiness of the modern self unable to transcend its solitary condition. Subjective freedom left individuals a prey to doubt and scepticism. Unlimited freedom and the unconditioned will possessed an aimless, valueless character.

What Quinet sought amounted to a reorientation of the human mind in its relation to nature and to social existence. Subjective freedom needed to be anchored in history, rooted in becoming, in the intersubjective social world of religions, laws and institutions. By locating individuality within the sanctified territory of history the dangers of indeterminacy and the unlimited will could be avoided. By turning to history Quinet sought an ethical underpinning for individual action, a way out of the negation of nature and the denial of value to other selves. How was the exercise of freedom to be made meaningful? Quinet began by reminding individuals that their actions were part of a general history of striving. Self-conscious freedom had meaning in virtue of its relationship to a history of individual and collective struggles. Freedom was not therefore circumscribed to the pursuit of individual goals, and the individual, despite his acute sense of separateness, remained part of mankind. Humankind is a collective entity, an 'impalpable being, always moving, always changing', a being whose activity motivates and explains the life of the individual existences which it contains and absorbs (*I*, 12). The inner void, the sense of meaninglessness, the *mal du siècle*, all arise from the experience of a subjective freedom alienated from humanity. Once the self realises that individual existence is part of the human collective adventure then serenity begins to take the place of anxiety and unease: 'When I saw [the] immense assembly of centuries and diverse peoples I felt with joy that I was not alone in time' (*I*, 58). Quinet described how he was drawn by a 'marvellous sympathy' to his fellow human beings (*I*, 58). Inner peace was attained when he recognised that the past lived on within him and constituted his being. By means of a mystic communion with other selves, the fractured self rediscovered its plenitude. Within himself Quinet almost became a time traveller, listening 'in the depths of [his] soul to the dull sound of past centuries' (*I*, 59). The freedom which constituted selfhood was rooted in the history of the collective soul of humankind. The past was rediscovered in the present, the inward relocated in the outward.

However, while the triumph over time and the acknowledgement of identity in difference were consoling experiences, the process of merging with the past contained dangers: the surrender of selfhood, the loss of liberty, the fusion of self with other. Of these risks Quinet was well aware: 'I was no longer living in myself but in the confused mass of nations and diverse existences which preceded me; and I gave myself up to them so much that I thought for some time that my personality was going to be absorbed into the universal consciousness of the human race' (*I*, 59). Submission to the past could become destructive of the values of freedom and selfhood. On the other hand the error of modernity had been to carry the principle of subjective freedom to excess and conclude that free individualism could be sufficient unto itself and dominate reality (*E*, 539). By introducing the concept of humanity Quinet released the self from the limits of subjectivity and restored the sense of community. Henceforward the individual felt protected by the 'authority of mankind' (*I*, 70). But Quinet's intention was to strike a difficult balance between reason and history. He sought to redefine the context of freedom without undermining the notion of personal independence which was central to his political philosophy. To this end he left his readers in no doubt that love of humanity should inspire in them a renewed striving, a self-sacrificial sense of duty, rather than feelings of self-satisfaction leading to an abandonment of effort.

Man's moral development was far from accomplished (*I*, 67). Much work remained to be done.

Quinet thus related the problems of the individual self to the idea of humankind in its historical development. However, in order for the actions of humankind to become truly meaningful, the history of humanity was itself construed as the realisation of a divine purpose. History was understood in terms of appearance and reality. Beneath the apparent chaos of events lie divine thoughts. This is history as understood by Cousin – to whom Quinet dedicated his translation of Herder – history envisaged as the external envelope which contains divine ideas. At first sight events appear confused and unstable, especially when they are contrasted with the seeming permanence and immutability of the universe. History, however, is shown to be not a random sequence of events but an orderly process which has its real foundation in the infinite. Quinet distinguished between the real and the ideal, between the necessary and the accidental. God is the ruling power of history. Humankind is 'moved by an invisible hand' (*I*, 34). Events take on true being in so far as they can be shown to correspond to the progress of the ideal. The serenity which is achieved when the individual communes with mankind springs from an identity of essence, a shared participation in the unfolding of spirit. Individual existences and collective entities are finite vehicles for the realisation of a higher purpose which guarantees meaning and which, by implication, justifies revolution and violent change.

Quinet was happy to cite Saint Augustine and Bossuet as precursors in the writing of genuine philosophy of history but he leaves us in no doubt that in his view all human history is potentially sacred history, to the extent that it participates in the revelation of the divine. The different ages are distinct but they are unified by something which transcends the life of determinate communities – the development of the infinite. In other words, the distinction between sacred and profane history gives way to a perspective which embraces the past in its totality and identifies the development of intelligence and the progress of the human spirit with the content of revelation. World history tells of the extension of freedom. However, the movement of history also corresponds to the progressive revelation of reason and justice. Like Guizot and Cousin, Quinet at this stage in his development wanted to harness world history to liberal ideology. He wanted to show that history was rational and intelligible, to demonstrate that the growth in freedom which structures the process could be articulated with social purposes and ethical ideals, and in this way be related to general concerns. Freedom constitutes the essence of the self but Quinet was not promoting unlimited freedom in the sense of the Marquis de Sade. He wanted men to be free as citizens, he wanted the exercise of liberty to serve public as well as private goals.

This line of argument leads the reader towards the conclusion that the locus of the concrete actualisation of freedom, justice and reason is the liberal nation-state. For the moment, however, let us emphasise the central point that for Quinet history possessed a coherence which derived not from the retrospective gaze of the historian but from the fact that phenomenal reality was held to be the mode of existence of a higher power immanent in time. It follows from this that no serious history can be written simply by amassing facts about the past; that would be a history of dubious veracity focusing upon 'ephemeral contingencies' and transient individual existences (*I*, 17). Genuine history requires that events be related to the truth which they are manifesting. Quinet searched for the rational element, the thought or idea which the civilisations of the past had expressed. His difficulty lay in reconciling his commitment to individual freedom with a view of history conceived as the unfolding of the divine. He wanted simultaneously to acknowledge the power of the infinite manifesting itself in time and to protect rationality and human liberty. At times he seems to remove the initiative from man, suggesting that the real subject of history is universal life. Could history have been different? Was everything determined after all? Sometimes this seems to be the case: 'every city appears when its day has come and in the form in which the world requires it' (*I*, 68). Indeed Quinet went further and claimed that the order which he found present in history was mirrored in nature: 'in passing from the science of things to the science of wills, you merely see in analogous and purer forms the same order, the same stability which presented themselves to you in the contemplation of the physical world' (*I*, 38). History was described as the 'highest power of nature'; nature and history together form 'the changing figure of an indivisible unity' (*E*, 535). Contraries are transcended. The self is at peace since it feels that it belongs to the order of nature whose regularity and legality are mysteriously reflected in the unfolding of history. Harmony and order replace discord and division.

The full implications of Quinet's position are revealed in an essay published in 1830, *De la nature et de l'histoire dans leurs rapports avec les traditions religieuses et épiques*. This piece testifies to the increasing influence of German philosophy, notably that of Schelling. Here nature and history are directly associated with the life of the Absolute which objectifies itself as nature and comes to consciousness of itself in the course of world history. History is defined as 'the consciousness of the universe or the organ by means of which the universe reveals itself to its author' (*DLN*, 400). What Quinet termed the 'cosmogonic idea' first manifests itself as unconscious nature and eventually achieves self-awareness in the form of human society. Quinet did not deal with the ontological status of the idea or with the inner logic of its externalisation. However, he took as given the primacy of the ideal over the real and the belief that reason is at work in both the immutable laws of nature and in the unfolding of world history. The idea, first incarnated in nature, is raised to conscious expression by humankind. The aims of historical communities are defined not by individual goals and private interests but by general ideas which take the form of collective aspirations and desires. The outworking of the idea is identical with the elaboration of the historical existence of the collectivity in question. A mathematical rigour determines the operation of this process although individuals are not conscious that the final goal of their activity is the actualisation of the idea. What needs emphasising with regard to Quinet's view of history is the extent to which he ascribes a vital role to nature, something which may strike us as bizarre, bearing in mind his insistence upon the centrality of freedom.

Quinet, like Cousin, posited a form of pre-established harmony between the human and the natural. This was not a matter of the environment exerting a formative influence on social groups, of vague comparisons between national characteristics and landscape, of the determining power of climate as described by Montesquieu. In Quinet's eyes space and time were manifestations of the Absolute and not merely a priori categories of the human understanding. (Quinet talked in a Schellingian way of the ideal identity of nature and history.) What was suggested is as follows: the Absolute objectifies itself as physical nature, unfolds its essence, externalises its ideal reality in the form of a series of material environments dispersed across the earth. The idea struggles to express itself as unconscious nature but needs the human mind in order to know itself fully and thereby return to itself as spirit. A civilisation is represented as an emanation of the world soul, a totality whose internal relations include both mind and nature. Quinet took up the widespread notion that collective entities have purposes and missions but claimed that the idea which the collectivity represents is in harmony with its environment. This provided him with an explanation of the dynamics of world history; migrations of peoples have supposedly occurred when collective entities have journeyed to new locations in quest of the natural setting which corresponds to their idea. It is insufficient therefore to hold that we can give an adequate account of historical change in terms of willed freedom meeting the resistance of an inert universe. In reality, Quinet explained, man is neither the slave nor the master of nature; he is the interpreter of its meaning, the decipherer of its symbols. Man perfects, completes and spiritualises nature which he raises to the ideal. From the standpoint of the Absolute the distinction between spirit and nature is replaced by transparency and the circulation of divine energies. Historical events and material objects alike can be viewed as symbols because both are sustained by the Absolute. Humankind lends nature a voice, re-speaks nature, re-presents it and actualises its potential. By unifying nature and history Quinet involved the physical universe in the upward movement of history. However, the process of assimilation, of incorporation of matter by mind, is a complex one.

Humankind co-operates with nature in order to further the Absolute's journey to self-awareness. Primacy is ascribed to the idea and the religious consciousness seems to be the point at which the Absolute partially apprehends itself at various stages in its self-development. A religion is more than a social phenomenon. It is 'a cosmogonic idea, the cry of all the universe, a word long contained within creation and which now each object pronounces through the mouth of a people' (DLA, 121). What this means is that the organising idea which structures collective life arises at least in part from external nature and receives its most complete expression in religion. The idea of God produced by each religion is the fullest realisation possible of the ideal content latent in nature at that point. The collective actualises the idea but, as indicated above, the divine ideas or thoughts are dispersed in space across the globe. In this way Quinet – unlike Guizot, Thierry or Saint-Simon – placed nature at the heart of history. He was much

closer to the metaphysical idealism of Cousin. History, the progressive movement of mind and reason, reinstates the natural even
when appearing to displace it, recovering nature as value even
while it transforms it and assimilates its substance. However, this
also means that each civilisation can only realise a partial truth or
express an incomplete idea. Each civilisation marks a stage in the
return of nature to spirit, a stage in the Absolute's journey to
self-knowledge. In practice history takes the form of a westward
movement of peoples and religions. Different natural environments are unconscious, objective representations of divine
thoughts or ideas which are then given conscious, subjective
expression by certain collective entities. But only at the end of
history, when all the potential ideas of God have been imagined
and actualised, can there be a complete reconciliation of mind and
nature. At that point the meaning of the earth will be exhausted
and the Absolute will achieve self-knowledge. Quinet's approach
is well captured in a passage in the introduction to *Le Génie de
religions* (1842):

> each location in nature, each moment of duration having its
> own genius, represents the divinity under some particular
> form; from each form of the world arises a revelation, from
> each revelation a society, from each society a voice in the
> universal choir; there is no point lost in space or time,
> which does not figure for something in the ever-increasing
> revelation of the Eternal. Creation, at first separated from
> its author, tends more and more to reattach itself to him by
> the ties of the spirit; and truly the earth gives birth to its
> God in the travail of the ages.

(OC, I, 15)

For Quinet, therefore, the history of the world was essentially
the history of these different ideas of God. On one level the ideas
are constructs of the collective mind in interaction with its past
and its surroundings. At a deeper level they are moments in the
journey of the Absolute to self-knowledge. We have seen how
the ideas which constitute and organise social reality take their
origin in nature. A civilisation is a totality which binds the human
to the natural in a synthesis which embraces both mind and world
and reveals their deeper unity. The history of a culture is the
actualisation, the outworking of the idea, the difficult incarnation
of thought in the sphere of action.

Quinet's method initially made the collective essence appear passive, as mind, receptive to the external world, realised the promise latent within nature. However, Quinet also wanted to present humankind as a desiring subject. He likened humanity to Ulysses journeying through time in search of Ithaca. The movement of history is not simply a response to external factors. The collective will, like the Absolute of whose essence it partakes wishes to externalise itself. The dynamism of history arises from man's desire for the Absolute. Infinite desire is at once subject and object of the historical process. The movement of peoples across the globe amounts to a humanising of the environment, an appropriation of nature by mind. Religion is the powerful symbolic discourse which unifies man with nature. However, the idea of God is more than nature reflected in consciousness. Nature gives form to the 'convoitise de l'infini' (*OC*, I, 10), to the desire to possess the Absolute which ultimately constitutes man as the subject of history. Religion unifies the individual with the social by objectifying as a common ideal the unrealised potential contained within the collective essence. Religion is the central human experience because it projects into the future a model to be imitated, a goal to be achieved, a dream of immortality which contains the vision of a new social world. Collective energies fill the emptiness of the future, bringing hope as well as meaning to suffering humanity which strives unrelentingly to grasp the infinite within the bounds of finitude. As human reason develops and intelligence increases, existing religious forms cease to be adequate to new needs. No religion can contain absolute truth; all are subject to decay and attrition for such is the law of humankind's advance. The gods, symbolic representations of human desires, are overthrown, discarded, abandoned. New ways of imagining and representing the divine presence in nature and in history are invented. However, such sentiments should not be viewed as anti-religious. Quinet did not want to free the world from God. He wanted to distinguish between the Absolute on the one hand and the transient faiths of history on the other. He retained the philosophical framework provided by metaphysical idealism and did not conclude, after the manner of Feuerbach, that religion could adequately be explained as the expression of an alienated human consciousness worshippped as divine.

Quinet's overall view of history brought together elements which we have seen in the work of Cousin and the Saint-Simonians.

Like Cousin he considered that an accumulation of historical detail did not amount to truth and that the real meaning of the historical process lay in the outworking of a metaphysical principle. Like the Saint-Simonians he understood history as a history of cultures, of governing ideas whose rise and fall reflected the advance of man's intelligence. However, Quinet differed from both Cousin and the Saint-Simonians on a vital point; he placed the idea of active freedom at the centre of the argument. He grew progressively wary of Cousin, especially after the philosopher joined the ruling order of the July Monarchy. In a series of outspoken articles Quinet turned on eclecticism, denouncing it retrospectively as a defeatist and un-French philosophy, the intellectual counterpart to the humiliation of Waterloo. Quinet championed a reassertion of the French revolutionary spirit and repudiated Cousin's endorsement of the judgement of history as final.

For Quinet, freedom remained constitutive of the self. At the same time his awareness of the inner emptiness of the modern individual meant that he could understand the Saint-Simonians' dissatisfaction with aspects of modern individuality and appreciate their yearning for a new social principle. However, Quinet was never converted to the new faith. His loyalties remained with the revolutionary tradition and when he envisaged a new social order he did so in terms of an extension of democratic ideas within the nation-state, not in terms of a unified humanity revelling in the power of industry to transform nature. Quinet was temperamentally ill-disposed to Saint-Simonian ideas of hierarchy and obedience which aped Catholic models. His thought was just as oriented towards the future as was Saint-Simonianism but he was more of a seer than a social scientist. And when he turned to history the search for meaning involved more than the ritualised intoning of the Saint-Simonian mantras of organic and critical periods. For Quinet the content of history was resistance to authority; he was unlikely to be convinced by a Saint-Simonian reading of history which colluded with political authoritarianism.

Quinet explains the modern crisis in terms of the working out of the consequences of Christianity. In practice this means that if we want to understand the meaning of the society arising out of the French Revolution we need to view it in relation to the general development of the Christian culture of the west. Christianity, as I have already noted (p. 144), is taken to mark the birth of self-consciousness (although the pre-Christian religions are recognised as having prepared the way). The change wrought by Christianity was irreversible and it put an end to the harmony of the Classical world. Christianity revealed the inward presence of spirit and freedom. Henceforward man would never again be at rest, never be at peace with himself.

Quinet's view of European Christian civilisation followed his general approach to the history of religions according to which the life cycle of a religious idea began with unquestioning faith and ended in the triumph of critical reason. At the inception of a religious period the self was overwhelmed by the divine, lost in God; only gradually did individuality disengage itself and assert its independence. Reason and art progressively subverted the authority of faith. In Quinet's work this movement from religion to science, from the divine to the human, from the general to the particular, from the collective to the individual has the status of a historical law. The erosion of belief was inevitable. However, when the old beliefs have been destroyed and the gods have faded from memory a new faith is born. Quinet represents the Middle Ages as a theocentric age obssessed with the idea of death, as a period when the concern for an other-worldly spiritual life led to a corresponding denial of value to material reality. Humankind was humbled before a transcendent deity who seemingly sat in judgement on creation. In a number of his writings Quinet evoked the slow passing of the Middle Ages, the painful questioning of former certitudes. As the medieval religious world view gradually lost its dominant power over men's minds, so the presence of the infinite was progressively reinscribed within time, relocated within nature. The collective, anonymous inspiration of medieval Christian art was replaced by personal projects and individual desires. The Gothic spire gave way to Brunelleschi's dome. Changes in the representation of the human figure in Italian painting from Cimabue to Raphael disclosed a new valorisation of terrestrial reality. Individuality was emancipating itself from religious authority.

At times in the 1830s Quinet adopted an elegiac tone with regard to the loss of the consolations of faith. However, the fact remained that the gods were transient representations of the desire for the infinite; as the human intelligence grew and reason expanded, so religion declined. The individualism of the Renaissance and the Reformation undermined the cohesiveness of the medieval religious and political order while heightening the conflicts between self and world, between self and society. Subjective freedom increased further as a result of the advances made by science and philosophy since the seventeenth century. In 1789 this process culminated in the ending of arbitrary political rule and the overturning of the old religious order. None the less, in Quinet's writing it is never a simple matter of reason displacing faith.

In an article of 1831 Quinet left his readers in no doubt that the French Revolution was justified. He commented that the Revolution's mission was 'to say farewell to the religious world' (*DLA*, 118). The new regime, founded upon reason and individual rights, corresponded to the moment when modern man heroically took charge of his own destiny. It marked the end of the sacerdotal Middle Ages; henceforward God would no longer be present, 'in the form of Christ', to direct human affairs (*DLA*, 118). However, we should not construe this view of the liberation of human reason as necessarily anti-religious, or even as anti-Christian. First, we should note that in this article the English and French Revolutions are both presented as political consequences of the Reformation. Second, we should remember that although subjective freedom was characteristic of the crisis of modernity the principle of individuality was integral to the Christian idea. Third, we need to bear in mind that while the revolutionary assertion of selfhood removed the individual from dependence upon tradition, when viewed from the perspective of Quinet's general philosophy the desire of the ego to assume authority and independence was itself an expression of a historical moment in the unfolding of spirit. Thus the this-worldly revolutionary project of social construction which sundered Frenchmen from their past was both legitimate and necessary. Quinet remarked that the Revolution was the moment when man demonstrated what he could achieve without God; however, by this he meant without any external authority rooted in divine sanctions. The infinite was still present in nature and in history even when its presence was concealed, obscured, veiled by the assertion of the will and the triumph of reason. In the present Quinet looked forward to a rebirth of religion but by this he meant the relocation of revolutionary freedom within the life of nature and the currents of history. Individuality remained the fullest realisation of humanity but in order to avoid distortions, personal freedom had to rest upon an awareness of the interconnectedness of all things.

However, before describing the rather ambiguous ways in which

Quinet treats the question of man's return to God – he lacks the cocksure confidence of the Saint-Simonians that the 'definitive epoch' was at hand – we need to look further at some of the comments he made about French identity and the French Revolution in the 1830s. His work before 1830 indicated that his sympathies lay with the liberal opposition but at that stage his writing was not overtly political in character. In the wake of the July Revolution he made his commitment to the democratic opposition clear. He also revised his broader intellectual allegiances, developing a critical evaluation of German thought and articulating a prophetic fear of the threat that a Germany united under Prussia would pose to France. The orientation of his thought moved from a generally humanistic cosmopolitanism to a more aggressively militant nationalism. He felt he belonged to a lost generation condemned to inaction by 1815, deceived by the false promises of eclecticism, disappointed by the failure of the July Revolution radically to change society.

Quinet believed his contemporaries were afflicted by a new strain of the *mal du siècle* which he termed 'le mal de l'avenir', 'the sickness of the future' (*A*, 10). Unlike their predecessors who had felt burdened by the ruins of a lost past the victims of 'le mal de l'avenir' lived in a heightened state of anguished expectation, unable 'to bear the weight of the future in the void of the present' (*A*, 10). The present was viewed as an interregnum, as a painful period of transition. But transition to what? There came no clear answer, although, in Quinet's case, the desired future would undoubtedly include a reassertion of the values of the revolutionary period. Quinet, however, made no attempt to restrict the true meaning of the Revolution to 1789, 1791 or, for that matter, to 1793.[5] In his view all the regimes from the Constituent Assembly to the Empire were moments in a single process. The Revolution was an assertion of the national will which sought to actualise ideals of universal application. It achieved the destruction of the old order and moved humanity forward in the direction of 'a new period in the history of the world' (*DLR*, 465). Quinet spoke of French energies creating a new Europe and he associated the revolutionary idea with nationhood and democracy – although he provided no clear definition of what the term democracy actually implied. In fact he devoted almost all of his attention to the Empire and he represented Napoleon, despite his failings, as the heroic embodiment of the revolutionary age of democracy, as a world-historical individual in the Hegelian sense. Napoleon represented 'the development of individuality in modern times' (OC, VII, 157). In other words he illustrated the power of the modern self to mould and fashion the world in accordance with its desires.

In his epic poem *Napoléon* (1836) Quinet's intention was to use the figure of the emperor in order to convey how the freedom of the will could be used positively or negatively. Such freedom was used productively when it was made to serve rational and universal ends. On the other hand when Napoleon the private man displaced the agent of universal progress he fell from grace. Napoleon thus embodied in extreme and exemplary form the dangers of an unrestrained freedom which only recognised its own finite desires as legitimate. In order to be properly used, modern liberty needed to be rooted in the national will which was an expression of historical forces. The attraction of the imperial myth for the young Quinet lay precisely in its capacity to unite revolutionary freedom with an active assertion of the national will. Rather than recall an idealised 1789, Quinet evoked a violent communion on the battlefield, a transcendence of self through participation in action. The Empire reconciled revolutionary individualism with collective purpose. The class conflict which bedevilled the France of the 1830s and 1840s seemed in retrospect not to have sullied the nation during the Empire. Quinet even regretted that he had not had the opportunity to die in the 'holy battles of 1814 and 1815' (OC, VII, 142).

The Revolution remained unfinished and its objectives unfulfilled. The onward march of democracy had been halted in 1815. Quinet wanted to revive national energies by a return to the revolutionary idea. In 1833 he admonished the citizens of the bourgeois monarchy, taking them to task on account of their pusillanimity, contrasting their submissive conformism with the spirit which had earlier animated the doughty soldiers of the *Grande Armée*. Not for Quinet the argument that 1830 marked the end of history, the triumph of a unified Third Estate, the long-awaited establishment of constitutional rule. On the contrary, he saw a country divided by class hatreds, rent by divisions which only a revival of the revolutionary spirit could heal. The forward movement had been arrested in 1815. There had been a brief revival in 1830 but after three days of insurrection conservative forces had regained the upper hand. Far from wanting to effect the closure of history, Quinet wanted to stimulate national energies in order to challenge the bourgeois order. The democratic potential of the Revolution remained unactualised, present to consciousness only as an idea. Unlike the Saint-Simonians who understood both 1789 and 1830 as the climax of a negatively individualistic critical period, Quinet insisted on the Revolution as foundation. It contained 'a system of facts to be accomplished' (DLAER, 28), by which he meant a democratically organised nation-state. In no way could Quinet share the Saint-Simonian view that a regime based on reason and individual rights was a mystification. Far from being an ending, July 1830 was a frustrated new beginning, 'a fact of civilisation which served the accomplishment of an unfinished period' (DLAER, 6).

But this desire for national revival and a return to revolutionary idealism was an integral aspect of Quinet's more general longing for a broader religious renewal. We would be ill-advised to separate the political and religious elements too sharply. Both are grounded in his understanding of the meaning of history. I have indicated already that Quinet saw a revival of religious sentiment as an answer to the negative consequences of scientific and philosophical individualism, a phenomenon which – however historically necessary – had banished God from the world. Instead of consciousness standing over against its object Quinet proposed a synthesis of knowledge which recognised the presence of the divine in nature and in history. One suggestion he makes is that a future religious renewal may take the form of an interchange between mind and the natural world in North America (DLA, 124–6). Elsewhere he speaks of a 'cosmogonic gospel' presently emerging from the sacred texts of Christianity: Jesus is identified with infinity and the church with the natural world (A, 10).

These ideas were not elaborated in a very cogent fashion but what Quinet said points towards a post-Christian pantheistic creed (albeit couched in Christian language), a new Christianity which is this-worldly, life-affirming and engaged in an effort to actualise democratic values. Quinet leaves us in no doubt that traditional Catholicism – like the monarchy which it underpinned – belongs irrevocably to the past and that recent attempts to rejuvenate the faith – such as that undertaken by Lamennais – will fail. Quinet's brand of Christianity denied original sin and asserted the belief in progress. All the same, he found no difficulty in claiming that what he was advocating amounted to a loyal transformation of Christianity in accordance with modern needs. Quinet's new

Christianity rejected coercive authority; it defended individuality while seeking to relate the activity of the self to collective purpose. Above all it was a passionate religion of reason which recognised the inevitability of abandoning the traditional symbols of faith. The loss was painful but irreparable. However, Quinet was not seeking to resurrect the dry rationalism of the eighteenth century. In his case reason did not stand in opposition to life. Its processes legitimated the imagination in its quest for a poetic truth which, by transcending limited human perspectives and adopting the standpoint of absolute identity, might yet create a new mythology.

Quinet talked in somewhat gnomic terms of humankind in travail giving birth to a new god. It is difficult to see quite what this can mean other than a wish for his contemporaries to sub-scribe to his own philosophical views: a Christianity transformed into a religion of universal life which re-established links with external nature and other selves. Antagonisms between subject and object would be transcended when viewed from a perspective which overcame difference and asserted identity. However, despite the importance attributed to restoring communication between man and nature this area was not central to Quinet's later thought. He kept his attention instead on the need for the self to re-establish links with other selves. Although this process can of course take the form of interpersonal relationships, with indi-viduals coming together through the experience of love or friend-ship, Quinet focused upon the wider context of the social and political world. Moral autonomy needed to be reconciled with social values in a manner which avoided both self-validating egoism and coercive forms of external authority.

Quinet's philosophy of history underpinned his politics – but political activity itself became for him an expression of the religious life. In an unpublished essay written after the funeral of Benjamin Constant in 1830, he observed that in the modern world religious feeling took the form of commitment to the idea of freedom. God no longer manifested himself in nature but in politi-cal liberty.[6] By this Quinet probably meant that whereas the developmental process had now ceased in the natural universe, the unfolding of the divine principle continued within history where it took the form of the extension of reason, justice and freedom. History taught that nations actualised the designs of providence. Each collective ego or national spirit was the embodiment of an idea. France was both the Proteus of modern liberties and the bearer of a new social principle (*DLAER*, 36). France was the agent for the advance of European civilisation, or as Quinet put it rather more dramatically, France gave birth to the future (*LPDA*, 262). The reader was left in no doubt that in a world which had gone beyond traditional forms of religious belief the return to God would involve the general transformation of social relations and the revival of the French national spirit.

It was in the lectures delivered at the Collège de France between 1842 and 1845 that Quinet articulated in detail his understanding of history from the birth of Christianity to the French Revolution.[7] The burden of his argument was that the legitimacy of the French Revolution lay in the fact that it marked the actualisation of the principles of Christianity.[8] In this way Quinet, like Saint-Simon, presented to his audience a 'new' Christianity which was supposedly at one with genuine Christianity, a Christianity no longer betrayed by the churches but realised in social life. Quinet united his commitment to individual freedom with his belief in nationalism, investing France with a messianic mission. He did this in a more cogent manner than in his earlier writings and his argument struck a responsive chord in those who opposed the policies of the July Monarchy.

The lectures amounted to a call for action, for a return to the revolutionary idea, and they caused serious embarrassment to the government which finally succeeded in silencing the troublesome professor in 1845. Quinet's lectures showed that he remained preoccupied with the renewal of society and that he persisted in envisaging this process in religious terms. Political revolutions, in order to be successful, needed to be grounded in religious revolutions and Quinet quested after the new religious idea which would both unify society and consolidate the claims of individual freedom. There were, however, differences between Quinet's stance at the Collège de France and his earlier work. Instead of the cosmic Christ we have a representation of Jesus as the embodiment of active individuality. This reflects a significant shift in emphasis away from Germanic abstractions and totalisations and in the direction of a positive valorisation of individuality. A clear indication of this change had been provided in 1838 when Quinet attacked David Strauss's *Leben Jesu* on the grounds that it employed Hegelian speculative philosophy in a manner which dissolved Jesus's individuality, preferring instead to exalt an impersonal humanity. Quinet, in contrast, made the experience of individuality by the historical Jesus the condition for the manifestation of the divine presence:

> if the idea of the God made man has a sense comprehensible for us all, irrefutable for us all, it is in showing us that within each conscience dwells the Infinite as well as in the soul of the human race, and that the thought of each man can spread and dilate until it embraces and penetrates the whole moral universe.

(OC, III, 339)

Selfhood and Christhood were one but the individual only participated in the divine life by means of effort and struggle. What distinguished Christianity from earlier religions was that it was the revelation of inwardness, the apotheosis of the personality, not of the external world. Such statements, to be sure, echo formulations which we have met in Quinet's earlier writings. However, in the lectures of the Collège de France years Quinet gave less prominence than previously to the relation between mind and nature. The thrust of his argument in the 1830s had been that history was to be understood as the recovery of a hidden order of meaning embedded in the physical universe; nature traced the contours of history and shaped the human desire for the infinite. According to this interpretation the natural environment of Europe mysteriously corresponded to the realisation of Christianity and the suggestion was that at some stage in the future the world spirit would leave the shores of Europe and emigrate to North America. This line of argument pointed unmistakably in the direction of a post-Christian, post-European future. In the 1840s the ideas of Christianity and Europe regained their centrality.[9] The future lay in France rather than North America, in human relations rather than in a mystic union of mind with nature. External nature was expressly associated with the pre-Christian religions which represented the Old Testament of humankind. Medieval Christianity corresponded to the New Testament, to the age of the Son. By uniting Christianity with the ancients the Renaissance inaugurated the reign of spirit (OC, I, 358). In this manner Quinet described the temporal stages of the self-manifestation of the triune God. The age of spirit proceeded from the Father and from the Son, from the pagan and the Christian past. The Romantic expectation of religious and social renewal

161

was thus set in a context which recalled both millenarianism and the three ages as described by Joachim of Fiore.[10]

'L'Esprit', spirit, was the guiding concept in Quinet's thought of the 1840s. It underpinned both his nationalism and his conception of the personality. Spirit is a force present in the world and it is action rather than knowledge which now seems to be the end of history. Matter offers resistance to spirit but it is not devalued. On the contrary spirit needs its material incarnation in order to realise itself in the form of action. God as spirit reveals himself in the life of the individual. Quinet, however, argues that we only participate in the life of spirit by dint of an unrelenting effort. Individuals are in an important sense self-creations. The individual's spiritual nature realises itself in freely determined practical activity in the moral sphere as opposed to the contemplation of infinity or the mystic's union with the godhead. Particular responsibility rests with those individuals such as Galileo, Kepler and Voltaire who are presented as the heroes of the religion of spirit. In Quinet's view, the pursuit of scientific knowledge and philosophical truth is an intrinsically religious activity; like Saint-Simon, he accused the Catholic Church of acting against the interests of spirit, of behaving in an un-Christian manner. But while championing the individual Quinet does not neglect the collective. He reaffirms his belief that peoples, races and nations represent ideas. The origin of the ideas is obscure but their reality cannot be denied. They come from God and inspire collective action: 'When Providence wants a thought to enter into the world and for ever to remain there, it makes this thought the soul of a new race' (OC, III, 166). Nations have collective personalities, they are embodiments of ideas, centres of value. A nation is a manifestation of Spirit in the world and each nation has a mission to fulfil. Nations are the real agents of progress and patriotic feelings should not be suppressed in favour of generalised humanitarian ideals. Expanding on ideas found in his earlier work, Quinet presented France as the nation with the most important mission to fulfil. We learn that while decadent Catholicism could only aspire to universality by extinguishing the fertile spirit of nationhood, France can unite the nations in the service of spirit. France can be viewed in religious terms as the Christ of nations, charged with a redemptive mission.

In Le Génie des religions Quinet described how religious ideas, the reflection of external nature in human consciousness, were the

generative cause of history before the coming of Christianity. In
Le Christianisme et la Révolution française he moved on to explain
how the Christian idea of God (the conjoining of the Greek
awareness of the presence of the divine within man with the
Hebrew belief in a transcendent personal deity) organised social
and political reality. However, the Christian idea of God – Jesus
as God-Man – took concrete form in different ways. The Christian
idea was initially embodied in Jesus himself who is presented with
tender admiration as a centre of spontaneous spiritual activity, an
enemy of the restrictions of formalised religion. Jesus evidently
represents the values which Quinet was defending: life, creativity,
personality, movement, action. We are shown Jesus inspiring the
disciples by his deeds and by his moral strength. Quinet then
moved on to discuss the early church and the formation of Christian doctrine. This amounts to an analysis of how organised Christianity came to define in intellectual terms its notion of the divinity.
Quinet's thesis is that the dogmas of the church moulded social
reality. Medieval ideas of the relationship between spiritual and
temporal power are held to flow directly from the belief in the
two natures of Jesus. Ideas control events. We are told that Saint
Augustine effectively mapped out the parameters of social organisation for the Middle Ages: in comparison with the weight of
Augustinian theory, the barbarian invasions were only a secondary
cause in the development of feudalism (*OC*, III, 78).

Quinet viewed the increase in papal authority as a sign that the
church was moving away from the true message of the Gospels.
He finds evidence of the spiritual decline of the church in the
Crusades, the crushing of the Albigensians, the Inquisition, the
burning of Joan of Arc, the despoliation of South America. The
figure of Gregory VII stands out as a lone exception in Quinet's
exposition; here was a pope who genuinely stood for unbending
moral and spiritual authority. But by the end of the Middle Ages
spiritual energy had drained away from the church. In the seventeenth century French Catholicism was already a spent force,
divided against itself, as the Jansenist controversy demonstrated.
In *Les Jésuites* (1843) and *L'Ultramontanisme* (1844), Quinet
argued that post-Tridentine Catholicism gave legitimation to
absolutism and brought sterility to Spain and Italy. The true spirit
of Christianity was elsewhere, developing outside the church. The
onward movement of liberation, begun by the Reformation and
extended by the philosophers of the Enlightenment was completed

by the French Revolution which overthrew a spiritual order which was already bankrupt and moribund.

History, the outward manifestation of ideal forces, is called upon by Quinet to legitimate the French Revolution and the democratic nation-state. He did not present individual rights and freedoms as abstract inventions of Enlightenment reason but as the long-awaited inscription of the Christian message. The Reformation, in the shape of Luther, had accorded to the living individual 'the freedom, the authority, the intrinsic value which the church only accorded to the dead' (OC, III, 170). Unfortunately – Quinet echoed Saint-Simon on this point – the Reformation remained unable to escape from a regressive desire to rebuild the primitive church. The French Revolution gave new force to the Reformation's assertion of the freedom of the individual from external authority. Selfhood proceeded from the divinity. Conscience, 'the inner God hidden within each one of us' (OC, III, 209), was sacred and inviolable. Moreover, the Revolution went beyond the Reformation because it accepted that the promise of Christianity should no longer be displaced into an other-worldly afterlife but be actualised here and now in social existence. Christ, Quinet declared, 'is incarnated in history century by century' (OC, III, 79). The Middle Ages actualised the idea of Christ on the cross. The Revolution, by extending the gains of the Reformation, inaugurated the real age of spirit, actualising Christianity within society, realising 'that eternal evangel which Italy had prophesied since the twelfth century' (OC, IV, 465). The Revolution embodied in law and in institutions the rights of individual conscience. France was the instrument of spirit and God's Kingdom could be realised now, on this earth. The decadent church, on the other hand, was the agent of resistance, of impurity, of matter: 'The church had become the stone which enclosed spirit in the sepulchre; . . . the angel of France lifted the stone; spirit revealed itself' (OC, III, 56).

Quinet's fondness for religious language and rather extravagant comparisons should not blind us to what he is saying. He is using symbolic language in order to effect a movement of desymbolisation.[11] In so doing he is being consistent with his earlier stance: post-revolutionary modernity involved both separation from the traditional religious view of the human condition and a return to God, a rediscovery of his inward presence. So when Quinet mentioned the Second Coming he did not envisage the Son of Man literally returning in glory. He was using the Christian imagery to convey something different; the notion that the realisation of the Kingdom would involve a new age of striving, a further development of the inwardness of spirit (*OC*, III, 49). The new order would not be a supernatural one. Indeed, in Quinet's terms, to interpret the supernatural literally is to collude with matter, to limit the creativity of Spirit. The Word which liberates allows interiority to triumph over exteriority. The divine was not something set over against the world of finitude; the divine was present within time. The traditional language of the supernatural was appropriate when describing the power of Spirit manifesting itself in history provided that it was not taken literally. Hence Quinet's willingness to talk of the miracles wrought by the Revolution, to describe its wars as holy and its soldiers as Crusaders. Religious imagery was ennobling and moving but it was figurative in character and did not designate any supernatural reality.

Revolutionary Christianity did not take its source in Christianity as defined by the church; it originated in the historical Jesus who embodied the fertile activity of spirit in the world. Thanks to the French Revolution the idea of the God-Man, the conjunction of Christhood and selfhood within the personality, was finally realised and universalised after a gap of 1,800 years. Moreover, since revolutionary Christianity – like Jesus himself – drew life and inspiration from the inward presence of the divine within the human, it had no need to rely on sacred texts and the authority of the Bible. The Revolution had gone beyond the Reformation. Man no longer needed the support of external nature or of biblical authority. He knew God directly, inwardly, and he externalised the divine within the sphere of practical existence. The Word, freed from bondage to the letter, became creative, inscribing itself in social reality, engraving its substance in new texts, in laws which objectified in the discourse of universal reason the legitimate rights of human subjectivity. The Revolution thus marked the long-awaited realisation in social life of the Christian idea of God. In that climactic moment it seemed that everything was possible. In his discussion of the energy of the Convention Quinet evoked a moment when the distance between thought and action, between word and deed, was replaced by immediate actualisation. There seemed no longer to be a divide separating theory from practice. The difficult labour of time was elided.

However, although the Revolution was the culmination of the

history of the Christian west it did not inaugurate God's Kingdom. Simultaneity gave way to succession. Dissent and freedom of thought were violently repressed in the name of liberty and human goodness. Quinet's analysis of why the Revolution went wrong is based on the idea that in France political transformations were hindered because they could not build upon earlier religious transformations; that the Revolution, lacking a Protestant base, was unable to make its advances secure. Whereas in England and in North America democracy relied upon a firm Protestant foundation, in France the Revolution had to deal with an intolerant church which was opposed to all claims made in the name of freedom. This incompatibility was the source of much chaos and confusion. The Revolution misunderstood the nature of its enemy and made misguided attempts to rally the church to its cause. The Civil Constitution of the Clergy was presented by Quinet as a failed attempt to emancipate a church which was incapable of recognising that the Declaration of the Rights of Man was in truth an expression of God's will (*OC*, III, 227). Although the Revolution had become the legitimate spiritual power, in the sense that its authority was sanctioned by Quinet's interpretation of history, it had to face a resolutely hostile institutional embodiment of religious authority. Moreover, it was not only the church that remained caught in the habits of the past. The revolutionaries themselves fell victim to the authoritarian mind-set inherited from the Catholic past.

Quinet praised the Convention for its energetic defence of the nation, for its achievements in reforming education, science and national administration, but he also pointed out that the men of the Convention were dominated despite themselves by the intolerant spirit of the religion which they rejected. Quinet's own brand of revolutionary Christianity valorised the inward depth of spirit which externalised itself as action and social practice. Seen from this vantage point, the revolutionary cults of the 1790s seemed dangerously backward-looking; so many self-conscious constructs, pale imitations of Catholicism, reassertions of the outward, formalised religious practices of the past, examples of sterile imitation, not of fertile invention:

> Sadly, at the very moment when [the men of the Convention] thought they were at their most revolutionary they fell back into the shadow of the church. These abstractions put

in the place of saints, these seasons, these virtues instead of ecclesiastical festivals, was all this not a constant imitation of Catholicism? The same desire to strike the senses, the same faith in images, in surfaces.

(*OC*, III, 230)

Quinet recoiled when he described the Convention's wish to reintroduce a state religion. Here was the Catholic denial of freedom of conscience re-emerging in a different guise. Robespierre became a dictator, a revolutionary pope. The Committee of Public Safety violated the sanctity of individual conscience by requiring citizens to surrender to the state the precious essence of their personal being (*OC*, III, 231). The Revolution, which had begun by going beyond the achievements of the Reformation in terms of individual freedom regressed wildly; punishing dissent, proclaiming its own exclusive truth, instituting a new orthodoxy supported by the machinery of the Terror. The Convention disastrously confused means and ends but in Quinet's eyes it did not irrevocably compromise the enterprise of renewal. During the Empire the army spread the message of 1789 beyond the frontiers of France. However, like the men of the Convention before him, Napoleon fell victim to the insidious influence of the past. Once he accepted that his authority needed consecration at the hands of the Catholic church his fate was effectively sealed. He was ensnared by the symbols of the past and embarked upon a misguided attempt to build an empire which imitated medieval models. Quinet none the less still held that revolutionary freedom was vanquished at Waterloo along with imperial despotism. In *Le Christianisme et la Révolution française* Waterloo was presented as the Golgotha of modern times, as the defeat which began thirty years of suffering, humiliation and living death for the French people. However, Quinet earnestly believed that like Christ, France had to undergo this period of suffering in order to fulfil its redemptive function, and that like Christ, France would eventually be resurrected.

The relation of man to God was clearly crucial to Quinet. His attitude can be contrasted with that of Saint-Simon. For the author of *Le Nouveau Christianisme*, God, if he existed at all, was of little significance. What mattered was the power of organised religion to structure social relations. Quinet's case was very different. He considered that without the idea of God there could be no history, no freedom, no ideal. And his God, simultaneously immanent and mysteriously transcendent, existed in contradistinction to human constructions of the divine. But while Quinet affirmed God's existence his approach raised questions as to God's nature and the final destination of creation. Was it enough to consider that we know God inwardly and by examining what He has done in history? Matters were reasonably straightforward when Quinet spoke a recognisably Christian language. His application of the trinitarian formula to history allowed his readers to place what he was saying about spirit in relation to Christian ideas of creation and incarnation. When he adopted a vocabulary closer to Cousin or German idealism his position likewise possessed a degree of coherence and clarity: he suggested that God was at one with divine reason, the power which structures and orders reality. God was the source of the legality of the universe and the guarantor of the meaning of history.

Quinet usually represented nature and history as manifestations of divine thought, suggesting that beyond appearances lay the reassuring ordering presence of thought or reason. The power of mind sustained phenomenal reality. In *Ahasvérus*, however, he raised the possibility that at the core of things lay a cosmic life force, beyond all human categories of good and evil, indifferent to the concerns of men. At the close of his epic he introduced the figure of Eternity, the power that lay behind the transient gods of history. Eternity emerged as a life-giving force, relentlessly creative. However, Eternity was far removed from the sovereignty of divine love as understood by Christianity. Eternity was amoral, capricious, at times irrational and vindictive. It asserted its will in a manner which demonstrated that it did not depend on anything outside itself. It cried aloud its solitude and its transcendence – this was not the Absolute which by a movement of internal necessity objectified itself as nature and history. Was God as understood by the Christian tradition the real subject of history after all? The act of creation now seemed a gratuitous gesture, a device for overcoming the tedium endured by the cosmic self. In other words the character of the absolute self recalled the extreme forms of subjective freedom. Could such a power sustain history as an unfolding of meaning?

That Quinet had doubts on this score is revealed by the way in which, in *Ahasvérus*, he compared history to a dream in the mind of God, to a game, to a dance. What was the status of history if behind the surface of events lay not the rational unfolding of divine ideas but an unlimited freedom identified with absolute egoism? Was man's only line of defence the deployment of irony and parody? At the centre of creation lay an intensity of life which seemed less the sovereignty of reason than the relentless rampaging of the cosmic will. Was history any more than a hoax? Quinet's vision, which probably drew on Spinoza, Fichte and oriental religious traditions, left no room for man to engage in dialogue with the imperious cosmic energy. Man was cast in the role of Job. Eternity was life-giving but it was hard to see how it could provide a foundation for the development of reason and justice. On the other hand, if Eternity were judged to be the power which constituted history, was this tantamount to inscribing 1793 as a cosmic principle, to asserting that history was the creation of a violent and irrational will to power, the product of passion, not reason?

Too often literary history minimises the anguished uncertainties which accompanied the Romantics' expressions of confidence in nature and trust in history. Alfred de Vigny was not alone in entertaining an ambivalent relationship with nature. Michelet, as we shall see, saw nature as simultaneously creative and destructive. Like Quinet he understood history as the development of freedom and selfhood, as a process which involved the progressive reduction of dependency upon nature. However, as we have already seen, in Quinet's case this process of disengagement from nature was not an authentically human achievement. First, the entire global environment seemed to have been shaped in order to guide human evolution. Second, and more significantly, Quinet attributed to nature the function of revealing the idea of God to man. How could human freedom invest history with meaning if the driving force of cultural evolution – transformations in the representation of the divinity – rested wholly upon impressions which the mind received from the external world? In the 1830s and early 1840s Quinet, like Michelet, understood the significance of the Judaeo-Christian tradition in terms of the overcoming of the eastern identification of nature with God. Human freedom and selfhood really began when the idea of God ceased to be identified directly with the visible universe and no longer filled the content of consciousness. Quinet, however, never satisfactorily resolved the question of the ontological status of nature in relation to history. He did not address the problem of nature in philosophical terms and left the disturbing image of Eternity to haunt the minds of his readers. In the 1840s he moved away from his earlier willingness to locate Christianity within a framework inherited from the philosophy of identity. Unfortunately he did not properly work through the consequences of his new position.

Quinet's writing of the 1840s presents us with an image of history as the creative embodiment of spirit. The presence of the eternal within time drives the process in which mind progressively triumphs over matter, freedom over necessity, liberty over authority. The ideal has primacy over the real. Divine life animates the historical process. Its energies course through time. Nations and individuals alike are channels of spirit, agents of the infinite. The study of history became Quinet's way of expressing the mystery of the incarnation. History was at once human and divine. Our knowledge of God seemingly arose from our knowledge of what He has done in history. He is known through the category of action, not of substance. There are different degrees of incarnation (individual and collective) and the highest was made manifest in the person of Jesus Christ. History as a single whole was an Eternal Evangel, filled with the divine presence which shaped events. The role of the historian was not therefore the humble labour of sifting and evaluating evidence in order to distinguish truth from falsehood. The historian, or more properly the philosopher of history, took on what amounted to a sacerdotal function, revealing God's presence in events. In Quinet's view this was a role that the church could no longer fulfil – which is hardly surprising given the absolute certitude with which he reprimanded the church for failing to recognise what he termed the divine necessity of the Reformation and the French Revolution! The holy is therefore revealed in history, not in scripture. Did this imply that in future times the historical text would itself become holy writ, the new and unimpeachable source of authority? Was history henceforth to be worshipped? The extent to which Quinet was in fact willing to go down this road was evidenced in a passage where he explained that if the philosophy of universal history were fully developed it would be identical with universal religion.

And yet, while knowledge of the past disclosed the presence of the divine, this knowledge could itself become a burden, weighing on the present, inhibiting action. Quinet was keen to close off the possibility of any unproductive imitation of past reality, for even the greatest achievements of the past could enslave the present. All imitation involved a movement away from spirit in the direction of matter and unfreedom. Historical knowledge was liberating in so far as it identified time with life, not with death. But this was time irradiated by the active presence of eternity. The past which reasserted itself simply as past bore death, not life, for life had moved on, leaving behind only the material shell of existence. To yield to time in this sense was to validate a simulacrum of presence, to align one's being with an arid emptiness which was movement without life, repetition, pure externality, a beguiling shimmer dissimulating an immobilism. Quinet accused the Jesuits of materialising spirit. The pull of the past was similar. If not properly used, the past became a malign and deceitful force resembling life but actually stifling life. The past acted on the present like those dead gods which became parasitic on the men who created them and whose substance they devoured. In order for the past not to hinder the present it needed to be constantly illuminated, transformed by spirit. In that way the negativity of the past was itself negated and the creative power of eternity was released. Mankind progressed when the power of the future was active in the present transforming the past.

The negative pull of the past was exerted in a variety of ways. Sometimes the process was largely unconscious. The Revolution's catastrophic reproduction of Catholic models of authority was a case in point. On other occasions the prestige of the past expressed itself more directly. Quinet ascribed Italy's failure to achieve national self-determination to the seductive power of political myth in the shape of the people's fascination with idealised images of the papacy and the Holy Roman Empire. But the influence of the past could also take the form of more self-conscious and seemingly well-intentioned types of imitation such as the Reformation's understandable but inappropriate wish to recreate an ideal of primitive Christianity. In fact, in Quinet's eyes, any wish to escape the past, into a lost golden age, was a delusion which denied the onward and irreversible movement of time. The past was at best a temporary refuge since by definition it could not offer anything adequate to present needs. Quinet urged his listeners to create a new world, to avoid repeating the past. Even the French Revolution was not something to be idolised, to be uncritically imitated. Neither was the revolutionary state something to be venerated as if it were a religion (OC, III, 266). Quinet remarked that although the Revolution marked a sublime effort to grasp the divine it was none the less not identical with 'justice, the Eternal Evangel, Absolute Religion' (*OC*, III, 265). The past, however admirable, should not be allowed to absorb the life of the present. Neither, in Quinet's view, should men respond uncritically to the blandishments and false beguilements of those who promoted visions of an ideal future society. The idea of the future, if wrongly applied, could be just as inimical as the past to the spirit of genuine change. All too often the wish to bring an ideal future into being amounted to a displaced desire to return to the past. In the plans of the Saint-Simonians Quinet detected the presence of the past masquerading as the future. Their view of the future amounted to a disguised restatement of the Catholic desire to '[suppress] all the individuality of modern man' (*OC*, III, 269). Freedom was at stake and Quinet was in no mood to find excuses for the Saint-Simonians – no allusion here to their idealism, sincerity or compassion.

Quinet directed his listeners to concentrate on the focal point of present reality, illuminated – but not overwhelmed – by knowledge of the past. Spirit was on the side of creation, not on the side of the forces of imitation and repetition which trapped the activity of mind in the negativity of matter. However, Quinet's argument did not suggest a denial of the past in the manner in which the men of 1789 had repudiated history in the name of reason. In his view an ethical imperative could be derived from history, provided that the past was grasped as a manifestation of the divine, as a leaving behind of the resistance of matter, as a work of reconciliation. Quinet had a clear sense that society was not as it ought to be but he laid responsibility for improvement on the individual self and the collective self together fulfilling their destiny as embodiments of spiritual energy. He called upon individuals to resist the temptations of material satisfaction which engendered immobilism. It was the willing self which could produce a better world, not the compliant self which moved with the surface currents of time. Quinet decried material progress if that meant simply the extension to all citizens of the lifestyle of the bourgeoisie. He proposed a stern morality of self-discipline which regarded conflict and negation as necessary elements in humankind's spiritual advance. Hence his dislike of compromise and moderation – as evidenced in eclectic philosophy or *juste milieu* politics – which too often signalled a cowardly accommodation with the world as it was. Only by an intense inner effort could man produce the creative energies needed to transform reality. However, by dint of such mental and moral heroism the human could give birth to the superhuman (*OC*, III, 263).

Quinet rejoiced in the Revolution of February 1848. France regained its self-respect and the spirit of 1789 was revived. The government of the Republic restored Quinet to his chair at the Collège de France where in March 1848 he delivered a rousing speech, praising the masses whose actions had served the fulfilment of God's design for humanity. Quinet now abandoned his academic career and became an active politician, sitting as a left-wing member of both the Constituent and Legislative Assemblies. However, the high hopes of February 1848 proved to be short-lived. As events unfolded the intensity of class antagonisms was revealed and the continuing power of the church over the mind of the masses became apparent. During the uprising of June 1848 Quinet served as a colonel in the National Guard, defending the area around the Panthéon against the insurgents. (He blamed Bonapartist elements for stirring up the rebellion.) His understanding of history was deeply affected by 1848. In that year he began publishing under the title *Les Révolutions d'Italie* the lectures that he had delivered during his early years at the Collège de France. The first volume was completed before February 1848. The latter two, appearing in 1851 and 1852 respectively, bore the imprint of recent events. Here his general thesis was that the Italian people had been unable to achieve national unity because they remained enslaved to the past, unable to detach themselves from social ideals inherited from the papacy and the Holy Roman Empire. Quinet departed from the admiration usually accorded to Italian municipal freedoms by liberal historians and presented instead the Italian republics as prisoners of their Catholic past. He drew a distinction between the enfranchisement of the Communes in Italy and the operation of the process in northern Europe. He made the church principally responsible for Italy's failure to develop into an organised nation-state. The violence and factionalism of Italian history arose from the nation's Catholic education.

How relevant was the Italian example for nineteenth-century France? Quinet was well aware of the differences between France and Italy. He recognised that for centuries the French state had given political embodiment to a sense of collective identity which Italy still lacked. However, there were also disturbing parallels. Italy and France were presented as peoples originally enslaved by

Rome and subsequently placed in submission to the church. In both countries the temperament of political leaders and the character of the population reflected Catholic habits of intolerance transmitted from the past. In both countries class conflict threatened social cohesion. In his earlier writings Quinet had warned of the dangers posed by class divisions within France. After the sad experience of 1848 he drew two related conclusions. First, the masses were sorely in need of education. Second, there was an absolute incompatibility between Catholicism and the French national spirit. Henceforth he would admit no compromise whatsoever between Catholicism and the revolutionary idea: 'the Catholic principle is incompatible with modern freedom' (OC, IV, 550). Quinet looked on in horror as the new republic acted in ways which contradicted its very principles, notably by seeking an accommodation with clerical interests. In Le Christianisme et la Révolution française he had warned of the power of the past to enslave the present. The aftermath of 1848 confirmed his worst fears. Once bound to the church, the republic jettisoned its principles by sending the military expedition to crush the Roman republic. The passing of the Falloux education laws simply completed the submission of the state to the church.

In Les Révolutions d'Italie Quinet showed himself to be less confident in France's regeneration and much more aware of the factors which conspired to hinder the actualisation of freedom. He now saw that it was not just a question of the past weighing on the present; the events of 1848–51 forced him to recognise the existence of a human propensity towards voluntary servitude. Citizens seemingly colluded with the forces of reaction which were ranged against the idea of democracy. To be sure France was not quite in the same predicament as Italy. France after all possessed the national statehood which for Quinet was a prerequisite for freedom. However, France remained tied to Catholicism. In Le Christianisme et la Révolution française Quinet had been reasonably confident that by reconciling the objectives of individual freedom and association France was going to realise true Christianity. However, in the wake of 1848 and 1851 he was noticeably less sanguine about the future. A new realism prevailed when it came to sizing up the chances of transforming French society. During the July Monarchy Quinet had stressed the need for self-discipline in the hope that his ideas would eventually triumph. The course taken by events during the Second Republic led to some sober reconsideration. Quinet repudiated what he called the 'favourite idea of modern liberalism' (*OC*, IV, 387) – that ideas possessed a life of their own and could not permanently be crushed by force. History, he now realised, taught a quite other lesson. He concluded that in order to make ideas a reality a willingness to act was required, by which he meant a willingness to use violence where necessary. Looking back to 1789 Quinet observed that if revolution was the desired goal, then its supporters had to will the means to achieve it, including the use of terror (*OC*, IV, 190).

Quinet would nuance his views some years later in *La Révolution* (1865) but the direction of his argument was clear. It was one thing to master the past by interpreting it as a progressive unfolding of purpose, quite another to conclude that new ideas would be accepted and introduced without pain. As we can see, Quinet had by now gone well beyond the liberal defence of freedom as an absence of coercion by state power. The events of 1848 raised an essential question: how should a society which claims to be just and tolerant deal with forces which deny pluralism? Quinet plainly thought that it was incumbent upon the state to intervene to protect essential freedoms against those who invoked toleration in order to suppress liberty. The events of 1848 revealed the catastrophic consequences of a revolution willing to compromise with Catholicism.

Quinet was driven into exile by Louis-Napoléon's *coup d'état*. In the years which followed he devoted his attention to exploring why some revolutions succeeded whereas others failed. He treated the revolt of the gladiators under Spartacus in a drama of 1853, examined the foundation of the Dutch republic in 1860 and revised his estimate of the French Revolution in 1865. His writing of these years demonstrated a more sober treatment of history. Quinet had contributed to the construction of the Romantic myths of Napoleon and the Revolution. His work after 1851 involved an element of demythologising, a restoring of events to the world of fact. In the 1840s he had presented the unfolding of history as the mode of being in which freedom revealed itself. He had reminded his students how difficult it was to escape from the pull of the past but he had nevertheless suggested ways in which historical knowledge could serve the cause of liberty. In the climate of the 1850s Quinet came to view the liberal and socialist historians of the July Monarchy as accomplices in the decline of the nation. He correctly perceived the extent to which liberal history was a history of fulfilment whose legitimacy was unlikely to survive the collapse of the constitutional monarchy. He argued his case in an important essay of 1855, *Philosophie de l'histoire de France* (*OC*, III, 353–422).

Quinet fully recognised how the remaking of French history in terms of the ascension of the Third Estate had given retrospective legitimation to the liberal state and the constitutional monarchy.[12] He himself had never accepted that the regime of 1830 marked the culmination of French history. In the 1830s and 1840s his thought had been overtly future-oriented, prospective in character (he criticised Hegel precisely for refusing to address the question of the future). Historical knowledge, far from confirming the *status quo*, was viewed as a prelude to action; once the past had been grasped in its potentiality as well as in its actuality it became possible to espouse the movement of creation which engendered the future. For Quinet the Revolution of 1848 was a moment of hope because it signalled that progressive forces were again on the move. The failure of the Second Republic substantially altered Quinet's own views on history, but the fact that the February Revolution had taken place at all was proof enough in his mind that the liberal historical project was now obsolete. However, being disproved by events did not absolve liberal historiography of its wider responsibility. In *Philosophie de l'histoire de France* Quinet launched a broadside against the liberal representation of the past. It was now Augustin Thierry's turn to be charged with disfiguring history in the name of politics, with mutilating the record of events the better to endorse Orleanism. It was now liberalism, not royalism, which stood accused of concealing the truth about the past, of rewriting defeats as victories.

Quinet formulated a broadly based critique which included socialist as well as liberal historiography. Both were held to be guilty of lending to events an impression of inevitability. Quinet was particularly enraged by the historians' propensity to countenance the crushing of freedom where it got in the way of state-building and centralisation. Liberals who made excuses for the policies of Louis XI, Louis XIV and Richelieu had in fact compromised the political future of the nation.[13] Quinet considered that such amorally optimistic theories which explained away instances of tyranny and repression, on the grounds that they contributed in some manner to a general levelling process, in fact undermined the struggle for freedom in the present. He was angered when the failure to advance the cause of freedom in the past was justified on the spurious grounds that change would have been premature. Socialist historians were especially taken to task for repudiating the very germs of liberty which lay within the national past; Quinet cites Buchez and Roux's justification of the Saint Bartholomew's Day massacre in a way which lent succour to Catholicism. The socialists' ill-conceived hatred of individualism led them to deny the value of the Reformation and enter into what amounted to an objective alliance with the Inquisition. In their desire to present history as an increase in equality they endorsed the suppression of liberty.

But what was left once the myths of liberal and socialist history had been stripped away? After 1851, while not disowning his general view of the discipline of history as a moral discourse on society which served the republican ideal, Quinet urged a reappraisal of method. In no circumstances could the Second Empire, organised around the personal authority of Louis-Napoléon and supported by the church, be held to constitute the good society. Hence the need to re-examine the discourse on the national past. Recent events had discredited the salvatory, optimistic and self-justificatory national narratives. It was as if the defeats of 1848–51 had inaugurated a different perspective on the past, comparable in some ways to the emergence of Romantic historiography in the wake of the French Revolution and the First Empire. For Quinet the coming to power of the new imperial regime cast serious doubt on the broader question of whether meaning could be sustained by the reference to history. Could the Second Empire, a regime which he likened to a new Byzantine age, provide a vantage point from which to disentangle the past? Class conflict and the collapse of parliamentary government had dealt a severe blow to Thierry's image of a unified nation reconciled with itself. It had also given the lie to the integrative project dear to progressivist historiography. The establishment of the Empire became the measure against which theories of history were henceforth to be judged. The nature of the regime meant that the historian could no longer see his function as that of reunifying the fragments of the past in the form of a progressive, revelatory movement. Moreover, the re-emergence of arbitrary rule undermined belief in the rationality of history in general.

Quinet none the less retained his belief in the development of freedom and individuality, and continued to explain historical change in terms of intellectual realities as opposed to economic forces. What largely disappeared from his work was the over-powering sense of purposeful historical dynamism, the confidence in the indwelling of active spirit. The presence of freedom was now something to be discovered and treasured, something fragile, something to be grieved over when lost. As *Les Révolutions d'Italie* had demonstrated, force could – and did – eradicate right. French history was now largely viewed as a series of defeats, most notably that of the Gauls by the Romans. Freedom it would appear, always found it hard to take root in France. The French people were no longer the unchallengeable embodiment of virtue. Instead Quinet described a nation ever willing to lay down the burden of freedom when promised increased material well-being. The French were rebellious in character but at the same time they were not reluctant to abandon liberty and submit to religious or political authority. Liberal and socialist historians had com-pounded the problem because in their work they had all too often been guilty of the very failings which Quinet now held to be common among the French: an immoderate worship of success, a lack of pity and an indifference to freedom. In other words, in Quinet's estimation liberal and socialist historiography re-inforced the least positive aspects of the French character. Defeat and conquest had produced something akin to a slave mentality.

Could history be rewritten in a way which defended freedom and challenged the authority of the Second Empire? As a first step, the myths produced by Quinet's contemporaries would have to be abandoned. The historians of the Third Estate had produced unifying narratives which presented the development of France as a continuity. In the 1850s and 1860s Quinet proposed a very different view of national history, one which foregrounded rep-etition and recurrence rather than continuity and development. The truth of history could no longer easily and confidently be related to the activity of a higher power manifesting itself in time, embodying itself in the collective destiny of the French people. Quinet was now suspicious of the attempt to draw a distinction between the significance of a historical personage within the con-text of his own time and his meaning within a grand narrative. Quinet's goal had become the preservation of the differentiated nature of historical reality. In the 1840s history had seemed an

'Eternal Evangel'. Spirit endowed events with a meaning which was simultaneously human and divine. Revolutionary France was envisaged as the agent for the realisation of Christianity. After 1851 the note of religious enthusiasm was noticeable by its absence. The events of 1848–51 not only overthrew liberal certainties – Quinet's diagnosis was correct on that score – they also brought about a general failure of history as a discourse of legitimation. After 1851 it was as if the divine presence no longer filled history, no longer inflated the succession of events with its transforming power. The meaning of events could no longer be determined in relation to an overarching developmental metaphysic, to a discourse which distinguished between accident and essence, appearance and reality, form and substance. The divine seemed to retreat from the collective sphere and take up residence within the inner world of the moral conscience.

Having laid aside his hopes for a radical religious transformation of the moral and social worlds, Quinet set out to secularise and demythologise history. To couch the representation of history in religious language was now considered to have been an error – although it should be said that while Quinet charged others with this failing he uttered no personal *mea culpa*. In the 1840s he had clearly felt that he was using the language and the symbols of faith in accordance with the needs of spirit, that he was renewing their content inwardly, returning them to life. However, there was always an element of risk: the transforming agent might betray its spiritual nature, coalesce with externality and submit to the traditional meanings carried by the symbolic forms. Had Quinet made an error in enveloping his interpretation of history in religious language? He did not say so directly. However, there can be no doubt that in his writing of the 1850s and 1860s his approach to history was reframed. Events were understood in human terms rather than evaluated as divine punishments. Quinet ceased to invoke providence. The French were no longer the chosen people. As confidence in the power of the god of history to sustain collective truth ebbed away, so the use of religious modes of expression became less and less appropriate. Quinet was now much more sparing in his use of biblical imagery. He was suspicious of the power of language to disguise reality, to say one thing and mean another. The use of figurative or symbolic language produced a certain instability of meaning and at the same time invited a range of interpretative strategies. Quinet wanted to close off these possibilities. The historian as the voice of conscience saw his task as liberating the determinate human meaning of events, however unpalatable. France was in a parlous condition and recovery required that certain unpleasant truths be faced.

In *La Révolution* matters came to à head. Quinet still endorsed the spiritual meaning of 1789, still admired what the Revolution had tried to achieve. However, he no longer presented 1789 as the Christian idea achieving fulfilment in history. He now saw France in 1789 as a nation 'obliged to deny its history', required to reject a past which contained nothing but absolutism, despotism and arbitrary rule (*LR*, I, 27). The heroic stature of the Revolution sprang from the magnitude of the task it faced in trying to establish the rule of law. However, from the standpoint of the 1860s Quinet was struck as much by the abortive, monstrous aspects of the Revolution as by the courageous attempt to invent a new order. Viewed from the vantage point of the Second Empire, it was difficult to see how the Revolution could be judged to have been successful. Quinet noted the vast disproportion between the sufferings occasioned by the Revolution on the one hand and what had actually been achieved on the other. His explanation of why the Revolution had not succeeded was part of the wider demythologising process. Instead of being represented as the founding moment of modernity the Revolution was portrayed as a failed attempt to escape from the past.

In Quinet's view a successful political revolution needed to be rooted in a religious revolution. However, in France this proved impossible since Protestantism had been crushed and Catholicism was resolutely hostile to change. The French could not find sustenance in the national past. They were the descendants of the Gauls and still lived in mental subjection to Rome. Despite their best intentions they were unable to overthrow habits of mind produced during centuries of servitude. The Jacobins restored despotism and centralisation. The revolutionary cults were but poor imitations of the religion they were intended to replace. We have heard much of this before. In the 1840s Quinet had warned against the seductive power of the past and had denounced the errors of the men of 1793. However, there was a qualitative difference between the mood of the 1840s and that of the 1860s. In the 1860s there was no longer an alternative history of hope to fall back on, just as there was no sense of the bubbling up of a different future.

The past was seen as a dead weight or, more depressingly, as an invisible magnet determining the way in which Frenchmen behaved. During the July Monarchy Quinet located the meaning of his epoch in the unfolding of the potential of the revolutionary idea within time. He had spoken in extravagant terms of Napoleon as the possible precursor of a new religion and related the emperor's destiny to the implementation of a providential plan. After 1851 the myth of the emperor crumbled and with it the spiritualist philosophy of history which attributed symbolic meaning to events and sustained the transformation of historical agents into messianic, mythical personages.

Brooding in his Swiss exile, Quinet could not bring himself to recognise in the flawed French Revolution a substitute religion or a new church. Not for him the mobilising myth of the Fête de la Fédération so dear to Michelet.[14] He no longer subscribed to the belief that the masses made history, inaugurated the Kingdom. By inserting the French Revolution into a national history of discontinuity and repetition he destroyed, even more effectively than did Tocqueville, the notion that 1789 had effected a radical break with the past. Quinet called into question central elements within revolutionary ideology. He declared that the execution of Louis XVI had been a mistake, that the Terror had not been necessary to ensure victory over foreign foes. By dismantling the intellectual system which justified the Terror he deprived the revolutionary experience of the crucial dimension of redemptive suffering. Transgressive acts of violence had changed little of real substance. Quinet drew out of the history of the Revolution a sense which defied the truth as defined by left-wing orthodoxy and his book incurred the wrath of other republicans who accused him of betraying the cause.[15] Reason, not belief, became his criterion of interpretation. Historians who had distorted the reality of the past were held to have contributed to the current climate of moral confusion. Was Quinet implying that history should henceforth concentrate on facts and their relations in a spirit which recalled eighteenth-century scientific method? That would be going much too far, although history as conscience was certainly at odds with the form and the content of history as divine discourse. Instead of fulfilling the exalted function of deciphering the meaning of events so as to reveal their divine meaning, Quinet now saw it as his duty to judge the past in moral terms without invoking an overarching transcendent purpose. However, what agency could henceforth serve as a mediating presence between self and society if history were no longer available as an ideal supported by a providential intention?[16]

6

Jules Michelet (1798–1874): history as resurrection

Michelet's output was phenomenal: histories of the Roman Republic, of France and of the French Revolution, a translation of Vico, textbooks, a life of Luther, an examination of the codes of medieval justice, polemical works attacking the Jesuits and the Catholic priesthood. The list is extensive and for the most part I have been alluding only to his publications of the Restoration and the July Monarchy. Between 1851 and his death – a period which falls largely outside the scope of the present book – he maintained this high level of activity, bringing out works of history, volumes of natural history as well as popular books on matters of morality such as *L'Amour* (1858) and *La Femme* (1859). Moreover, he was all the while consigning his private thoughts and musings, his dreams and his anxieties, to his *Journal*, and this, in printed form, runs to several thousand pages. Michelet's reputation as France's greatest historian is secure.[1]

He grew up in Paris, in difficult circumstances, the son of a printer with revolutionary sympathies whose livelihood had been ruined by Napoleon's censorship laws. As a child Michelet lived in an environment without luxuries. He was an introverted youth. The solitude of his adolescent years was broken by an intense friendship with a schoolfellow of the same age, Paul Poinsot, who died in 1824. As a young man Michelet displayed a vast appetite for knowledge. In later years he was troubled by the thought that his commitment to his historical studies had led him to neglect personal relations. Indeed, when his first wife, Pauline, died in 1839 he was overcome with guilt and remorse: 'My *second wife*, history, appeared before 1830. The first, poor Pauline, was quite neglected' (*J*, I, 357).

Michelet was always ambitious. He was successful in competitive examinations and embarked upon a teaching career. He obtained posts in secondary schools and, in 1827, he was appointed to the Ecole Normale where his responsibilities initially covered courses in philosophy as well as history. After 1830 his career developed in two distinct but complementary directions. He was appointed by the new regime to head the historical section of the National Archives under the overall direction of Daunou. In this role Michelet oversaw the classification of documents and helped establish procedures of verification which supported the Romantic historians' claim to be authoritative and scientifically accurate. At the same time he continued teaching, both at the Ecole Normale and at the university, replacing Guizot on a temporary basis at the Sorbonne. In 1838 he was elected to the Académie des Sciences Morales et Politiques and in the same year he was appointed to the chair of History and Moral Philosophy at the Collège de France. In that position he found himself at the centre of the church–university polemics of the 1840s. He was suspended from his chair in January 1848 but triumphantly resumed his teaching in March of the same year. In 1849 he married for the second time. His young wife, Athénaïs Mialaret, inspired in the historian a passionate devotion. However, Michelet again incurred the displeasure of the government. His lectures were suspended in 1851 and in 1852 he was officially removed from his post at the Collège de France.

The case of Michelet illustrates how by dint of scholarly effort someone of lowly origins could rise to occupy a position within the elites of Restoration France. The educational reforms of the Revolution and Empire had borne fruit, enabling clever young men to rise in society. It was the right moment for Michelet to make his mark; history was being organised as a discipline, institutionalised and professionalised. Michelet used his gifts to great effect. He was also what we might call a skilled academic operator, adept at obtaining friends at court and securing support within centres of intellectual power. The historian who is remembered as the embodiment of revolutionary history was not averse to cultivating influential contacts and in the years before he achieved great eminence he was disinclined to alienate the authorities. In 1828 he was made history tutor to the 9-year-old granddaughter of the reactionary monarch, Charles X. After the July Revolution he was chosen to fulfil the same function under the

Orleanist monarchy; on this occasion his pupil was the Princess Clémentine, the daughter of Louis-Philippe.

Michelet had his convictions but he was circumspect. In 1832 his friend Quinet burnt his bridges with the regime by openly accusing the new government of betraying the hopes of 1830. Michelet thought such a frontal attack unwise and advised against it. This reluctance to declare his hand was a fair reflection of Michelet's temperament. He did not lack backbone but he was decidedly not a man of action, not a politician or an agitator. The radicalism which increasingly informed his writing did not lead to the construction of a public persona – although his many supporters wished, especially in the weeks following the Revolution of February 1848, that he would play an active role in government. In this respect Michelet differed wholly from Quinet. However, in terms of ideology he shared much with the friend he had known since 1825. Both men were preoccupied with the religious meaning of the present age of transition, both were concerned with the definition of national identity in the wake of the French Revolution. But whereas Quinet wanted to write a great epic poem, Michelet set out to provide his fellow citizens with the narrative of national identity which the historians of the Restoration had promised but not delivered. He was an admirer of Thierry, a pupil of Villemain and a protégé of Guizot. But he was also their rival, determined to demonstrate the superiority of his own achievement. Michelet's ego was enormous. Not content with making Paris the fulcrum of the intellectual world he added an annotation: 'Moi-Paris'.[2] His work came to be dominated by the conviction that the meaning of French history lay in the struggle between the Revolution and Christianity, between justice and grace, between right and arbitrary rule, between equality and privilege. He made no pretence that the historian should divest himself of his convictions in favour of assuming a stance of specious even-handedness. In his mind good history was written by practitioners who were committed to the cause of right and truth.

Michelet's two main subjects were France and himself – although the relationship between them was not always clearly or adequately acknowledged. French reality consisted of qualities and values which evolved and came together to form an identity. The historian recovered less a definable national essence than a collective desire which became reflective and aware of itself in the historian's own writing. Michelet presented the activity of history-writing in terms of self-sacrifice, as a process which involved the casting aside of particularity the better to serve the public good. Among the most positively valorised terms in his vocabulary were 'general life' and 'generality', values which stood in opposition to individuality. The historian who partook of the general life of humanity transcended the limitations of his impoverished self and approached an ideal reality incarnated in the collective. Michelet observed that 'all that is noble moves away from individualities towards abstraction'.[3] Self-worth, paradoxically, was in this manner tied up with the transcendence of self.

However, identification with the past was not easily achieved and much mental rigour and moral effort were needed before the impure evanescence of personal existence could be left behind. In order to investigate the mysteries of the past Michelet felt he needed an equivalent of the Golden Bough mentioned by Virgil in the *Aeneid*. In fact he found what he was seeking by turning inward, by drawing on his own emotions: 'We need the Golden Bough. Where shall we pluck it from? From our own heart. Through his personal sorrows the historian experiences and reproduces the sufferings of nations; he renews them in order to console them' (*J*, I, 378).

Michelet abandoned any sense of the historian as a straightforward chronicler of events. He became a maker of meanings, but he carried out this task in ways which were disturbing and unsettling. Initially the historical project was formulated in terms of a disinterested duty to humankind, as a way of escaping the servitudes and tribulations of individual existence, as a method of purifying the ego. The act of identification with the past seemed to involve the annulment of individuality in order for the succession of events to be saturated with thought; but later, as Michelet's investigations expanded, his writing took on a vatic, revelatory dimension. He imprinted upon his interpretation of the past a series of symbolic oppositions, shifting sexual polarities. The historian gathered up the fragments of the past in a passionate intensity, hoping that his embrace would lend them new life. The act of writing history involved more than intellectual reconstruction. It was an impassioned act of re-creation.

Personal life and the life of history fused in Michelet's imagination in ways which liberated the act of writing. In 1840 he published the fourth volume of his *Histoire de France* which contained a description of the dance of death. In his *Journal* he explained that he had been able to evoke the past with such truth and intensity because he had drawn upon personal emotion, on the grief he had experienced after the death of his wife in 1839. Grief had liberated the complex energies and desires which reanimated the movements of the *danse macabre* and granted Michelet access to the hidden passions of fifteenth-century France:

> My wife died and my heart was torn to pieces. But from that very sundering there arose a violent and almost frenetic energy: I plunged with a dark pleasure into the death of France in the fifteenth century, blending with it those fiercely sensual passions that I found equally in myself and in my subject. It was not without reason that someone wrote that the fourth volume was the product of an immoral inspiration. That is what gives it its strange power.
>
> (*J*, I, 361).

Out of compassion the historian took upon himself the irrecoverable losses of humankind: 'The historian's harsh fate is to love, to lose so many things, to begin anew all the loves, all the bereavements of mankind' (*J*, I, 288). Michelet wrote that he loved death. In fact he loved death passionately in the hope that he might bring forth life. He remarked that loving the dead was a form of immortality. He had the body of Pauline exhumed and contemplated her remains. But what truth, what meaning might emerge from the spectacle of dissolution and decomposition? Was Michelet's entire historical enterprise driven by impulses he would rather deny? By an impure commerce with the dead?[4]

Michelet sought to reconcile the authority of the self with a belief in history as a meaningful process of development tending to the achievement of greater freedom. In 1827, in his opening lecture at the Ecole Normale he defined his approach. He observed that man, as an object of knowledge, could be studied from two points of view, as an individual or as a social being. Michelet's intention was to investigate both dimensions simultaneously (*LVR*, 144). He was dissatisfied with the notion of the individual subject as defined by French Classical thought. Like Quinet he was alive to the limitations of Cartesianism with its assertion of the authority of reason and its definition of true knowledge as that which could be formulated in clear and distinct terms. Descartes's influence was held to lie behind the Enlightenment's distrust of history.

Cartesian philosophy ascribed freedom and mastery to the self but at the cost of reducing the value of custom and difference.

Michelet challenged the view that self-examination was the only path to truth. He was concerned to rehabilitate the social dimension of the self. To be sure, he reaffirmed the value of the singularity of individual experience but at the same time he sought a form of self-interest, an individualism which escaped the confines of an eighteenth-century sensationalism which, in its more extreme forms, amounted to a self-enclosed hedonism. Michelet considered that the moral life could not be fully explored in terms of sensationalist psychology alone; other types of knowing and different reference points were required in order to reveal how individuals and social groups co-operated in the building of a human world. In 1825, in a speech delivered on the occasion of a prize-giving at the Collège Sainte-Barbe – where he was at that time employed as a teacher – Michelet explained that the individual was not a self-enclosed unit but part of something much greater, an element within the collective being of humankind. In his lecture he described how transient individual selves contributed to the life of the species by modifying and enriching the collective mind, what he termed 'la pensée commune' (*LVR*, 115). Individual lives took on meaning in so far as their activity helped advance the movement of progress. Awareness of collective identity and historical continuity mitigated the individual's sense of unfulfilment. Michelet, who found himself less and less able to place his trust in traditional forms of Christian theism, shared Quinet's belief that history could henceforth be relied upon to disclose meaning and purpose: individuals perished but each generation contributed to the growth of thought, of mind. Humankind advanced by developing, accumulating and transmitting knowledge.

Michelet drew from this his conviction that history should be placed at the centre of the educational process, a point he made forcibly in his speech of 1825, at a time when government policy, far from wishing to promote historical studies, was seeking to reduce the already limited place occupied by history in the curriculum of secondary schools. Michelet, on the other hand, believed in the absolute centrality of history. In his view the purpose of education was to transmit the knowledge of the past to the present generation and thus prepare for the future. It was an error to suppose that the self could inhabit an apartness, a realm which lay outside the community of history. Reliance upon the authority of Cartesian reason deprived men of that necessary sense of community and solidarity which was bolstered by the study of history.

Paul Viallaneix has described how Michelet's thought was nurtured on the humanitarian strand of Enlightenment philosophy, on Voltaire, Rousseau, Diderot and Montesquieu. In their writings Michelet discovered, not a narrow individualism, but the ideas which had inspired the revolutionary leaders' attempt to build a fraternal society reconciling freedom with equality. The historian considered himself to be the heir of the liberating currents of eighteenth-century thought which had emancipated the individual and challenged traditional social divisions. In the 1820s he shared the liberal mind-set of many of his generation, impatient with the conservatism of the Restoration. Like Quinet he admired Constant and looked to Cousin and Guizot for intellectual leadership. In his later work, however, he questioned the adequacy of the liberal stance and his central loyalty came to lie with the idea of national community as defined by the experience of the Revolution. He shared the revolutionaries' admiration for the ancient republics but his sensibility was that of the new generation for whom the certitudes of the *philosophes* had to be revised in the light of experience. In a celebrated passage he later described how, as a child, he was taken to visit the Musée des Monuments Français, set up by the Convention under the direction of Alexandre Lenoir, where were kept works of art from the medieval period which had been rescued from the destructive excesses of revolutionary vandalism. The young Michelet responded with feeling to these illustrations of the French past in a way which suggested that he would be ill-disposed to the idea that respect for antiquity necessarily went hand in hand with a denial of the national past in the name of enlightened reason. It would be more accurate to say that for Michelet forgetting the past amounted to the obliteration of meaning, to a form of death. Through the relation to the past men coped with their separateness and became fully aware of their humanness, binding themselves emotionally to humankind.

In Michelet's eyes history was the central human science, the core discipline. Inevitably he came up against the argument that historical knowledge lacked certainty, hence value. Was it not at best a highly imperfect science since its conclusions could not be tested? However, while Michelet agreed that historical truth was difficult to establish and admitted that facts were open to interpretation and falsification, he maintained his position that history should none the less be considered the central science of man. Reflection and Cartesian self-analysis were unable to grasp inter-personal experience or account for the way in which individual lives were shaped by different communal histories, languages, cultures and environments. Self-knowledge was held to be incomplete if it was elaborated without historical awareness. Enough knowledge could be ascertained about the past in order for its importance for mental and moral life to be assessed. Although history could not aspire to the same degree of certainty as mathematics or the natural sciences it none the less contained truths which individual reason was powerless to discover.

Without denying the value of psychology or rejecting considerations of personal motivation, Michelet found himself drawn, like Quinet, to the impersonal forces of beliefs, customs and laws. History was not a novel, not a literary space upon which an author projected imagined worlds produced within his own consciousness. History told of the real struggle of men to master their environment. It traced the process of constructing social forms which were the visible expressions of human values. The fact that historical knowledge was experimentally unverifiable was not therefore a reason to conclude that all reasonable men should retreat into historical scepticism. The historical enterprise was a worthwhile attempt at meaningful reconstruction. It involved taking risks as well as assessing the credibility of the testimony which had been handed down. The suppressed text of history needed to be brought to life in its difficult complexity and its singular beauty.

Michelet joined Thierry and the liberal historians in their repudiation of an outmoded history which amounted to little more than a list of battles and royal genealogies. However, Michelet went further than Thierry or Guizot in his understanding of his own role. In Michelet's eyes his own writing transcended that of his contemporaries. His relationship to the past was more intense, more vital, more personal. He distanced himself from contemporary practitioners – in his view Thierry exaggerated the role of race while Guizot was too preoccupied with institutions. Michelet was proud of his uniqueness: his history was neither narrative after the manner of Thierry nor analysis after the manner of Guizot; it was, in his own terms a 'resurrection' of the past in its fullness (OC, IV, 12). His work broke with that of his predecessors because it was a totalising, integrative project. In the 1869 preface to his completed *Histoire de France* Michelet proclaimed his originality, contrasting his production with the work of Barante, Guizot, Mignet, Thiers and Thierry. But this self-proclaimed originality had been achieved at a cost, for in Michelet's eyes the true historian of France shouldered an awesome responsibility. He was charged with restoring lost generations to life, with redeeming time. He was an intermediary between the living and the dead.

History offered a sense of community because it reminded individuals of that part of their being which arose out of their participation in social life. Each individuality possessed value but self-knowledge had society – and humanity in general – as its inescapable horizon. In this Michelet remained closer to Guizot than to Auguste Comte who, while also turning to history as a tool of post-revolutionary reconstruction, defined his sociological approach as one which ascribed primacy to the social. For Michelet the social inhabited the substance of the individual but did not coincide with it. Michelet's sense of history was shaped by his appreciation of the inadequacy of both Cartesian rationalism and Lockean empiricism. He discovered within the probabilities of history the source of moral norms and he did so in a way which implicitly challenged philosophy's claims to provide universal knowledge in the form of conceptual thought. In his view no enterprise of self-knowledge could ignore the collective dimension which was in part constitutive of individuality. However, Michelet's approach should not be viewed as a subversion of philosophy by history. Rather he wanted to bring the two disciplines together. In fact he recognised that all history-writing presupposed an underlying philosophy – even when it was not overtly articulated.

For Michelet the meaning of the present incorporated the past, as the meaning of individuality encompassed elements of communality. Events were understood as giving expression to an inward reality, to an intellectual substance which animated change and was defined collectively. The goal of the historian was to grasp this inner truth, access to which lay as much by way of the exploration of literature and culture as by the scrutiny of events. History came to possess its own spirituality and function as the source of moral life. Like Quinet, Michelet acknowledged the presence of the divine within time as a power tending towards greater freedom. The order of history was at once humankind's self-creation and the manifestation of a metaphysical principle.

Michelet's position in the 1820s was clearly influenced by Cousin's interpretation of history. However, Michelet never fell under Cousin's sway to the extent that Quinet did. He remained alive to the dangers inherent in Cousinian determinism and sensed the implicit illiberalism which lurked behind the idea that collective entities externalised a hidden intellectual content. Cousin, as we have seen, related collective consciousness to environment and viewed both as the elaboration of an idea which provided a complete explanation of the development of a social group. Michelet rejected Cousin's amoralism and distrusted Hegelian abstraction. Michelet wanted to bring together individuality and communality in a manner which supported the value of universal benevolence. He made the people a collective subject but he envisaged the social will as being refracted through the individual lives which built sociality. Michelet held that human fulfilment was not achieved in isolation but through the experience of association; love and self-sacrifice were integral to genuine community.

Michelet's thought oscillated between the public and the private, the personal and the impersonal. Moral individualism was an unchallengeable value but on its own it was insufficient. The subject desired to know itself immediately and totally but found that it could neither forge personal integration nor discover meaning without having recourse to the mediation of history. At first sight Michelet's distrust of the capacity of individual reason to reach the truth unaided recalls the Catholic traditionalists' critique of Enlightenment liberalism. Michelet, however, sought an intellectual framework which restored collective values without repudiating individualism. He recognised the essential role played by general ideas which bound individuals together within a network of beliefs, practices, duties and obligations but he regarded the authoritarianism of the Saint-Simonians and the anti-individualism of the traditionalists with equal distaste. Communality needed to be built differently, by reaching back into the national past and making available to citizens an awareness of the processes which formed collective identity. In Michelet's writing history became a power which actualised justice, a progressive force which required individual invention, energy and effort. The content of history was the advance of reason and law, justice and freedom.

Michelet looked to currents of thought which offered a defence of historical knowledge against the criticisms made by Cartesianism. His main inspiration in this area was the Neapolitan philosopher Giambattista Vico whose *Scienza nuova* he began translating in 1824 with Cousin's encouragement. However, he also discovered congenial ideas in the work of other thinkers, notably among the philosophers of the Scottish Enlightenment – Thomas Reid, Adam Ferguson, Dugald Stewart – authors whose writings were widely disseminated in liberal intellectual circles during the Restoration. The attraction of Scottish philosophy lay in its answer to the subjectivism and scepticism of Locke and Hume. Scottish philosophy argued in favour of an appeal to the principles of common sense, to those shared ideas whose truth was acknowledged as self-evident by members of a community. Here was a justification of the value of the collective which did not lead to a reactionary reassertion of an unchanging set of traditional values. Michelet's reading of Vico reinforced this attitude. According to Vico truth resided, not in abstract reason, but in common sense which was 'a *judgement* without *reflection*, shared by an entire class, by an entire people, by an entire nation or by all mankind' (*OC*, I, 434).

'It is infinitely probable that the common sense of a great mass of men is the truth. *Vox populi, vox Dei*. Common sense is divine meaning' (*LVR*, 170). This statement from a lecture of 1831 is significant since it testifies to Michelet's belief that the collective consciousness, while not infallible, none the less should be taken seriously as a repository of wisdom. In a similar vein he observed that 'the individual is prone to errors into which it is rare for the species to fall' (*LVR*, 170). In practice this meant that the escape route from subjectivism and solipsism lay via an exploration of history and collective life. This was not to express an uncritical admiration for the past or to assert its superiority over the present. It amounted rather to a defence of the historical project as an exercise of critical judgement which accepted that expressions of collective consciousness deserved consideration as legitimate forms of social knowing and perceiving. History contained genuine and worthwhile, if not absolutely sure, knowledge.

In arriving at these views Michelet owed much to Vico, a debt which he always freely acknowledged. In the introduction to his *Histoire romaine* (1831) he presented Vico as the great precursor, as the forerunner whose ideas anticipated Wolf, Niebuhr, Creuzer, Goerres and Gans. Michelet's abridged translation of the *Scienza nuova* appeared in 1827, the year which also saw the publication of Quinet's translation of Herder's *Ideen*. Michelet was responsive to Vico's contention that history was to be understood as the creation of men and thus knowable in a manner different from nature which was the creation of God. He was influenced by Vico's theory of the three ages (gods, heroes, men) which he saw as providing a key to understanding human development. He was impressed by the way in which Vico identified the stages with changes in mentality. Transformations of the human mind were externalised in a variety of imaginative, social and political forms. Michelet agreed with Vico's view that it was natural and appropriate for the primitive mind to be imaginative and literal; its way of thinking corresponded to a collective, popular creativity. Only later did rationality replace imagination, embodying itself in abstract as opposed to mythic or poetic ways of thinking.

Michelet viewed myths, legends and epic poetry as phenomena deserving serious study. They were not to be despised by the philosopher as simplistic and outmoded. Like Quinet, Michelet considered that it was appropriate for the truths of the past to be expressed in poetic or imaginative form. To ascribe value to myths and legends did not amount to questioning the value of reflective consciousness; it would be more accurate to say that it was a returning of individual reason to the world of collective representations. The historian used literature and religion to trace social destinies because they bodied forth general truths. Commenting upon the uncertainty of Roman history, Michelet pointed to the essential truth which was contained within myth and popular poetry. Such forms of writing, he declared:

> are ordinarily the true national history of a people, such as its genius has led it to conceive. It little matters whether it accords with the facts. For centuries the story of William Tell has aroused enthusiasm in Switzerland. We find textually the identical story in Saxo [Grammaticus], the ancient historian of Denmark. The story itself may well not be real, but it is eminently true in the sense that it conforms perfectly to the character of the people which has put it forth as historical.
>
> (OC, II, 64)

As these remarks indicate, Michelet's approach was comparative, looking for similarities in the ways in which different traditions developed. The use of the comparative method endowed the project of uncovering hidden meanings with scientific legitimacy.

Michelet distinguished between form and content, between

194

exterior and interior. From Vico he learned that the processes of history could be grasped not so much by attending to the sequence of events as by studying beliefs and laws, by treating evolving institutions and religions as expressions of the self-transforming human intelligence. Myths and legends possessed value because they were translations of collective truths expressed in imaginative form. They contained a deep wisdom for they testified to universal consent. At the same time they communicated a sense of the transcendent and, as we shall see, these views had a strong bearing on what Michelet would have to say in his *Introduction à l'histoire universelle* (1831). Vico's great achievement was to have revealed the human content which lay behind myths and religions, symbolic discourses of collective identity and purpose, emanations of a group mentality as opposed to individual creations. Vico allowed Michelet simultaneously to rehabilitate the collective imagination and celebrate the science which swept away the supernatural in order to reveal the human:

> When man desired to have men-gods, it was necessary to heap whole generations in one person. . . . The peoples remained prostrate before these gigantic phantoms. Philosophy raises them up and says to them: That which you worship is yourselves, your own conceptions. [Hereupon] these strange and inexplicable figures which floated in the air, objects of a puerile admiration, redescend within our reach; they quit poetry to enter science.
>
> (*OC*, II, 341)

However, whereas Vico situated his thesis within a Christian perspective which tried to accommodate traditional notions of the workings of divine providence, Michelet, like Quinet, was more open to the relativist implications of the *Scienza nuova*. Furthermore Michelet had confidence in the collective being of humankind, in its potential and in the progressive triumph of the principle of freedom. This meant that while he shared Vico's view of human nature evolving through stages, he neglected Vico's theory of repetitive historical cycles, adopting at first linearity and subsequently the optimistic image of the spiral ascending.

History, for Michelet, constituted a movement away from the natural towards the artificial, from the concrete towards the abstract, from the imaginative towards the rational. But at the same time he did not doubt that history possessed an inner spiritual, ideal meaning. The study of the past communicated a sense of the transcendent, an awareness that a purpose, a divine intention, lay at the heart of things. For Michelet this transforming presence passed through loss and death into renewal and eventually became identified with the revolutionary impulse. However, this spiritual reality operated inwardly, in the form of the development of mind, not externally in the form of an intervening force. This was Michelet's understanding of the message of the *Scienza nuova:* '*Humanity is its own work.* God acts upon it but through it. Humanity is divine, but no man is divine' (*OC*, II, 341). Humankind, in Michelet's words, was its own Prometheus, creating itself in history (*OC*, IV, 13). He envisaged history in terms of the rise and fall of cultures and religions. This process took the form of a movement from concrete poetic expression to prose and abstraction:

> humanity starts from the symbol, in history, in law and in religion. But, from the materialised, individualised idea it rises to the pure and general idea. Within the motionless chrysalis of the symbol is operated the mystery of the transformation of spirit; this grows and spreads as far as it can; it at length bursts its envelope, which then falls, dried up and withered.
>
> (*OC*, II, 341)

The advance of history involved the progressive triumph of the spirit over the letter. However, while Michelet was committed to modernity and to rationality he was acutely aware of the solitude, the apartness of the modern self. He was concerned that the freeing of modern individuality from the power of traditional religion seemed to lead to the pursuit of pleasure rather than to the actualisation of justice. He was aware that the post-revolutionary world could no longer proclaim a simple return to nature as a universal source of morality and in his writing nationalism came to replace religion as the centre of feelings of belonging and community. Michelet took myths and legends seriously, and to that extent his work reflected the nostalgia for idealised, unified cultures which informed much Romantic writing: heightened subjective freedom reinvented for itself lost paradises of association, playgrounds of spontaneity. However, Michelet's thought was different. His Romanticism did not look backward to an idealised harmonious past. It integrated the democratic and revolutionary projects in a way which associated the desire for social unity with the theory of the general will. Knowledge of the past was necessary and valuable but Michelet did not consider that the past could provide us with a workable blueprint for the social organisation of the future.

Michelet's general views were first expounded in his *Introduction à l'histoire universelle* (1831). Here we encounter the purified ego which has transcended nature and escaped from stratified social forms but none the less quests after reintegration. The modern self experiences a deficit, a sense of loss. In order to rediscover its wholeness it requires the support of history as a guarantor of meaning and needs an idea of society as a principle of validation. Michelet's text, like quite a number which appeared in the wake of the July Revolution, testified to a moment of profound crisis in French spiritual life. Like the Saint-Simonians he viewed the period since 1789 as one of analysis and criticism and, just as much as the followers of Enfantin, he longed for the work of social reconstruction and recomposition to begin. The travail of the present was explained in terms of the pains endured by humankind as it transformed itself, abandoning one system of belief in order to adopt another. As in the case of Quinet, the underlying question was whether a revived Christianity would be adequate to meet new needs. The religious crisis of the present reminded Michelet of the moral condition of humanity when paganism was giving way to Christianity. He ended his *Histoire romaine* with the following dramatic pronouncement:

> Epoch of uncertainty, of doubt, and mortal anguish! Who then would have thought that it was one day to return? This second age of the world, begun with the Empire, almost two thousand years ago; it appears as if it is near its close. Ah! if it be so, may the third soon arrive, and may God keep us suspended a shorter time between the world which is closing and that which has not commenced.
>
> (*OC*, II, 621)

At this stage in his life Michelet remained sentimentally attached to Christianity. Without Christianity humankind seemed in danger of losing its bearings. Michelet recounted how, on a recent visit to Rome, he had kissed the wooden cross which stood in the Colosseum. He was unsure. Was Christianity still perhaps 'the sole refuge for the religious soul'? (*OC*, II, 236)? Many of

Michelet's contemporaries experienced similar feelings of anxiety: an epoch was ending but what would replace it? Having observed that in Fichte, Byron and the French Revolution, western civilisation had reached its extreme form Michelet wondered whether the future of the west might not lie in restoring links with the orient (*OC*, II, 295). However, he did not dwell upon this decidedly Saint-Simonian notion which had as its disturbing subtext the rehabilitation of matter and the acknowledgement of the feminine. Michelet focused instead on society as the legitimate embodiment of the religious impulse in the modern world. He was particularly reluctant to turn to nature as a consoling form of substitute faith. Nature struck him as profoundly indifferent to the human predicament. In 1831 he recorded his reflections as he watched his young daughter standing on the shore at Le Havre facing the awesome power of the sea. As he surveyed the scene Michelet turned away from the frightening abyss of nature and sought instead to embrace the social world as a new source of religious truth: 'It is to you that I shall turn for aid, my noble country. You must take the place of the God who is escaping us and fill in us the incommensurable void which Christianity left when it died' (*J*, I, 83).

Michelet judged that the cross as traditionally understood was no longer the unique symbol of salvation. He spoke of a 'social God' gradually revealing himself in the very exercise of human freedom (*OC*, II, 255). The divine was to be made present in social and political life: 'the city is our only refuge. May it transfigure itself into heaven' (*J*, I, 83). Humanity became the agent for incarnation, for the progressive manifestation of the logos. Like Lerminier in his *Philosophie du droit* (1831) or Lamartine in his *Voyage en Orient* (1835), Michelet was tending to identify the historical development of human reason with the progressive unfolding of the divine. Awareness that God was present in the historical life of humankind became for Michelet a sign of hope. His text of 1831 suggested that the problems of subjectivity could be solved by participating in the unity of the new social form. This would mark the end of dislocation and dispersion, the beginning of a higher synthesis:

> it is above all by virtue of the social sense that mankind will return to the idea of universal order. Once order has been experienced within the limited society of the *patrie*, the same

idea will extend to human society, to the republic of the world.

(*OC*, II, 256)

The consequence of Michelet's argument was that the nation became the visible church of the religion of humanity. Within nationhood the advent of the Kingdom was sacramentally present. Michelet's view was that although Christianity had created man's moral being by freeing him from the religions of nature it had subsequently retreated from engagement with the world. A new religion of action was needed, a religion which placed energy at the centre of the self and of society. The aim of Michelet's new social religion was to actualise unity and equality, and the agent for the realisation of this purpose was the French people:

> If it is our social sense which is to bring us back to religion, then the organ of this new revelation, the interpreter between God and man, must be the people with the most highly developed social sense. The moral world had its Word in Christianity, son of Judaea and Greece; France will explain the Word of the social world which we see beginning.
>
> (*OC*, II, 256)

The *Introduction à l'histoire universelle* of 1831 was the earliest published expression of the historian's new sense of France's destiny. In 1869 he wrote that he conceived the project of writing his history of the French people in the illumination produced by the July Revolution: 'During those memorable days, a great light appeared, and I perceived France' (*OC*, IV, 2). The events of July 1830 determined his intellectual development and focused his political commitment. He noted that only at the close of 1830 did he really begin to exist, to be, to write. This was something of an exaggeration since he had already published his translation of Vico and his historical textbooks, but it remains true in a deeper sense. The July Revolution, which Michelet enthusiastically endorsed – although he was always wary at a personal level of transforming thought into a commitment to direct action – crystallised his ideas and empowered him to conceive of a new form of national history. He described the 1830 Revolution as the July lightning flash. It not only brought down an unpopular regime and forced a king to flee, it illuminated the historian's sense of his own vocation.

The study of 1831 needs to be placed in this emotionally charged context. This short book provides an overview of world history conceived as a westward movement of culture and religion, beginning in India and concluding in France. Michelet defined the content of universal history as the eternal conflict between freedom and necessity, between spirit and matter. He offered a version of the general picture with which we are familiar from our reading of Cousin and Quinet. The argument runs as follows: humankind originated in India where human beings were dominated by their environment, overwhelmed by external nature. Oriental pantheism was a religion of submission and immobility. As humankind journeyed westward, freedom and consciousness increased as dependency upon nature decreased. Persia and Egypt marked important stages in this process. However, the real break with the religions of nature came with the Jews who proclaimed the unity of the deity. In Greece men came together in city states. The divine was humanised and individuality asserted as a value. Greece witnessed the replacement of family and tribal identities by the superior notion of the city. This meant that the feeling of being bound by birth to a social group was replaced by a new identification of self with an ideal community grounded in the principle of rationality. The city was superior because it transcended nature; it was artificial, an invention of mind. Rome developed the idea of law but Roman society was eaten away by the cancer of slavery. Rome's authority was finally undermined by the popularity of oriental cults during the later years of the Empire. After enduring repression and persecution Christianity eventually triumphed. The new religion drew its strength from the fact that it fully embraced the cause of mind and wholeheartedly repudiated the oriental identification of nature with the divine. The Christian spirit was embodied in what Michelet called 'the miracle of the Middle Ages' (*OC*, II, 237).

According to Michelet, world history described a flight from nature which was also a struggle against matter. The content of history was the growth of liberty and 'the progressive triumph of *self*' (*OC*, II, 238). In crude terms – and Michelet's presentation is pretty schematic after all – Asia stood for the enslavement of spirit to matter, whereas Europe stood for the victory of reason, liberty, equality, justice and law. Europe was valued for constituting social worlds which had progressively emancipated human beings from biological and environmental determinants.

These matters will be looked at later (pp. 205–7) in relation to the *Histoire de France*. For the moment I want to concentrate on Michelet's treatment of the leading nations of modern Europe – France, Germany, Italy and England.[5] His thesis was that the individual nations had taken over the spiritual work which had been accomplished by the church during the Middle Ages. However, the extent to which national cultures have fulfilled their destiny varies. Two factors come into play: a) the extent to which the nations have succeeded in emancipating themselves from inherited racial characteristics; b) the degree to which they have managed to transcend the limitations placed upon them by their respective geographical environments. On the basis of how well each nation has performed in these two areas Michelet comes up with his hierarchy of states. France is placed at the summit and is portrayed as the agent of change, the herald of progress. England, on the other hand, comes off very badly indeed. The English are roundly lambasted for their materialism and denounced for placing a higher value on privilege than on social unity. The contrast between the two nations is stark. In France unity has been achieved. In England racial divisions persist and provide an explanation for class conflict in the nineteenth century. Germany, on the other hand, although inferior to France, fares significantly better than England. Michelet used a series of stereotypical Romantic views in order to categorise the Germans as a people distinguished by abnegation and naïvety, by a love of poetry and a feeling for nature. Germany is Europe's India, a country of thought, not of action. Italy, by way of contrast, is presented as the land of art, jurisprudence, urban values and practical skills. Most significant from Michelet's point of view, however, is his contention that Italy and Germany alike have failed to fuse local identities into a unified national consciousness. Instead they have allowed divisions to persist, divisions which reveal nature's power covertly to master human reality.

In France, on the other hand, the force of racial and environmental determinants has largely been overcome. France is not a race but a nation, the highest manifestation of the European idea of freedom. The example of France is held to give demonstrable confirmation of Michelet's main proposition that 'the mixing of races and opposing civilisations is the most powerful source of liberty' (*OC*, II, 247). Racial differences and antagonisms have cancelled each other out. The cohesion of French society rests upon shared intellectual and moral qualities which have in turn allowed the nation to take charge of its destiny and actualise a higher form of social unity. France is freer, less natural, more artificial than the other nations of Europe. This character finds political expression in the democratic spirit, in the extension of rights and the ending of privileges. In the modern world France has a mission of supreme importance to fulfil:

> France desires freedom in equality, which is precisely that which constitutes the social genius. France's liberty is just and holy. France deserves to initiate the freedom of the world and to bring together for the first time all peoples in a true unity of intelligence and will.
>
> (*OC*, II, 253)

France represents reason, mind, right and freedom. The nation has emancipated itself from its dependence upon nature and become a centralised, homogeneous entity. France represents prose, not poetry:

> France is the land of prose. . . . Now, whoever speaks of prose speaks of the least figurative and least concrete form [of thought], the most abstract, the purest, the most transparent form [of thought]; in other words the least material, the freest, the most common to all men, the most *human* [form of thought]. Prose is the final form of thought, that which is furthest removed from vague and inactive *rêverie*, that which is closest to action. To pass from dumb symbolism to poetry, and from poetry to prose, is to progress towards enlightened equality; it is an intellectual levelling. In this way the heroic aristocracy emerged from the mysterious castes of the orient. In the same way modern democracy emerged. The democratic genius of our nation appears nowhere better than in its eminently prosaic character, and furthermore it is by dint of this [prosaic and democratic character] that France is destined to raise up to equality the mind of mankind [*le monde des intelligences*].
>
> (*OC*, II, 250)

The view of French history outlined in the *Introduction à l'histoire universelle* was developed at greater length in a textbook which Michelet brought out in 1833, his *Précis de l'histoire de France*. However, we do not need to attend to the *Précis* since the first two volumes of the *Histoire de France* appeared later in that same year. This monumental project was not completed until 1869 and eventually ran to seventeen volumes. Here at last was the history which liberals and republicans had been calling for, a history of the people, of the nation, not simply a list of battles or a recital of the triumphs of royal diplomacy. Michelet wrote with passion and fluency, re-creating past reality in a way which immediately appealed to his contemporaries. Some readers were unhappy with the way in which he related events to general ideas but many were impressed by his skill in drawing new meanings out of historical facts. Liberal Catholics such as Frédéric Ozanam (1813–53) were not unsympathetic to his approach. Michelet wanted to trace the building of national consciousness and the creation of political unity. France was his subject and he declared France to be a living person. But in his writing France was not a fixed essence, an idea externalising itself in the world after the manner of the philosophy of Victor Cousin. Michelet's approach was subtler. France did not pre-exist as an ideal before its material manifestation as a collective entity. The meaning of France coincided neither with the Gauls nor with the Franks. France arose out of definable histories and particular environments but in a significant manner France made and remade itself over time. Thus, at a crucial moment in history, France defined itself in and through the wars with England. Frenchness arose from a sense of collective identity born of conflict with the hereditary enemy:

[France] was Catholic and feudal before it became French. England harshly forced France back upon itself, compelled France to retire into itself. France searched, dug deep, descended into the depths of the life of the people; and what did it find? France. France is indebted to her enemy for the recognition of herself as a nation.

(*OC*, VI, 182)

It was only by telling France's story that the meaning of the nation could be grasped. Truth arose from the narrative. However, as the *Introduction à l'histoire universelle* had already strongly indicated, France's contribution also needed to be located within the wider context of the conflict between freedom and necessity which lent purpose and direction to all of human history.

The *Histoire de France* is an intriguing and in some ways a perplexing work. The later volumes reflect changes in the historian's stance, mostly shifts in his position on the religious question. He also revised the text of the earlier volumes for republication. Thus we find that the chapter sympathetic towards Gothic architecture, originally published in 1833, was subsequently relegated to the status of an appendix. We can also trace Michelet's growing self-confidence: in later editions he jettisoned his original dedicatory preface to Thierry, Guizot and Simonde de Sismondi. The publication of the *Histoire de France* was interrupted in 1844 after the appearance of the sixth volume. Michelet then concentrated his attention on his *Histoire de la Révolution* which came out in seven volumes between 1847 and 1853. Publication of the larger work was resumed in 1853 and continued over the following fifteen years.

In the first volume of the *Histoire de France* (1833) Michelet reopened the question of the role of race which, as we have seen, had been central to political debate during the Restoration. Michelet did not challenge the usefulness of current speculations on the role of race as a determinant of national psychology. What he did was reject the idea that history could be fully explained in terms of the persistence of permanent racial characteristics (the theory associated with the name of Augustin Thierry and applied by his brother Amédée Thierry in his widely popular *Histoire des Gaulois* (1828)). Michelet's view was more nuanced. He accepted that the Celtic genius made an important contribution because it bequeathed to the French nation a confidence in the power of reason and a distrust of mysticism. Likewise he readily admitted that druidism contained several positive features – an awareness of the personality and a notion of immortality which predisposed the Gauls in favour of Christianity. However, Michelet was careful not to ascribe a monopoly of the highest virtues to the Celts and he eschewed completely the wilder shores of celtomania. The Gauls were presented as a poorly organised and ill-disciplined tribal society to which Caesar brought superior Roman ideas of government. Far from signifying a tragic setback, the Roman occupation of Gaul marked a definite movement forward, a movement away from nature; the time had come for a society to arise in which man would 'no longer devote himself to man but to an idea; and firstly to the idea of civil order' (*OC*, IV, 181). Progress required the abandonment of clans in favour of more general forms of social organisation. Michelet rejected deterministic forms

of explanation which he considered insensitive to the movement
of history:

> France has formed itself out of [different racial elements],
> which might have resulted in a quite different mixture. Oil
> and sugar consist of the same chemical elements. But all is
> not given, once the elements are given; there remains to be
> accounted for the mystery of a special and particular exist-
> ence. And how much the more ought this fact to be taken
> account of, when the question is a living and active union,
> such as a nation; a union, susceptible of internal development
> and self-modification! This labour, these successive modifi-
> cations, through which our country is moving and develop-
> ing are the subject matter of the history of France.
>
> (OC, IV, 182)

Over time France had mysteriously constituted itself out of a
combination of Celtic, Roman, Greek and Germanic elements:

> Let us not exaggerate either the primitive element of the
> Celtic genius, or the additions from without. The Celts have
> contributed much no doubt; so have Rome, Greece, and the
> Germans. But who has united, fused, converted [dénaturé]
> these elements, who has transmuted, transfigured, formed a
> single body of them, who has extracted out of them our
> France? France itself, by that internal labour and mysterious
> production, compounded of necessity and of liberty, which
> history must explain.
>
> (OC, IV, 182)

Rome was a civilising force when it overcame the introverted
disaggregation of Celtic society. But Rome was built upon slavery
and the Empire eventually fell before the advance of Christianity.
The barbarians became the agency which allowed Christianity to
accomplish its task of refashioning society in the name of unity
and universality. However, when it came to assessing the contribution made by the Franks Michelet once again refused to be
shackled by received opinion. He challenged the entrenched view
that the invaders embodied the spirit of Germanic independence.
He suggested instead that they perhaps owed their success to a
quite different quality – to their readiness to unite and to submit
to discipline.

Michelet claimed that among the successive waves of invaders who crossed the Rhine the Franks were the barbarians with the most discipline and the least individuality. In practice this meant that the Franks constituted the social group within the Germanic peoples most ready to abandon its symbolic formulations in favour of prose and reason. They thus fitted neatly into Michelet's ideal construction of France. What mattered most to the historian was the emergence of a truly unified French state. He had no time for what he judged to be flawed or half-hearted attempts at social integration. Thus the Carolingian empire received short shrift, being described as a deceitful unity in which real differences were concealed by dint of forcing antagonistic elements together in an unstable union. Feudalism compounded the problem by inaugurating a period of disintegration in which society collapsed into contending local powers. Feudal lords made their own laws, established fiefdoms which mirrored the disposition of the countryside – a further submission to nature, to matter. The feudal system tied man to the earth, fixed his social position within a system of dependency, promoted immobility. Most importantly, feudalism, in so far as it led to division, worked in favour of matter and against spirit. Michelet expressed gratitude that at this critical juncture in French history the precious idea of unity had been preserved by the church – even though episcopal power was itself limited by feudal power. Christianity represented hope:

> Matter tends to dispersion, spirit to unity. Matter, essentially divisible, seeks disunion and discord. Material unity is a contradiction in terms. In politics it becomes a tyranny. Spirit alone has the right to effect union; it alone *comprehends*, embraces, and, to say all in one word, loves. As has been so well put by the metaphysics of Christianity – Unity implies Power, Love and Spirit.
>
> (OC, IV, 328)

The message of Michelet's first volume was that France had constructed its own destiny in history, that the French people were in large measure a self-creation, the product of a melding of different races and traditions. He began his new volume with a section entitled 'Tableau de la France' which was designed to show how France overcame the second form of determinism, that represented by environmental constraints. The feudal division of the country marked a regrettable acceptance of the power of geographical factors to control the form of society. However, the values which

Michelet ascribed to France could not long be contained within the restricted embodiment of a series of local powers. Progress resided in the movement away from nature, away from purely local loyalties and in the direction of a broader allegiance to the modern idea of the *patrie*, 'an abstract idea which depends little on the senses' (OC, IV, 384). In Michelet's terms history effaced geography; over the centuries the people invented a new national space in which the ideal triumphed over the real, the general over the particular. France became a collective entity in which individuals moved and had their being. Whereas in the opinion of a good number of liberals localism signified individual resistance to the arrogance of central authority, Michelet identified it with obstructive, self-oriented egoism, with the misplaced desire to privilege limited objectives over the national interest: 'Individual man is materialistic; he spontaneously attaches himself to a local and private interest; human society is spiritualistic; it tends unceasingly to free itself from the miseries of local existence in order to attain the lofty and abstract unity of the *patrie*' (OC, IV, 384).

In the 'Tableau de la France' Michelet took his reader on a tour of the provinces, describing their geography and their inhabitants. He was alive to diversity but he valued homogeneity more. At first the range of different environments appeared to confirm the negative values of feudalism (inequality, self-centredness, territorial divisions). However, the principle of centralisation gradually arrested feudalism's tendency to disperse power. In terms of geography the centre lacked the strong particularities of the regions but its lack of physical distinctness was compensated for by Paris's role as intellectual centre, drawing reconciliation out of antagonism, fusing centre with periphery. In the end the disharmony produced by natural barriers could not resist the process of unification by mind. In Michelet's judgement political centralisation was an intrinsically progressive movement – even when the agent for its actualisation was a monarch of the likes of Louis XI. Territorial difference was negated in favour of a public space within which individuals were joined by sympathy and common beliefs.

Michelet placed a high value on the contribution of the medieval church which he viewed as the vessel in which the inheritance of Roman law was protected. The church defended the idea of right against force, of unity against division. Gregory VII drew from his faith the moral authority which allowed him to resist the secular world. The First Crusade brought individuals out of their localities and generated a new sense of community. Humankind 'began again to honour itself in the lowliest conditions' (OC, IV, 444). The power of feudalism was starting to fade. The enfranchisement of the Communes signalled a growth in the ideas of liberty and equality. The twelfth century marked a significant moment of change. Abélard, whose philosophy Michelet relates back to Pelagian ideas of freedom and reason, conceived of a more human-centred universe. Heretical movements such as the Vaudois and the Albigensians emerged to test religious cohesion. By the thirteenth century a new violent spirit was abroad. A climate of instability reigned in which neither pope nor emperor inspired confidence. It was a time of confusion and disarray. On the one hand the influence of lawyers and jurists was growing. On the other there was an increase in what Michelet called mysticism, a mood of religious enthusiasm encouraged by the crusades that bore 'a frightful fruit, hatred of the law' (OC, IV, 650).

Michelet had arrived at the central moment of crisis within medieval Christianity. The Gothic spire embodied the quest for the infinite, the striving for the divine, but the cathedral also testified to a peculiarly medieval preoccupation with death, suffering and self-immolation which seemed to cherish ugliness and decay. Whereas Michelet had been happy to consider Christianity as the civilising power which organised Europe after the fall of the Roman Empire, he considered that by the later medieval period the church had become allied with non-progressive forces. The thirteenth and fourteenth centuries saw the establishment of the Crown as an effective central authority in France. Philippe le Bel constructed the first non-feudal monarchy. The Great Ordinance of 1357 marked an extension of power in a republican direction. However, Michelet saw this as premature. He expressed concern on the grounds that the Ordinance appeared to be giving 'the supreme authority to the people when there was as yet no people' (OC, V, 498). In his view the authority of Crown and state needed to be made secure before other developments could take place.

Michelet brought out individual volumes of his history until 1844. These told of peasant uprisings and urban conflict; they described with great effectiveness the ebbing away of medieval ideals. Much space was devoted to the struggle between Louis XI and the Duke of Burgundy. However, Michelet's concern throughout remained the achievement of national unification. It was during the wars with England that the French finally fully realised that their identity was different from that of the English. At that crucial moment France 'saw itself for the first time as a nation and in prosaic form [in the shape of Froissart's *Chronicles*]' (*OC*, V, 275). The new national spirit took concrete form in the person of Joan of Arc. For Michelet Joan was the embodiment of the heroic spirit, an active force, the personification of the nation. After the expulsion of the English a period of national reconstruction began. However, the church had declined into scholastic abstraction. It had condemned saintliness in the form of Joan. The time of medieval Christendom had passed.

Freedom for Michelet was never pure in the sense that it always involved an overcoming of the world of matter. The struggle could take different forms. There was the opposition between mind and external nature. There was also the more traditional notion of the conflict between spirit and flesh, between body and soul. In 1830 Michelet gave his students at the Ecole Normale a clear warning against the Saint-Simonian theory of the rehabilitation of the flesh: 'The body is always the enemy of human freedom. . . . The soul must struggle until the body is its slave'.[6] Statements such as this indicate the extent to which in the 1820s and 1830s Michelet's morality of effort could share common ground with Christian ethics. He understood Christianity as a constructive dualism which freed the personality by portraying the body and the senses as the enemies of the mind and the will. Christianity lay at the origins of moral freedom and for this reason, whatever his spiritual doubts and longings, Michelet was unwilling to follow the Saint-Simonians in their rejection of the old faith. To deny the significance and continuing relevance of Christian teaching amounted to denying the meaning of history. On the other hand, the role played by Christianity in the past was not sufficient reason to secure its position in the present.

In the 1840s Michelet's thought would cohere around the opposition between Justice and Grace, between Revolution and Christianity. In the 1830s, however, he was much less extreme. He recognised the positive role played by the church in the past and he looked for some way in which Christianity might yet renew itself. We have seen already how Michelet's democratic nationalism suggested that God, the desired object, would henceforth appear in social relations. Humankind was moving towards a new

idea of God known in action. The freely undertaken movement
of individual selves to join with other selves (sympathy and fraternity) was an act of volition (liberty) which took place within a
framework of law (equality and justice). Since God as spirit was
active in the world the movement towards a freer and more equal
society could also be portrayed as a movement towards God. God
was no longer absent or non-existent. He was present and known
as freedom and right within the political and legal worlds. But
was it enough to hold that in the nineteenth century moral and
political freedom gave expression to the divine presence, that the
divine would no longer be hidden in images, communicated in
symbols transmitted from the past? Could such views be reconciled with Christianity? Michelet's attachment to Christianity
remained strong. In his *Histoire romaine* he encountered Christianity at its beginnings. In his *Histoire de France* he followed the
role of religion in the Middle Ages. In his *Mémoires de Luther*
(1835) he found Christianity in crisis. Michelet commented that
in whatever direction he turned he met Christianity, barring his
way, preventing him from passing on. However, the depth of his
filial attachment to Christianity was evident in the analogy he
drew in the *Mémoires de Luther*:

> To touch Christianity! Those alone hesitate not to do so,
> who know not what it is. . . . For myself, I recall the nights
> during which I held vigil at the bedside of a sick mother; she
> suffered from remaining long in the same position, she wanted
> help to change her position, to turn round. My filial hands
> hesitated – how could I move her limbs so full of acute pain?
> (*OC*, III, 240)

Christianity was sick, perhaps mortally ill. Should the religion be
left to die? In the 1830s Michelet was generally reluctant to pro-
nounce Christianity dead. His attitude changed in the early 1840s
when he realised that the church, far from being on the point of
extinction, was an active force blocking the social and political
changes which he wished to see implemented. From that moment
he ceased to be concerned whether tenderly and respectfully
'moving the limbs' of ailing Christianity might threaten its existence; he decided instead that the time had come for the son to
use transgressive force in order to hasten the demise of the mother.

We must now turn to a central question which has emerged
upon a number of occasions in the course of our exploration of

Michelet's thought: the role attributed to nature and the physical universe. In his work of the 1830s nature was understood primarily as unfreedom, as the negation of spirit. The beginning of the *Introduction à l'histoire universelle* declared that the motive power of history arose from the conflict between freedom and determinism, between mind and nature: 'With the beginning of the world commenced a war which will end only with the world, and not before; that of man against nature, of spirit against matter, of freedom against necessity. History is nothing other than the account of this interminable struggle' (*OC*, II, 229). The progressive liberation of humankind lent meaning to existence. History could be interpreted as the actualisation of God's intentions by human will. At the centre of Michelet's philosophy lay the notion of separation. Nature denied, or to put it rather differently, Nature absent, lay at the heart of history, as a lack propelling humanity onward. The subject separated itself from nature, from the universal, but simultaneously longed for reconciliation. In Michelet, as in Hegel, we see the unhappy consciousness struggling to escape from alienation and division. To unite with nature was a temptation, but it amounted to a form of death wish since it entailed the abandonment of mind and freedom. On numerous occasions Michelet portrayed the embrace of nature as seductive but bearing death. His depiction of nature was highly sexualised.[7] Nature represented an overpowering profusion of life but at the same time constituted a threat. Nature was the mother to be denied, the lover to be escaped. In a note recorded in his *Journal* Michelet imagined mother nature desiring an incestuous relationship with humankind, her offspring:

There is a strange sensuality in solitude. It is a *tête à tête* with the all-lovable and all-fecund, but also with the dangerous, the resistant, the homicidal [feminine] ... both mother and lover, incestuous mother, who creates us and proposes to seduce us, makes us enjoy her, caresses us, intoxicates us and kills us: Nature, *O stepmother* [*unnatural mother*]! ... Must it be that so many tears wept in the desert have not yet purified this incestuous Circe? I would like to see her pure and divine. But I sully her with my desires, or she sullies me with her caresses. She is certainly divine. What then! is there adultery and incest with God?

(*J*, I, 119)

Nature threatened history, conspired against freedom. The great goddess stood at the beginning of things, in the terror of origins. Michelet mentioned Maya, Isis, Ceres, Persephone: 'Queen of heaven, she is the night from which light emerges and into which all life returns; mysterious union of life and death' (*OC*, II, 276). Nature represented creative power without rationality and direction. By refusing the emancipation of her children nature became a bad mother or a cruel stepmother, enticing them into abandoning the risks and potential gains of human time in favour of reintegration into cosmic time, a union in which death and life became one. Hence Michelet's welcome for the overturning by Christianity of the power of the oriental religions of nature which had impeded the development of mind. In the *Histoire romaine* he used a discussion of Cleopatra to refer to the magnetic power of nature, to its capacity to absorb mind. Michelet identified Eve with the serpent. Christianity had broken the hold of the dissolute, Bacchic religions of nature. In time the good mother, the church, replaced nature, the bad mother.

History therefore involved not just a denial of nature but a denial of the feminine seen as the source of life but the enemy of mind. History was the power which brought freedom, reason, subjectivity and control into existence. History involved more than transforming the environment by labour or by art. In Michelet's writing of the 1830s history became an overwhelmingly masculine domain, embodying a purity, an elevation of spirit. History, Michelet later declared in *La Femme* (1859), was a word which the French language had stupidly placed in the feminine gender (*LF*, 148). History corresponded to the masculine world of reason and conceptual thought, striving and freedom. History was an ejaculation of mind.[8] Nature had a different sexual identity, life-giving but mind-threatening. The impure energies of nature subverted the claims of reason; life stifled mind.[9] Michelet's approach thus demonstrated how philosophical discourse configures history as masculine while constructing a notion of feminine difference as negativity (although this never prevented Michelet himself from speaking in the name of women).[10] Nature remained associated with intoxication, madness, violence and sensuality. Nature influenced man but man moulded, reformed nature. Earlier in this chapter we saw how the notion of the progressive denial of the power of nature (the overcoming of the determinisms of race and geography) was used by Michelet in his historical writings to co-ordinate events which at first sight seemed to lack direction. The result was that the meaning of history was held to lie in the advance of consciousness and individuality. However, the extent to which women had access to these developments was, to say the least, unclear.

Nature was thus for Michelet the elemental form of otherness. He resisted what he saw as the pantheism of the Saint-Simonians because it submitted mind to matter. He was also suspicious of the seductive Schellingian proposition that spirit slumbers within nature. To present inorganic, organic and mental life as a continuum was not in his judgement a good idea. Michelet was not insensible to the poetic quality of Schelling's philosophy of identity but his intellectual reservations remained uppermost; he used forceful language, describing Schelling's philosophy as an act of adultery committed between matter and spirit, as a regression to the pantheism of India (*OC*, II, 240). Michelet's attitude needs to be distinguished from that of Quinet who in his early writings was closer to the Schellingian position. While Michelet feared that the spiritualising of nature might lead to the sacrifice of the moral life to the energies of matter, Quinet charged the poet with respeaking the word of nature in order to release its latent spiritual content. Quinet, as we saw in the last chapter, incorporated nature within his view of history as the coming into being of God. The human and the natural were linked by a network of correspondences, of analogies which expressed the hidden harmony of the cosmos. Michelet could not easily bring himself to trust nature. To unite with nature marked an abdication of the will, of reason, of the world of prose. In the *Introduction à l'histoire universelle* he was willing to admit that the inhabitants of a country in some ways reflected their environment and in his *Histoire romaine* he included some expressions which suggested the presence of correspondences between the human and the natural. However, these formative influences were not accorded a truly mystical status. In a brief review of Quinet's *De la Grèce moderne* (1830) Michelet significantly chose to praise his friend precisely because his writing had escaped the pantheism inherent in Schelling's philosophy of identity (*OC*, II, 685–6).

Michelet's thought had a puritanical, self-denying streak combined with an anti-feminine component. Maternal nature abandoned man once the idea of freedom manifested itself. Christianity was valued by Michelet because it advanced the cause of freedom by implementing the fullest negation of nature. Medieval Christianity proclaimed the nothingness of all finite things, placed death at the centre of life; it was as if it colluded with death in order to deny sensuality. In the *Introduction à l'histoire universelle* Michelet raised the possibility of reconciliation and identity as the end of history. However, he left the reconciliation of man with nature, of reason and desire, almost completely out of the picture. What we have instead is a dream of reconciliation, not between self and non-self, but between self and other selves in the form of a community unified by law, sympathy and love. Individuality as egoism was transcended. Individuality as humanity was preserved within a spiritual universal as opposed to being dissolved within a material universal. Michelet described world history as a movement from the arbitrary favouritism of the mother to equality under the law of the father:

> Man left behind the fatalistic nature-god, the exclusive divinity and unnatural mother who chose between her children, in order to reach the pure God, the god of the soul, who does not distinguish man from man, and who, in society, in religion, opens up to all men equality in love and at the paternal bosom.
>
> (*OC*, II, 238)

Justice was the principle of the masculine God of history. The orient had immolated the soul, sacrificed it to nature. The west, in the form of Christianity, asserted the superiority of moral infinity over material infinity; Spirit was incarnated within matter but was not identical to it. Therein lay the strength of medieval Christianity which used the story of Christ's passion to represent the suffering of the infinite within finitude. Michelet, who was drawn to Christianity after reading the *Imitation of Jesus Christ* as an adolescent, interpreted personal and collective experience alike by analogy with Christ's suffering:

> Yes, Christ is still on the cross; he will not descend. The Passion endures and will endure. The world has its passion, as has humanity in its long historic life, and each man's heart during the few moments it beats. To each his cross and his stigmata. Mine date from the day that my soul fell into this miserable body; which I finish wearing out in writing this.

My Passion began with my Incarnation. Poor soul what had you done to be burdened with this flesh?

(*OC*, IV, 701)

Clearly, this aspect of the Christian message still spoke directly to the condition of nineteenth-century man. Michelet denied that passion was exclusively pain passively endured. For him it was self-chosen suffering and as such 'active and voluntary'; it was a willed struggle against the impurity and dispersion of matter (*OC*, IV, 702). The soul incarnate in flesh could choose which course of action to follow; it could renounce its spiritual nature and satiate itself with human pleasure, or, as freedom, it could strive to overcome the limitations imposed upon it by nature, the cruel stepmother. However, rather than relate suffering to the doctrine of sin, Michelet proclaimed the sanctity of effort: 'This is heroic Passion; strength, the beginning of virtue' (*OC*, IV, 702).

No reader can fail to register the two-sided character of Michelet's treatment of medieval Christianity. At first sight Christianity, represented by the Gothic cathedral, seemed close to extinction. The cathedral had fallen into silence, the meaning of its symbolism had been lost. It had become an object of anti-quarian interest, deserted by the masses: '[The priest's weak voice] is powerless to fill vaults, whose ample span was built to embrace and contain the thunder of the people's voices' (*OC*, IV, 710). And yet, Michelet concluded his discussion with the assertion that Christianity and Christian art could not die: '[Christianity] may change its vestment, but perish, never! It will transform itself to live again once more. One morning it will appear before the eyes of those who think they are guarding its tomb, and will rise again on the third day' (*OC*, IV, 724). In historical terms Michelet described humankind outgrowing the Christian faith of the Middle Ages, outgrowing a restricted definition of the meaning of the passion. Philosophical reason, in the person of Abélard, had chal-lenged the authority of faith. Prose had overcome poetry. Spiritual life had not ceased but was developing beyond the confines of the ecclesiastical institution. Michelet noted the obscure awareness of 'an everlasting Christ, unceasingly renewed in mankind' (*OC*, IV, 723). He was drawn to Joachim of Fiore, to the 'Eternal Evangel' and the notion of the third age of spirit.[11] What seemed like the abandonment of Christianity corresponded in fact to its actualis-ation by the people. The incarnation had become generalised:

'God is not less God for having made himself mankind . . . the temple is not destroyed, because it has become as large as the world' (OC, IV, 723).

Like the Christian socialists of his time, Michelet concluded that the realisation of a more just and equal society was not antithetical to the existence of the transcendent realm. It was a precondition for ultimate reconciliation. At the close of the Middle Ages the Christian notion of self-sacrifice and redemptive suffering entered the generality of people where it attained its highest degree of perfection in Joan of Arc who was both the embodiment of the struggle of the French people for national identity and the last visible representation of Christ produced by the medieval mind. Due to Joan's heroic self-sacrifice, to her active passion, France was saved. In the person of Joan, Michelet found the figure of a female Messiah, rescuing France from the English, engaging with political reality, making history. However, we would be unwise to conclude that in the form of Joan the female principle had become the wholly legitimate subject of history. In Michelet's text Joan remained an icon of innocence and purity. If she was the female Christ, the new redeemer, she was still not fully woman in her humanness. Indeed, as Frank Bowman has observed, Joan remained the only feminised form of Christ approved of by Michelet.[12] In most circumstances the feminine denoted grace, not justice.

Michelet's analysis of the waning of the Middle Ages echoed his treatment of pagan religion in his *Histoire romaine*. He was describing a crucial moment of transition, a shift in sensibility when men discovered that what they took to be supernatural entities were in fact representations, figures, projections. The decline of the Middle Ages corresponded to the disintegration of an ordered system of symbolic meanings. In the end, commented Michelet, the papacy itself discovered that it was unable to decipher traditional symbols. Meaning had drained away, had been lost. In the *Roman de la rose* allegory triumphed over symbol. But the demise of the symbolic order was necessary in order for scientific knowledge to increase. In Michelet's terms this was a victory of prose over poetry, of abstraction over symbolism, of mind over matter. Symbolism had to be discarded in order for modern notions of equality and legality to emerge.[13] However, Michelet was painfully aware of the loss and suffering occasioned when symbolic forms were abandoned: 'Nothing is so cruel and ungrateful as prose, when it shuts its eyes on the old and venerable poetic forms within which it has grown up' (*OC*, V, 335). Moreover, the experience of being deprived of a sustaining system of meaning was not restricted to the transition from the Middle Ages to the Renaissance. It clearly extended to the present. Could the moral centre represented by traditional Christianity adequately be replaced? In discussing the Middle Ages Michelet was undoubtedly addressing the religious crisis of his own times. He unburdened himself in a passage which he suppressed in later editions:

> Indisputably morality today is more enlightened; is it firmer? This is a question well calculated to trouble every sincere friend of progress. None more warmly than the writer of these lines associates himself with the immense steps made by mankind in modern times, and with its glorious hopes. The living dust [i.e. the people] which the powerful trampled under foot, has acquired a human voice, has risen to property, intelligence and participation in political rights. Who does not bound with joy in seeing the victory of equality? . . . I only fear that in acquiring so just a feeling for his rights, man has lost some part of his feeling for his duties. One's heart bleeds to find that in the universal progress, moral strength has not increased. The notion of free will and moral responsibility becomes daily fainter. How strange! In proportion as the old fatalism of climate and of races which weighed upon antique man diminishes, it is replaced by an increasing fatalism of ideas.
>
> (*OC*, IV, 662)

According to Michelet, history was a dynamic movement which progressed through a series of stages. Nature, on the other hand, was life without moral sense, without a fixed purpose beyond generation. History opened up a space, a gap between mind and nature which was filled by the moral life. Thus far, when we have looked at this gap, this distance, we have seen it in terms of separation, of the negation of matter by mind, of the repression of the feminine by the masculine. However, there were times when Michelet was inclined to envision history more as an appropriation of nature than as a negation. These two aspects came together in the context of Michelet's understanding of symbols, and, in a broader sense, in his reading of history as a process of symbolisation and desymbolisation.[14] Many of the Romantic generation held that nature, as an expression of the divine, could be read as symbolic. The universe was charged with a hidden meaning which was decipherable in terms of correspondences and analogies. Michelet, on the other hand, although he evoked the notion of universal harmony, usually denied moral value to nature and thus closed off one of the Romantic roads to reconciliation and identity. He did none the less acknowledge that the primitive mind turned instinctively to the forms of nature in order to embody thought. This was Vico's notion of imaginative and figurative ways of grasping the world. Michelet went most deeply into this question in his *Origines du droit français cherchées dans les symboles et les formules du droit universel* (1837), in which he investigated the laws and customs of many different cultures in order to demonstrate a historical shift from symbolic expressions of legal duties and obligations to abstract definitions of right. His general thesis was used to support the particular case of France: the land of prose divested itself at an early date of the symbolism and poetry characteristic of Germanic law.

According to the *Origines du droit français* humankind originally made sense of itself and of the world by ascribing to external nature symbolic meanings. An intimate relationship prevailed at that stage between an ill-defined perceiving self and the world which surrounded it. Human beings were still so much a part of the life of nature that it appeared normal for human meaning to be attributed to the language of birds or to the rumbling of thunder. However, as humankind began to take some degree of control over its destiny language progressively lost its figurative character. Symbolic modes of thinking which used powerful concrete imagery became less and less appropriate as intelligence and self-awareness increased and history began to separate from nature. Symbolism was inadequate to the task of communicating the new forms of knowledge. In the end the idea escaped the prisonhouse of nature, left behind the imprecision of figurative language and articulated itself with clarity within the abstract discourse of reason. Michelet explained that the sadness of the human condition arose from the resistance which the external world opposed to the actualisation of ideas. But was nature irrevocably an irreducible otherness? In the *Origines du droit français* Michelet used an expression already employed by Quinet: he spoke of captured infinity. This suggested that the divine was present, bound within material reality. Humankind imprinted its meanings on nature but perhaps nature was, after all, in some way receptive, attentive. Did spirit inhabit the inwardness of the material world? Michelet did not concede that mind was an emanation of the life of nature, a manifestation of the world soul. He held fast to his view that mind grew by denying its origins and by inhabiting an anticipatory awareness of its own destruction. In a revealing comparison he described childhood as 'a heavy incarnation of thought, weighed down with milk, blood and poetry' (OC, III, 627). He added: 'Age cures us of childhood, as do prose and analysis, and above all death, the supreme analysis' (OC, III, 627). The progress of mind required separation, discrimination and self-awareness but death was the inevitable conclusion. Michelet had to find a way of making death itself fecund.

History as progress broke with the language of symbolism as part of the separation from nature and the abandonment of the regularity of cosmic, maternal time in favour of human – or should we say virile? – time. At this point we encounter the broader cultural dimension of Michelet's use of symbols. Symbols were not just the appropriate form of expression for the mind of primitive man. They were associated with religious epochs in general. Symbolism was suitable for rendering the obscure intuition of the holy, the power of the infinite. World history exhibited cycles which began with ages of faith and ended with the victory of human reason. In the 1830s Michelet, like Quinet, was preoccupied with the question of whether the symbolic world of Christianity had to be abandoned for ever. Was the world of politics and law sustainable without recourse to symbolic codes? Vico's three ages (Gods, heroes, men) suggested that symbolism cohered with the collective in the initial stages but that democracy and individualism ultimately excluded symbolic systems as traditionally conceived. The symbol mediated a world of oneness and community. Its position was undermined once authority was ceded by the collective to the individual. The act of rational interpretation drew new senses out of a tradition, an image or a text. It defied religious truth. We have seen Michelet identify France with a positive dynamic of desymbolisation, a movement from poetry to prose. However, he always handled symbols with respect and caution. Religious symbols were not inventions designed to exploit humankind's susceptibility to superstition. They embodied ideas and ideals which bound communities together.

As Michelet's treatment of the Middle Ages demonstrated, the great religious symbols were both vessels of meaning and movers of history. Identification with symbolic representations determined patterns of conduct. The very imprecision of the symbol allowed for a potential range of meanings, in this case concerning the crucifixion and the resurrection. Symbols seemed to possess a degree of independent life and their capacity to endure reflected their rich ambiguity. However, there were limits to their indeterminacy. The problem which Michelet and his contemporaries faced was to decide whether Christianity had run its course. Was it still possible for Christianity to transform the meaning of its symbols in order to accommodate modernity or was extinction rather than metamorphosis in prospect? Would arresting the process of transformation abandon men to an absence of meaning or liberate the possibilities of a new symbol? Interpretation, the work of reason, produced a knowledge laden with guilt because it contained the potential for an act of deicide. Looked at more positively, however, the instrumental language of prose, of analysis, dissolved the letter and emancipated the spirit. Prose was the least figurative form of expression; it was closest to thought (hence closer to the dream of a simultaneity of thought and action). The language of the symbol, on the other hand, was closer to nature than to mind, less artificial, more material.

As the *Origines du droit français* showed, symbols were originally the product of primitive man's ascription of human meanings to the external world. The symbol was a recapitulation of the incarnation, an instance of the fundamental duality of mind and matter, form and content. In a world without transparency and immediacy mind was constrained to inhabit matter in order to convey sense. But for Michelet, as we have seen on numerous occasions, the relationship with nature could never easily be one of identity. Matter, in the form of the external embodiment of thought, was always potentially invasive of mind, of reason. What united symbolic forms was precisely their dependency on matter. The extent of dependency varied but for Michelet there was inevitably an element of danger once thought inscribed itself in nature. It comes as no surprise to discover that in discussing symbolism Michelet again had recourse to sexual polarities. Architecture – the most symbolic form of art because the most material – was discussed directly in sexual terms. In India Michelet found two types of monument: womb-like cave structures and phallic pyramids 'seeking to impregnate the sky' (*OC*, IV, 712). Art mirrored the polarities of existence: male/female, man/nature, light/darkness, 'mortal life and fecund death' (*OC*, IV, 712). In so far as art imitated nature man ran the risk of submitting to matter, of conniving with the homicidal stepmother. But art could never free itself entirely of matter. The process of artistic creation, of spiritualising and humanising matter, carried risks. Thus when Michelet described the representation of vegetation within the stonework of the Gothic cathedral he included a reference to the veil of Isis (*OC*, IV, 711) in a way which suggested that the ambiguous death-bearing life of nature even infiltrated the liberty-asserting death represented by the building which symbolically expressed Christ's crucifixion. Architecture imitated, reproduced, even parodied man's divided relationship to mind and nature.

For Michelet the symbol had the potential to take on the ambiguity, the deceitful instability of feminised nature:

> Each symbol is an equivocation, as is all poetry. Is nature herself anything else? Look how she acts in the illusion of living forms, in this fertile sophistry, in which each object has a double meaning, ceaselessly translating [transforming] the beings, asking nothing better than to bring all things back to her, to mix together all life in one vast equivocation.
>
> (*OC*, III, 642–3)

This was Nature as Maya, life as illusion. At this point, however, Michelet added a new element, the presence of God, as the male principle, ordering and discriminating: 'God does not let himself be tricked. He untangles whereas [nature] mixes and confuses. Each creation is a distinction. He distinguishes ceaselessly, describing, defining, measuring, prescribing, the eternal *measurer*, the all-powerful jurisconsult!' (*OC*, III, 643). Here Michelet is saying that the organisation of creation depends upon the activity of a masculine power which is responsible for constructing meaning by instituting difference. In contrast to his standard representation of nature as overwhelmingly feminine he is suggesting that a maleness already inhabited the cosmos prior to the expulsion of humankind from union with the mother. Was the male principle the one cause through which all else, including the multiplicity of things, existed?

Unfortunately, Michelet tells us little about the male principle apart from the fact that it exists in a conflictual relation to the female principle whose generative work it reorders by separation. However, despite the lack of clarification, this reference is of importance. Desymbolisation clearly serves the male God. Man separates, discriminates, and by so doing emancipates himself from the power of nature. Man is critical intelligence, self-created subjectivity. Michelet was fascinated by the processes by which symbols were transformed and took on new meanings. He described the Roman judge using cunning to lend new interpretations to the written law, extracting meanings from texts.[15] Here was freedom not opposing nature directly but working with symbols, teasing new meanings out of old texts. In the end Rome effected the removal of the idea of law from the confusing language of symbol and represented it in the clarity of prose. On other occasions the possibility of transformative collaboration between text and interpretation – of seduction or incest? – was absent and it seemed that destructive action alone could found justice and emancipate humanity.

The strength of symbols lay in their capacity to accommodate change. The lack of an absolutely fixed signification was not just an illustration of the capriciousness of feminised nature controlling the form within which the idea was made manifest. It also meant that symbols could carry new meanings and discard old meanings, facilitate progress as well as impede it. The loss of access to symbols was highly significant because it amounted to the loss of the space within which shared collective identity was defined. Scattered fugitive identities tended to dispersion. But could individualities cohere and yet stay loyal to the claims of law and right? Could there be a new unifying idea, a poetry of history? It is worth recalling that Michelet was called 'Monsieur symbole' by some of his contemporaries. This was because he made sense of history by relating events and individual actions to ideas and to forces which exceeded them. But was the historical word on its own sufficiently powerful and unificatory to forge collective cohesion? Detached from the ambiguous comforts of the symbol, reason inhabited not oneness but differentiation, not generality but individuality; reason seemed destined to reinvent time in its own image, not as symbol but as history.

In his later writing Michelet would address the symbolism of the nation and the collective modes of its celebration. For the moment he emphasised liberation from symbols. If symbols united, it was at too great a cost, by absorbing the self-determining activity of mind. Michelet left his readers in no doubt that it was impossible to return to the poetic formulations which bound man to the ambiguities of nature. Nature was a text of life, not of meaning, an unstoppable process of substitution based upon equivalence. The real work was done by the desymbolisers, the translators of myth into history, of poetry into law, ultimately of thought into action. The symbol accomplished its destiny in its own death. However, Michelet rarely addressed directly the sublime moment of the death of symbol, of the triumph of analysis and separation over unity and synthesis. The evidence of history indicated that the demise of a symbol was more likely to be a lingering, drawn-out affair, painfully uncertain in its ending.

In the 1840s Michelet worked his way towards a new sense of the historian's role and an expanded definition of his responsibilities. At the same time he reviewed his understanding of the dynamics of history and formulated a modified periodisation, one which ascribed special significance to the Renaissance.[16] The *Introduction à l'histoire universelle* of 1831 had proposed what amounted to a linear view of history as a vector of progress arising from the never-ending struggle between man and nature, freedom and necessity. To be fair, Michelet did draw attention to the fact that nature was not just resistance. In a lecture of 1831 he echoed the idealist position held by many of his contemporaries when he explained that it was man's task to humanise the material universe. However, Michelet did not go so far as to view the reconciliation of man and nature as the real end of the process. He emphasised the control of matter by spirit. He concluded his observations with a telling comment: 'When matter will be nothing other than the expression of our thought, we will no longer run any risk by placing our love in nature' (*LVR*, 266). In these words the reader immediately recognises the authentic voice of Michelet. Nature, if not untouchable, was unlovable. Nature needed to be transformed by mind, mastered by man before it could be the object of genuine filial affection. Did that imply that the bad mother could only be redeemed at the cost of her surrendering, if not her generative power, then at least her ontological primacy over her offspring?

In the 1830s Michelet suggested that humankind resembled a dispossessed, abandoned, sometimes angry son who, by demonstrating independence of will, had largely reared himself in accordance with his own self-definition.[17] It was man who by his industrial and artistic activity endowed the material world with human

223

meanings. In the 1840s Michelet moved away from the conflictual interpretation and sought reconciliation. The desire for union took the form of the establishment of a love relation with the cosmos. However, in order to present nature as a worthy object of love Michelet needed to get beyond the ambivalent identification of nature with generation without moral meaning. Nature had to be reconceptualised as productive of meaning prior to its incorporation by mind. Could nature become the source of law and justice, and cease being antithetical to mind and freedom? This was the movement which Michelet's thought accomplished in the 1840s and which underpinned much of the writing on natural history which he produced during the Second Empire. Already, according to *Le Peuple* (1846), our moral being arose less from the domination of nature than from an awareness of the manifold interconnections which bound human existence to the fabric of animate and inanimate nature. Man still set out to control his surroundings but forms of collaboration now replaced confrontation narrowly defined. The maleness of the universal subject gave way to notions of androgyny. Instead of the political ideal of the virile community, Michelet foregrounded his idea of the people which was gendered as female or bisexual. Michelet discovered that the paternal bosom could not nurture society in its fullness, that the law could not adequately be approached in terms of male reason alone. In 1845 he expressed the wish that man might experience 'the law like a mother and live in her warmth' (*J*, I, 627).

We have already taken note of some modifications in Michelet's views. In the *Origines du droit français* (1837) he had been less antagonistic towards the material universe. In his treatment of Joan of Arc (1841) he had recognised the value of the feminine. The transformation of his perception of nature in the 1840s was accompanied by significant developments in his understanding of history. He located history within the cosmic processes of life which he henceforward characterised in a positive manner as maternal. However, we cannot gauge the import of Michelet's changing views of history unless we relate them to the intensely personal experience of bereavement, to the struggle involved in recognising – or refusing – the proposition that certain losses are irrecoverable.[18] Michelet's reassessment of the past was part of a struggle for meaning and value occasioned by a prolonged meditation on death. I have already alluded to the feelings of guilt and remorse which he experienced after the death of his first wife in

1839. The reality of personal annihilation led Michelet to reflect further on the status of the individual. We have taken note of the way in which he tended to associate sensuality with individuality while identifying generality with mind and reason. In August 1839 he observed that 'our perfect side is our general dimension [*notre généralité*], it is less ourselves. Our bad side incontestably belongs to us' (*J*, I, 311). He also remarked that when we love other human beings we love them in their individuality, as fallible and flawed creatures. Did death signify the release of the soul, of generality, from imprisonment within the flesh?

In August 1839 Michelet commented in his *Journal*: 'We must learn to die. After a life of individuality, we must begin a life of generality, if that is possible. But how bury, without a tear, such a dear part of one's heart?' (*J*, I, 314). How indeed? A few days later he had Pauline's body exhumed only to recoil at the sight of the decomposing corpse which was merging with the anonymous generality of matter. Could the irreparable loss of an individual life, the extinction of a unique person ever wholly be a good? Moreover, each individual life was implicated in the lives of others, and one death rent asunder the threads of life which bound human beings together. Despite his desire to value the general, to privilege universal humanness, Michelet found that the experience of Pauline's death simply threw into greater relief the solitude and insufficiency of the self. Reflecting upon what he had lost, Michelet evoked the memory of a love relation which surpassed humanness. Whereas sexual relations of a purely physical nature were held to be a surrender to nature and to the baser promptings of individuality, love could also signify a magical communion of self and other, mind and body: 'finding in each other a sweet forgetfulness of oneself, each evening dying within each other, dying and creating together, being gods together!' (*J*, I, 318). Love, 'this intoxicating death of self', was also a transcendence of self (*J*, I, 318).

Pauline's death left Michelet wanting to believe in some form of immortality but he again refused to turn to nature as a substitute divinity. Nature was still the cruel power which wove the intricate web of life only to shatter it without thought. Nature resembled life, but carried the seeds of death. History, on the other hand, which at first sight seemed to be the province of the dead, became for the historian a source of life and nourishment. In Barthes's phrase, Michelet fed upon the substance of history, becoming the 'manducator, priest, and owner of History'.[19] By embracing death in the form of history, by transmuting decay into growth, he forged a form of personal integration whereby union with the violent energies of previous centuries became a way to a higher form of knowledge. Michelet suggested that the historian could in a sense relive, rediscover within himself, the lives of the oppressed throughout history. He felt that his compassion was sufficiently vast to encompass the sufferings of all who came before him. History was more than an exercise of critical judgement, it became an enterprise of resurrection (*J*, I, 353). The word of the historian redeemed time. History, in the words of Edward Kaplan, allowed Michelet 'to deny death by absorbing *individual* life into the *general*'.[20] The motivation of the historian was the need to assert the value of life in the face of death:

> I need to prove to myself and to this humanity whose transient appearances I sketch that we are reborn, that we do not die. I need to do this because I feel myself dying ... I want, over and above the chain of these mobile lives, these instants that we call men ... I want to weave a fabric of ideas by which they perpetuated themselves, gave the lie to death, mocked nature.
>
> (J, I, 359)

Without history, it seemed, there could be no foundation of meaning. But, despite Michelet's tendency to identify generality with universality and abstraction, he was proposing recovering the past in its fullness rather than extracting from it an ideal philosophical history. If history was a way to discovering truth, then it was truth incarnate in individual lives, in events and beliefs, not truth bodied forth as a transcendental formula:

> History: violent moral chemistry, where my individual passions evolve into generalities, where my generalities become passions, where my peoples become me, where my self returns to animate the peoples. They address me in order that I may make them live. Alas! Am I really alive? Oh! brothers, I do not lack compassion, it is immense and painful. But do you believe that I can disentangle your pains from mine? I willingly take them into myself. But will I not confuse them? Will my individual life not take the place of your general life? Then, lamenting, they said to me, that it

was the same thing, that they and I were but one, that our hearts suffered in the same way, that their life lived in my life, that these pale phantoms were my phantom, or rather that I myself was the living, fleeting, phantom of peoples fixed in real existence and in changelessness.

(J, I, 362)

In these remarkable lines we can see how the historian established his identity – or controlled his fractured, heterogeneous identities – by drawing sustenance from the dead. The communion with the past was a passionate exchange of energy, not a consoling merging with a plenitude of being.

In May 1840 Michelet met Mme Dumesnil, the mother of one of his pupils. She became an object of tender affection for the historian. She brought love and meaning back into Michelet's life and her somewhat maternal presence certainly influenced a new responsiveness to the value of nature. However, Mme Dumesnil fell ill and her health rapidly deteriorated. Michelet, while caring for his sick friend, pursued his private meditations upon the historian's relationship to the past. In his diary he recorded a dream in which the dead pleaded with him to restore them to life. Without his intervention the past was incomplete. The historian's fusion with the past resembled an act of love, a death of self, but it was also a communion which permitted meaning to emerge. The historian fulfilled the role of Oedipus:

[The dead] need an Oedipus, who will explain to them their own enigmas whose meaning they do not possess, who will teach them what their words, their acts, what they have not understood, meant . . . we must make the silences of history speak, those fearsome organ pauses, when history speaks no more and which are precisely its most tragic tones.

(J, I, 378)

The writing self was fully identified with its object: 'What has history been made of, if not of myself? What will history be made of, what will it recount, if not myself?' (J, I, 382). The recovery, the reclaiming of the past, was a complex process in which the self at first seemed to be absorbed by the multitude of other selves but then expanded in order to fill the recesses of time and endow the dead with meaning. At first sight this appeared to be an excess of subjectivity, a dilation of the ego. However, we should remember Michelet's point that in order to be fully oneself one must first be transformed by death into what one really is. This was a way of restating the fundamental inferiority of individuality when compared with generality and universality. However, it also suggested that the historian who endowed the past with life wrote from the vantage point of personal death, of the annulment of self, dying to selfhood as in the act of love.

Michelet identified the meaning of his own existence with the accomplishment of the project of writing: 'It is necessary to live and die as a book, not as a man' (*J*, I, 330). He wanted to accept death as the power which released the good, which separated true life from the limits of individuality. But he also recognised that within the less good and the less true, within the transient life of individuality, all was not without worth. In the presence of the dying Mme Dumesnil Michelet found himself once again brought up against the problem of meaning. His anger again focused on nature: 'Nature: mother or stepmother? If she is a mother, why death?' (*J*, I, 388). However, Michelet now altered his perception of nature and convinced himself of the general fecundity of death: 'Death must be a childbirth. Absolutely it must be so' (*J*, I, 388). In the weeks that followed he expanded this intuition. On 9 May 1842 he noted: 'I had reached [the idea of] a God-mother, of death as birth' (*J*, I, 399). Maternity, understood as a cycle of life–death–rebirth became the beneficent power which presided over nature and history alike. All life took on a maternal aspect. To confirm his intuition Michelet turned to transformist biology, to the work of friends such as Etienne and Isidore Geoffroy Saint-Hilaire. Transformism lent legitimacy and authority to Michelet's new awareness of the unity of all things. Universal life was purposeful and meaningful and seemingly underwrote personal survival after death. Michelet now believed that the soul, 'far from dissolving into some generality, must, according to what we see in the ascending chain of beings, become increasingly individualised' (*J*, I, 402). In this way trust in the maternal synthesis of all things came to displace Michelet's earlier suspicion of nature. But if history were naturalised could it still remain the discourse of freedom?

Michelet's published work of the period currently under discussion included *Des Jésuites* (1843), *Du prêtre, de la femme et de la famille* (1845), *Le Peuple* (1846) and his *Histoire de la Révolution française* (1847–53). In *Des Jésuites* his main thesis paralleled that argued by Quinet in his corresponding lectures: the Society of Jesus reduced human beings to the status of obedient machines the better to control, manipulate and enslave them; Jesuitism was the enemy of progress in science and in law. However, like Quinet, Michelet still sought to draw a distinction between Jesuitism and the Christian spirit. He contrasted the creativity and fecundity of the Middle Ages with the life-denying immobilism of the Society of Jesus. He declared himself to be on the side of life and growth and he accused the Jesuits of representing fatalism and the rejection of all possibility of renewal. He reminded his audience that he, the son of the Revolution and the champion of freedom, had none the less opened his heart to the Middle Ages in a spirit of 'infinite tenderness' (DJ, 55).

Unlike the Jesuits who wanted to arrest time, Michelet considered that he espoused time in its creative dimension. He repeated his definition of 1831 that history was the progressive victory of liberty but added an interesting clarification: progress did not take place by destruction but by interpretation. The activity of interpretation presupposed both 'the *tradition* which one interprets, and the *liberty* which interprets' (DJ, 55). By denying validity to the work of interpretation the Jesuits manufactured their own sterility. They came to inhabit a spiritual vacuum, an unproductive realm where power was exercised in order to suppress selfhood, a realm situated outside the purposeful movement of history. *Des Jésuites* also reflected the new positive valorisation of femininity which we have seen expressed in the *Journal*. In the course of a critique of Jesuit educational practice – which he called 'education against nature' – Michelet evoked the notion of 'the maternity of Providence' and observed that God was a mother (DJ, 81). Maternity was now identified with the loving force, the divine power which encouraged the development of life, action and liberty. God as mother nurtured and did not disinherit her offspring. Michelet was plainly indicating that culture, in order to be beneficent, should follow the path of nature.

In *Du prêtre, de la femme et de la famille* Michelet widened his critique. Here his *bête noire* was the priest who, as director of conscience, took control of families, usually by means of exerting influence over the wife. Michelet reaffirmed his new-found commitment to maternal values. Maternal love was no longer perceived as stifling. It was held to nurture the independent heroic spirit: 'superior men are all *sons of their mothers*' (DP, 246). However,

Michelet was still not willing to deny Christianity completely. In 1845 he again wondered whether Catholicism might transform itself (*DP*, 263). But this was a last, lingering hope. The evidence of the *Journal* indicates that the substantive break with the church had effectively occurred in 1843. Michelet had lost Pauline and Mme Dumesnil. His daughter had subsequently married Alfred Dumesnil. In the wake of these losses he judged that he had also reached the moment of final separation from Christianity. In August 1843 he bade farewell to the past and placed his hope in the as yet unknown God of the future (*J*, I, 517). Three years later he published *Le Peuple*. He viewed this as a positive work, a step forward from the critical orientation of his recent production. He now openly proclaimed his commitment to revolutionary France, to the new principle which had succeeded where Christianity had failed:

> The Middle Ages promised union but only produced war. It was necessary for this God [the divine Word] to have his second epoch, for him to appear on earth in his incarnation of 1789. At that moment he gave to association its most extended and truest form, the form which alone can yet unite us, and through us, save the world.
>
> (*LP*, 217)

France had a messianic destiny to fulfil and for Michelet the new incarnation was indisputably collective, not individual, in character; the people – not a great world-historical individual, such as Napoleon – was the true agent for reconciliation and justice, the unifying power. The crucial point for Michelet – and he noted his disagreement with Quinet on this score – was that the French Revolution was more than the actualisation of Christianity. The Revolution 'infinitely surpassed both antiquity and Christianity' (*J*, I, 604).

Michelet was preoccupied by the solitude endured by the self. Only by transcending individuality could contact be made with generality in one or other of its manifestations. After Pauline's death he turned in anguish to the community as a potential source of solace: 'How I need to clasp hold of the *patrie*, to know and love France more and more!' (*J*, I, 310). In his historical researches he took note of the desire of human beings to come together in collaborative communities of equals. He found evidence of just such a wish for association within the Middle Ages – until the church altered its stance and lent its spiritual authority to the principle of divine-right monarchy. In Michelet's case the idea of association was at one with his concept of the people. Association did not denote a grand plan to reorder social relations in the light of abstract rules. (Michelet defended private property and had no time for the brand of socialist internationalism which denied the nation its central position.)

In the *Histoire de France* he described the slow construction of collective identity. He had a deep sense that the people were the real and rightful subject of history but that they had been betrayed by the church and the monarchy until the Revolution consolidated the popular spirit in the form of the nation. In 1847 he would begin publishing his own history of the Revolution. In 1846, in *Le Peuple*, he dealt with the consequences of the Revolution, with nineteenth-century France's failure to complete the building of the unified society which 1789 had appeared to inaugurate. For, despite its ringing nationalist sentiments, *Le Peuple* was not a book brimming over with confidence. It was written out of an anxiety that the nation, whatever its ultimate destiny and intellectual superiority, was engaged in a process of decline. Michelet's main concern lay precisely with the lack of association. Association, which he saw as both an ideal and as the natural expression of social relations among the people, seemed in danger of disappearing. In the first section of *Le Peuple* he described the class divisions consequent upon the industrial revolution and the abuse of power by the bourgeoisie. He launched a bitter attack on mechanisation which destroyed the individual's self-respect and led to debauchery, violence and unrest. He charted a pattern of dependency which brought different groups – peasants, industrial workers, manufacturers, shopkeepers, civil servants – into relations of exploitation and duplicity which encouraged isolation and egoism, the worst aspects of individualism. Love, instead of binding individuals together, became egoistic self-enclosed desire among the workers and heartless calculation among the rich. In the modern world industrial civilisation represented the unthinking, repressive forces of fatalism.

In 1831 Michelet had spoken of the coming into existence of a new social god. In 1846 he envisaged a community which incorporated his more recent thoughts on the relationship between nature and history and which reflected his commitment to the maternal ideal. France was mother, the people were a positive force. Contact with nature was beneficent, indeed essential for social harmony. Michelet had transformed his definition of individuality and rethought its relation to generality. Mind, freedom and intelligence were no longer enough if their activity excluded the value of the natural. This raised an important question: did historical knowledge risk becoming less important if the ideal form of association partook of the generative and healing power of maternal, cosmic time? It was evident that Michelet now placed his goal of establishing social harmony within a much grander perspective of reconciliation, one which included the natural world. His text contained a memorable chapter which urged respect for animals, too often brutalised by man. The divine seemed now to be present in all forms of life. Creation in its totality was a brotherhood. Michelet urged the rehabilitation of nature. How different all this was from the *Introduction à l'histoire universelle*! Michelet now expressed admiration for the Hindu sacred texts which preserved a sense of the universal brotherhood of all creatures, a bond broken by the classical world and reinforced by the Judaeo-Christian tradition. Jesus, Michelet pointedly observed, died for men, not for the animals which were consigned as impure. In practical terms, however, Michelet was less concerned with the concrete fate of the natural world than with the inclusion of nature as value within a new pattern of social relations. Friendship and love were now placed at the centre of his notion of association. Love was the force which bound citizens together. Friendship was made central and considered 'a means of progress' (*LP*, 200).

Michelet believed that human beings were naturally sociable, disinterested and compassionate. These were the values which in his mind were associated with 'le peuple'. Christianity, with its basis in the doctrine of original sin, denied this natural goodness and even branded innocent children as fallen creatures. Michelet's new religion of revolutionary nationalism was quite different. It sought to reach out to all who had traditionally been excluded or silenced. He urged respect for the wisdom of simple people and of children. Children were close to the spirit of the people, they were naturally good. However, this line of argument did not imply a wholesale rejection of culture and reflection in favour of an affective bonding with the natural world. Michelet remained committed to the intellectual progress accomplished by history. What was new was the desire somehow to conjoin the value of instinct with the power of mind. He revered the people whom he saw as embodying warmth and life but he also valued education – the need to develop an appropriate education for the people was a subject to which he often returned. Knowledge was necessary for the building and reinforcing of community. The child represented hope for the future but in order to fulfil its mediating role it needed a suitable form of education. In *Le Peuple* Michelet projected an image of himself as a man of the people who, having gained access to culture, wanted to raise up his fellows without causing them to lose their original energy and moral qualities.

Le Peuple became a book of impossible syntheses, between adulthood and childhood, masculinity and femininity, culture and nature, past and present, analysis and feeling, barbarian energy and moral rectitude, rich and poor. In place of the universal male subject of 1831 Michelet described a new ideal, the genius who reconciled contraries within himself by possessing 'the two sexes of the mind [*les deux sexes de l'esprit*]' (*LP*, 185). This mental bisexuality represented humanity in its fullness – although in reality it was generally viewed as an extension of masculinity rather than as a gain for femininity. (Michelet still placed women firmly within a secondary, supportive role, nurturing or inspiring the male.) The genius contained within himself the polarities of creation and for that reason was himself endowed with creative power, with the capacity to transcend time and succession: 'For other people everything drags itself along, slowly. The genius fills the gap, connects both ends, abolishes time, he is a lightning flash of eternity' (*LP*, 188). Furthermore, added Michelet, it was on the pattern of the divine soul of the genius, with its combination of male and female elements, that the social world should be modelled. We are given an inkling of the form that this process of creative imitation might take when Michelet presents the *patrie* as an object of love. According to *Le Peuple*, the *patrie* should function as a mediating presence, uniting citizens despite their many disparities of wealth and social condition. At the same time – and for Michelet this was vitally important – through a combination of love, friendship and education, the ideal of the *patrie* also encouraged a reduction of inequalities within the wider association. This fraternal ideal should not be isolated from Michelet's turn to maternal and natural values. The new religion of the French people represented a response to the plight of the alienated self because it offered the possibility of a return to oneness, a reconstruction of the all-important sense of belonging (*LP*, 200). It is noteworthy that in *Le Peuple* Michelet took care to situate the national spirit within nature, within a particular environment. According to the 'Tableau de la France' of 1833 the intellectual and moral force of the nation placed territory under the stewardship of mind. History, Michelet had remarked, effaced geography. In *Le Peuple* his attitude was at first glance similar. He described how the collective mind appropriated a space within nature which it then controlled and dominated. Collective self-identity was achieved and maintained by imposing order and human meaning upon land, upon the 'indifferent and dissolving nature which always wishes to mix together' (*LP*, 219). Organised human societies thus represented a concentration of mind, a victory for freedom and discrimination. However, Michelet had in fact modified his position and moved away from an unqualified commitment to masculine values. He was now more willing to place nature at the heart of society, to look for a harmony between man and world. Nature had become part of the symbolic home inhabited by Spirit. In *Le Peuple* he deepened his definition of the *patrie*, of the fatherland, by incorporating into his concept the value of nature and of femininity:

> The fatherland (the *motherland* as the Dorians so well called it) is the love of loves. It appears to us in our dreams as a young adored mother, or as a powerful wet-nurse who suckles us in millions. . . . What a weak image! Not only does she suckle us, she contains us within her: in ea movemur et sumus.

> (*LP*, 219)

Through the agency of the *patrie* the bond with the maternal principle was re-established. Michelet concluded that in order for the spirit of a people to be actualised it needed both a social organisation and an appropriate natural environment. We see evidence of this in his treatment of the peasant whom he presented as the backbone of France, the embodiment of revolutionary virtue. In his opening chapter he dwelt on the peasant's relationship to the land which he cultivated, and which, thanks to the Revolution, he now owned. According to Michelet the peasant sensed that the land he possessed was both nature and the product of human history; he loved this 'human land' like a living person (*LP*, 84). But by entertaining this love relation, this marriage

234

with the land, man was accomplishing something more than the
transformation of matter by his labour. It could be said that the
peasantry created the land by making it fertile. Michelet observed
that the land of France became productive because it was loved.
In this intermingling of human and natural meanings Michelet
approached his ideal.

Michelet's best-known work, his *Histoire de la Révolution
française*, appeared in seven volumes between 1847 and 1853. His
study belonged to a body of writing produced during the 1840s
– by Lamartine, Quinet, Buchez, Alphonse Esquiros (1812–76)
and others – which aimed to reassess the meaning of 1789 in the
light of France's current predicament.[21] Michelet's history was
intended to revive the memory of the Revolution in the hearts of
a divided people and spur them to reconciliation and to action.
His book was written against those socialist historians who worshipped Robespierre and glorified the Terror. Having put to one
side his general history of France, he turned to the moment when
the people finally achieved oneness and fundamental rights. For
my purposes the crucially important volumes are the first two,
those which appeared in 1847 and covered the years from 1789
until the attempted flight of Louis XVI in 1791. This period
contained the apogee of the Revolution in Michelet's eyes, the
moment when national cohesion was at last achieved. However,
unity did not endure. The threat to France from foreign armies
joined with the rise of Jacobinism to undermine the Revolution's
original disinterested generosity. Michelet admired the achievements of the Convention but he felt that the Jacobins imposed a
mechanical, unflinching order which was contrary to life and
inimical to the human spirit.

Michelet declared that the time for accommodation with Christianity was over. There was no room left for compromise: the
Revolution continued Christianity but it also contradicted it: 'It
is, at the same time, its heir and its adversary' (*HRF*, I, 8). The
Revolution was now Michelet's religion, superior to the failed
religion of Christ. He regretted his earlier willingness to rehabilitate the Middle Ages. He attacked Christianity for relying on the
notion of grace which he understood as an arbitrary principle that
took no account of effort or worth. The Ancien Régime anointed
tyranny in the name of grace, endorsed inequality in the name of
grace. The Revolution, by contrast, was the belated advent of
justice and law, powers which for Michelet were by their nature

divine: 'O Justice, my mother, Right, my father, you who are but one with God' (*HRF*, I, 81). Christianity was fundamentally flawed since it proclaimed the brotherhood of man but held to the doctrine of original sin which united human beings only in their fallen condition. The Revolution built a different kind of solidarity: 'I define the Revolution – the advent of Law, the resurrection of Right, the reaction of Justice' (*HRF*, I, 1). What this amounted to was Michelet's absolute conviction that fraternity could only be built upon solidarity freely chosen. Christian brotherhood was a sham which concealed intolerance and inequality. Fraternity by coercion, community by obedience on the Jacobin model, was likewise meaningless. True revolutionary fraternity was different because it involved communication and transparency, and recognised that individual rights were the basis of a unified society. Michelet wanted to remind the public that in essence the Revolution was neither class struggle nor Terror. It was a vast aspiration to peace, love and unity.

Christianity, whatever its apologists claimed, had not put an end to slavery. It preached a form of resignation which endorsed inequalities and hindered the achievement of social unity. In Michelet's eyes, the Revolution, unlike Christianity, took God's will seriously. The Revolution strove to actualise the ideas of love and union within a living communion of Frenchmen. The Revolution was authentically holy, 'sainte' (*HRF*, I, 80). The night of 4 August, the ending of feudal rights and obligations, was 'the first miracle of the new Gospel' (*HRF*, I, 289). Michelet repeatedly used such religious and biblical language, not in order to explain events as the fulfilment of Christianity but in order to ratify linguistically their sacred status. He seized upon the religious language which was available to him, even though he was celebrating works, not faith, France not Christ. We have noted a similar procedure in Quinet. But is this what we expect from Michelet, the desymboliser who read history in terms of reason interpreting, challenging, transforming and eventually overcoming religious symbols? Michelet now held that by 1789 the attempt to transform Christianity – 'reviving the spirit without killing the old form' (*HRF*, I, 291) – was already a forlorn hope. Was it wise in 1847 to use the language of one's opponents in order to recapture the essence of 1789?

Michelet expressed admiration for the intellectual forces which had kept hope alive by resisting the dead weight of the church in

the name of freedom of thought. Like Quinet he used the term
'pure Spirit', which he conceived as an ideal power seeking to
actualise itself in the world, to inaugurate a new age. Both Quinet
and Michelet rehabilitated the eighteenth-century philosophers as
agents of thought, as servants of the legitimate spiritual power in
the modern world. For Michelet the eighteenth century was a
heroic age, a time when mind struggled against an oppressive and
spiritually dead faith. The philosophers formulated the new idea
of right which the Revolution subsequently inscribed in law.
Henceforward justice would no longer live capriciously and arbitrarily in the sacred body of the king; it would dwell within the
collective body of the nation, inscribing itself in the principle of
popular sovereignty. The philosophers lent intellectual clarity to
ideas which had been circulating haphazardly over the centuries:

> With what slow steps does thought emerge from instinct to
> dream, to *rêverie*, and thence to the chiaroscuro of poetry!
> How long has thought wandered among children and the
> simple-minded, among poets and madmen! . . . And [yet]
> one morning that madness proves to be the common sense
> of all!
>
> (*HRF*, I, 29)

The ideas articulated by the philosophers were then actualised by
the masses. The Revolution amounted to a new revelation of the
divine, to the true advent of the reign of Spirit. The philosophers
bequeathed to the political world the idea that the living body of
the monarch was no longer the symbolic representation around
which the people coalesced. The new unity would be based on
access to spirit by all, on what Michelet called 'the union of hearts,
the community of mind, the profound marriage of feelings and
ideas which is made out of everyone by everyone' (*HRF*, I, 47–8).

Michelet placed his history of the early years of the Revolution
under the sign of unity. He began by underscoring the spontaneous and unanimous character of the elections to the Estates
General:

> Unanimous! There was a complete and unreserved agree-
> ment, a quite simple situation with the nation on one side
> and privilege on the other. And in the nation, then, there
> was no distinction possible between the people and the
> bourgeoisie. . . . Ah! who would not be touched by the

remembrance of that unique moment, which was our point
of departure? It was short-lived, but it remains for us the
ideal towards which we shall always tend.

(*HRF*, I, 88–9)

This apostrophe to the spirit of concord set the tone for Michelet's
history. Writing at a moment of social tension and political division he looked back to the Revolution as a lost age of unity. But
was it quite lost? Had not the historian the magical power to
resurrect the past? Michelet believed that the spirit of the Revolution was something which he could rediscover within his inner
being. It was the power which had enabled him to decipher the
course of French history. By recalling the memory of 1789 could
he make the spirit come alive anew in 1847? In Michelet's eyes
the Revolution remained true to itself from 14 July 1789 until the
national Fête de la Fédération in July 1790. During this period
the people were a united and irresistible force. At first sight the
fall of the Bastille seemed an impossible goal; it was achieved, not
by calculation and planning, but by an assertion of the popular
will, by what Michelet considered a spontaneous act of collective
faith in the revolutionary idea. The united people, sovereign in all
but name, had at last fully become the true· subject of their own
history. The people immediately converted thought into action.
According to Michelet, they were in essence a non-violent force,
empowered by love to transform the world. When violence
occurred, as at the Bastille, this was usually attributed to the
unreasonable resistance of the old order. And when Michelet dealt
with moments of vicious bloodletting such as the September mass-
acres he tried to exonerate the people as much as he could, usually
by blaming evil individuals for manipulating popular sentiments.
The Terrorists, he pointed out, were in the main from the middle
class and were not men of the people.

Michelet's ideal remained close to that described in *Le Peuple*.
The Revolution brought together mind and nature, town and
country, men and women.[22] It transcended the contraries which
normally structured existence. It marked the irruption of the
divine into historical time. The world was redeemed, recovered
by a God whose presence was made manifest in collective life.
The resistance of matter to mind was overcome. This sublime
moment was captured in the movement of the Federations in
which regional diversity was subsumed into the life of the *patrie*

or, as Michelet now described it, 'the great mother' (*HRF*, II, 152). In a celebrated passage, he used the image of dance, of the farandole, to evoke the movement of the Federations across France, unifying the people, overcoming barriers of localism and isolation. Unity and fraternity were in effect consubstantial. As in the 'Tableau de la France', Michelet placed Paris at the spiritual centre of the nation, constantly in communication with the periphery, reprocessing and retransmitting life, ideas and energy. The administrative reforms of the Revolution, the ending of internal taxes and tariffs, all contributed to a removal of obstacles, to a process of exchange which was ultimately founded on love, mutual recognition and sacrifice (and which was by implication opposed to narrow self-interest as defined by economic liberalism). The redrawing of the map of France, the replacement of provinces by departments, corresponded to Michelet's understanding of the duty of mind to reorder and reorganise matter. However, the Revolution also seemed to incorporate nature at a deeper level.

Michelet expressed regret that so much criticism had been levelled at the geometrical character of the new administrative divisions. In reply he went so far as to claim that the invention of departments, far from being dangerously artificial as argued by the propagandists of the Counter-Revolution, was a decision which re-established the bond with nature – were not many departments named after natural features such as rivers? Revolutionary man entered into a new relation with nature: 'Man had not only reconquered himself, he re-entered into possession of nature' (*HRF*, II, 163). Humanity which recognised its own inward divinity now grasped nature in its sacred dimension and came to know the world differently. Nature appeared as if in a new light, rediscovered by the fraternal gaze: 'Man perceived nature, seized it again, and found it sacred' (*HRF*, II, 164). Man, reborn in Revolution, felt the presence of God in the world of nature. For this reason the new revolutionary faith had no need of temples other than nature: 'No more artificial church, but the universal church. From the Vosges to the Cévennes, from the Pyrenees to the Alps, [spread] the single dome of the new cathedral' (*HRF*, II, 164).

For Michelet the Federations marked the miraculous triumph of the value of sociability. The key to this superior fraternal phase of the Revolution lay in a spontaneously arising disinterestedness and concern for the common good. (Clearly neither liberal self-interest nor Jacobin virtue corresponded to Michelet's definition of the true Revolution.) The Federations gathered up diversity within a higher unity where mind and matter interpenetrated one another. France achieved collective self-awareness. Individuals recognised the presence of their humanity, their generality in their fellow citizens. The newly unified people was as if endowed with the divinely inspired creative power which Michelet attributed to genius. The normal temporal order was disrupted. No longer were ideas slowly expressed, formulated and perhaps implemented. The people in revolution formed an invincible power which imposed its will. Thought was immediately transformed into action. Indeed existence had reached such a level of intensity that action preceded thought. According to Michelet too much attention had been paid to the deliberations of the Assembly and not enough to the creative role played by the masses. The balance needed to be redressed in favour of the people. He fervently believed that at this crucial moment in the revolutionary process the role of institutions was secondary. Theory arose from practice. The Assembly ratified the decisions of the popular will: 'the law is everywhere forestalled by the spontaneous surge of life and action' (*HRF*, II, 140).

As I have already noted, popular disorder of an unprovoked or violent nature was minimised by Michelet. What mattered was the image of France spontaneously organising itself, giving birth to the new order of law. Michelet claimed that even the new administrative division into arrondissements and departments had been prefigured in forms of spontaneous organisation, which reflected the people's desire for association: 'The law comes to recognise, authorise, crown all this; but it does not produce it' (*HRF*, II, 146). With reason he called his chapter on the Federations 'The New Religion'. He evoked a sublime moment of union, the transcendence of time and space in a collective act of love. Old attachments were forgotten:

> Time has perished, space has perished, those two material conditions to which life is subject. . . . A strange *vita nuova*, eminently spiritual, is beginning for France and making her whole Revolution a sort of dream, at one time delightful, at another terrible. . . . It knew neither time nor space.
>
> (*HRF*, II, 155–6)

However, the general Fête de la Fédération held at the Champ de

Mars in July 1790 was not the joyous culmination which the revolutionary spirit seemed to promise. Already, in what should have been the high moment of union, Michelet detected unease, division and early signs of conflict to come. Having reached what should have been the inauguration of the new age of union, Michelet found himself instead bidding farewell to the truly inspirational spirit of the early Revolution:

> Farewell epoch of expectation, aspiration, desire, when all dreamt of this day and longed for it! . . . Here it is! What do we desire? Why these worries? Alas! the experience of the world teaches us this sad fact that, strange to tell, but nevertheless true, union too often diminishes in unity. The wish to unite was already the union of hearts, the best unity perhaps.
>
> (*HRF*, II, 181).

What explained the mysterious vulnerability of the Revolution? Explanations in terms of the church, the Counter-Revolution or the Jacobins were considered correct but inadequate. Michelet's text suggested that what in large measure disrupted the consummation of 1790 was the very fulfilment of desire. The climactic moment when union became unity itself began the process of disintegration, the falling away into disharmony. The Revolution was a privileged moment, outside the time of history. Barthes wrote that for Michelet the Revolution ended 'historic time for good' and inaugurated 'natural time'.[23] Man and nature came together in a creative fusion, in a unified temporality. Historical time stopped on 14 July 1789 but access to the creative timelessness of eternity could not be sustained. Michelet identified life with aspiration, striving, movement, with desire seeking its object. The Federations, as the expression of the popular will, were charged with hope and potential. However, union fully achieved became unity and Michelet, although he longed for reunion, also feared the loss of self which identity demanded. Michelet sought an impossible unity which overcame but did not suppress difference. The Federations described a circular movement which reconciled wholeness with process, freedom with organisation. The ceremony at the Champ de Mars in July 1790 signalled an ending. Unity achieved resembled stasis. Michelet aspired to unity but his heart lay with history, with the suffering and drama of separation, with the movement of desire as yet unassuaged. And there was surely an additional concern. The very fact that the privileged moment did not endure raised the question of to what extent humankind was ever really in control of its destiny. Were human beings, impatient with their condition, condemned to wait upon sudden moments of revelation such as 1789 (or 1830)? If this were so, then what of Michelet's reading of human history as a Promethean story of collective self-construction? On one level the divine was present, immanent within the human, made manifest within social relations and institutional practices. At a deeper level the divine seemed inaccessible, unpredictable, like the figure of Eternity in Quinet's *Ahasvérus*. And from the standpoint of Eternity could the notion of the temporal incompleteness of the Revolution be said to hold any meaning of all? Should we commit ourselves to participation in the world or withdraw into contemplation, preserving a purity of distance between ourselves and the theatre of action? Despite the heroic assertion of the will was humankind's real destiny to prostrate itself before the natural order of things?

In order to explain the fall into historical time, violence and division which occurred after 1790, Michelet, like Quinet, focused on the religious meaning of the Revolution. He expressed regret that the Revolution had not fully recognised its own status as a religious principle. Like Quinet he drew attention to the error made by those who mistakenly considered that the church was amenable to reform. In Michelet's view the first age of the Revolution corresponded to the overcoming of the Ancien Régime and the promulgation of new laws. The second age, the social and religious epoch of fraternity and union, was only fleetingly realised. The incubation of the new idea was arrested. The fraternal spirit of 1790 was followed by the intolerance of the Terror and eventually by what Michelet saw as the intellectual stagnation of the Empire. The lightning flash of 1830 signalled a transitory renewal of popular union but this was followed by a further plunge into social conflict. What could console Frenchmen for their loss of hope? If history had reached its culmination in 1789 what was the meaning of the nineteenth century? The revolutionary union of mind and matter, male and female, thought and action had not been sustained, neither had it given birth to new life. The desired future had turned out to be still-born or monstrous. The relation of the nineteenth century to the Revolution could be read in several ways. The Revolution could be seen as either mother or as father to the present. Paternal values were associated with the aspiration to law; maternal values with the idea of the nurturing nation. Did this mean that the nineteenth century was cast in the role of the abandoned child, living on in a precarious afterwards, seeking to find its parents, to rediscover law and justice, to reunite mind and nature? This was surely the role which Michelet took upon himself to fulfil. He was spokesman for the Revolution and for his own time, for mother, father and son. He was triune after his fashion. By his historical writing he sought to create the conditions for a new and enduring union. The divine had only transiently been made manifest in the collective action of July 1830. Perhaps the historian could provide a glimpse of the desired world of harmony and use his word to reanimate it? Perhaps his word could spur readers into an engagement with social reality which would summon eternity back once again into time? Were writing and reading history new forms of prayer?

By textualising the Revolution the historian mastered succession and disclosed meaning, ordered time, used words to suggest acceleration or stagnation. Michelet's text aspired to be more than a mirror to events. It offered a chance to pass through multiplicity and succession to oneness and eternity. The historian adopted the standpoint of generality, dying to himself, to the life of individuality in order to fulfil his vocation. He engaged with the past 'with the disinterestedness of the dead' (*LP*, 73). The historical project rested upon an exchange of energies between the living and the dead.

Michelet's new revolutionary religion endorsed the sense of the collective which characterised all his thought. He responded to religions precisely because they mediated the power of generality which, incarnated in the body of history as well as in individuals, mysteriously transcended the world of succession, division and separation. Spirit, as a force dwelling in free individuals, needed to be reassembled in a form which at once fulfilled true individuality and escaped the restrictions of particularity. The Revolution was more than the proclamation of individual rights and liberal freedoms. By extending equal value to all citizens the Revolution displaced sacrality from its incarnation in the sacred body of the king (where it figured the saving presence of the divine Jesus) into the collective body of the nation.

Furthermore this new incarnation was characterised by purity

– always a significant word in Michelet's vocabulary – because it involved an intellectual and emotional union of hearts and minds expressing itself spontaneously in the sphere of action. Spirit flowed, circulated through the people. It was as if there was no longer a hiatus between intention and achievement, between theory and practice. However, while retaining his ambition to place individual value in relation to collective truth Michelet, by the late 1840s, had moved away from the linearity of the *Introduction à l'histoire universelle* towards the discontinuity of the *Histoire de la Révolution française* which valorised the rupture with the past, the denial of Christianity by the revolutionary faith. At the same time, however, we should never ignore the extent to which Michelet stayed wedded to his belief in achievement through work, not grace. History, although fractured by discontinuities and different sub-plots, remained a progressive movement, a positive narrative of struggle and collective self-assertion. The raising up of matter by mind required the intervention of the human will and it was this process which ultimately rendered history meaningful. Hence Michelet's continuing distrust of union if it should lead to an abandonment of selfhood. Despite his acceptance of maternal values he did not lose his fear of feminised nature. Could Michelet ever fully be reassured of the beneficence of nature? Nature, fickle and unfeeling, always threatened to devour history, to consume meaning.

Michelet had nevertheless clearly moved on from his *Histoire romaine* where he had valued Christianity for having overthrown the oriental cults of nature. His revolutionary religion was hostile to Christianity and it embraced nature: France was both community and environment, idea and matter. Henceforth the French nation was the necessary form out of which grander possibilities of union and reconciliation could emerge. However, the turn against Christianity and the assertion of the goodness of nature did not add up to a neat reversal of Michelet's earlier position. His attitude remained that in order for nature to become a truly positive force it needed to be completed by history, transformed by mind, regulated by reason. From the 'Tableau de la France' to the *Histoire de la Révolution française* he consistently related the formation of French identity to a triumph of mind and will over the fatalisms of race and environment. The peasant truly loved his land when he owned it and controlled it. The Federations hastened national unity by overcoming regional differences: 'Where are . . .

the old differences of place and race? Those geographical oppositions, so strong, so sharp? All has disappeared, geography is killed' (HRF, II, 155). This was strong language. In 1833 geography had been effaced by mind and history. In 1847 it was quite simply killed. In other words the actualisation of the revolutionary spirit required the symbolic killing, the annulment of nature. The natural world was called upon to die before it could be reinstated as revolutionary nature. Only when cleansed of Catholic royalism could nature find its place within the new symbolism of the revolutionary nation. The motive for this act of murder was presumably love. Revolutionary harmony required that maternal nature be organised by the paternal principle of law. Admittedly this was not yet the coldly inflexible law of the Jacobins. None the less, nature still had to pass through a symbolic death before being glorified by mind and history. Michelet thus constructed order and meaning out of the denial of the feminine and the death of the mother. Nature remained the repressed/desired origin, always threatening unless regulated by the masculine principle.[24]

For Michelet the divine idea, betrayed by the church, was at last made manifest within the united French people. He looked back with great feeling to the early revolutionary festivals which had taken place across France. In contrast to the ceremonies of the old religion these were happy affairs, celebrations of the moral force of the people. The festivals were joyous occasions which brought together young and old, men and women. Everyone participated. There was no longer any division between spectators and actors. The festivals organised by the Federations were moments of self-presence, of true communion. What Michelet termed the noble harmonies of family, nature and nation filled these assemblies with a genuine religious spirit. This was a lived religion which celebrated the indwelling of the divine within the human, equidistant from the sacraments of the old faith and from what Michelet pointedly called the 'cold image of abstract Freedom' (HRF, II, 156). The idea was fully self-present in this moment of communication and fraternity; it needed no representative material incarnation beyond its direct manifestation in life itself: 'No more conventional symbol. All nature, all mind, all truth' (HRF, II, 164). The opacity of existence yielded to transparency. Surely this moment marked the conclusion of the process of desymbolisation? The symbol was now man himself: an individualised, living being who also belonged to family and to nation.

But could the language of prose adequately render the fullness of the new harmony? Having described a festival at which Protestants and Catholics came together and buried their hatreds, Michelet added: 'All hearts overflowed; prose was not sufficient, a burst of poetry could alone relieve so deep a feeling' (*HRF*, II, 162). This was a shared moment of synthesis, not a distanced, self-aware act of analysis; and the spirit of synthesis, of unified collective life was naturally externalised in the language of poetry. The Revolution was more than a theory of rights, it was a new religion, a new church which bound individuals together fraternally – emotionally as well as intellectually. The legal language of rights needed to be completed by the religious language of belonging.

In his histories of France and of the Revolution Michelet created a new myth, the myth of the people. The desymboliser who had revealed the human meaning of the old myths himself charged history with a spiritual content. While nineteenth-century higher criticism struggled to determine what could be known about the historical Jesus, Michelet took the opposite road and represented history as miraculous – but, and this was the crucial point, in a divinely human, a natural, not a supernatural sense. We have seen a similar process at work in Quinet's lectures. History, the collective incarnation of the logos, was moralised, mythologised. The historian respected fact and chronology but used the power of rhetoric and symbol to enlarge reality in the direction of collective truth. In that way history was returned to the people. The reader might expect history to aspire to scientific exactitude and express a determinate meaning. However, as Lionel Gossman has remarked, conversion – not enquiry – was Michelet's aim.[25] His use of documents and authentic sources, his excursions into social and economic matters, his use of oral testimony, everything served the overriding goal of restoring contact with the sacrality of the past. The poetry of the Revolution, its transient achievement of harmony and the transcendence of contraries, mattered more than its politics.

According to *Le Peuple* the genius had the gift of seeing things in their completeness, their fullness. The historian was the mediator between past and present but also between sacred and profane time. Michelet wrote that through his writing he participated in all things. His text offered a further form of participation by making available to the reader the possibility of acceding in turn, at an additional remove, to the revelatory moment. In *Le*

Peuple he referred to France's superiority as dogma and legend. France was a religion. The historian recovered a shared desire, he articulated what the community already understood and felt; or perhaps it would be more accurate to say he reminded the people of something that they were in danger of forgetting. The life of Joan or Arc or the events of the Revolution were objective realities to be investigated but their true significance was revelatory. By its completeness and logic (*enchaînement*) French history was exemplary in its capacity to respond to what Michelet termed the exigencies of reason (*LP*, 229). The legends woven by the historian respected the world of fact but were none the less vehicles for the expression of a higher truth. The democratisation of society did not signify the end of symbolism but rather its transfer to the domain of the historian. Symbolism became a necessary mediation of generality, a way of uniting believers around a shared definition of the past. History became religion and since a demythologised religion was impossible the discourse of history became in effect the poetry of law. Michelet employed powerful metaphorical language to convey the presence of the divine. He used biblical references and symbolism. He was an impassioned writer. His declared intention was to be frankly and vigorously partial on behalf of what was true and right. He infuriated readers who expected dry, limpid, balanced analysis. He wrote with commitment and was present within his text. His repeated use of religious language and sexual symbolism reminded his readers that they were being asked to engage with different orders of reality. The work of the imagination complemented the lucidity of the historical intelligence.

Michelet's way of writing and his relationship to his subject matter meant that facts and events could be read in different ways. The historian was Oedipus explaining the enigmas of the past, communicating a knowledge unavailable before him, remaking the tissue of meaning. Michelet's historical world contained much more than just objective fact. Paris, for example, took on mythical proportions. It was less a definable urban reality than a laboratory of mental energies, the sensorium of France which received and integrated sensations. Michelet's text did not simply record events. It included them in order to translate them into a symbolic register. Historical facts contained several meanings, a lack of determinacy which was echoed in Michelet's style where the abstract and the concrete mingled to such an extent that Pierre Moreau, always an astute critic, described Michelet's text as a 'delirium of symbolism'.[26] Michelet sought to avoid the danger of the discourse on the past itself becoming a new fatalism, restricting liberty, impeding action. This was something which he detected in Herder, Schelling, Hegel, even in Vico (*OC*, IV, 662). He wanted history to be concerned with the future, with life – and there are moments when his work resembles the sometimes chaotic energies of life itself. Although Michelet's ideal was transparency and self-presence achieved in action, as a historian he was faced with process, with a succession of events. History was not pure thought, logic or conceptual discourse. Lionel Gossman has suggested that the historian was in fact the 'enemy of history, as he [was] the enemy of nature'.[27] Instead of celebrating the unity which he ardently desired the historian was obliged to devote his energies to describing time and dispersion, recovering epochs whose unfulfilment sorely tried his patience. Time in the end was redeemed because the historian restored it to presence. However, like nature, the past was refractive to mind and resisted appropriation. Its truth was not given directly in an unmediated form. It lay concealed within distorted accounts, buried in documents, hidden in legends, obscured by selective memory, damaged by the process of forgetting.

Michelet's gaze illuminated what it encountered, drew meaning and pattern out of the objects it reconstituted. But was it sufficient for reason to display the hidden truth? The power of figurative language was also required in order to convey the active passion of the Idea in its collective incarnation. However, by making history his new mythology Michelet ran a risk. The data of history comprised traces of actions, manifestations of the will, but reported events needed to be infused with the life of mind lest they acquire the fatalism of nature. In the symbol mind perceived both itself and nature, spirit and matter, idea and form. Michelet knew the danger inherent in all incarnation, that of spirit submitting to outward form rather than irradiating it. The poetry of reason which espoused the symbol accommodated a language which allowed for an ambiguity of meaning and in Michelet's terms this inevitably also allowed for a re-emergence of the feminine. Could the world of prose and law entrust its fate to poetry and symbol? In writing his history in the way he did Michelet took this risk. The religion of Revolution needed symbols in order to preserve faith and unify believers. He surely also knew that his own text would in turn feed humankind's inexhaustible appetite for interpretation. In any case Michelet took the chance and like Alfred de Vigny in a famous poem he tossed his message in a bottle into the rolling seas of humanity.

Michelet's courses were suspended in January 1848 by order of the July Monarchy. He had exhausted the patience of the authorities at a time of looming crisis. His lectures were a hymn to his ideal of the fraternal Revolution. He reaffirmed his faith in the masses. He called for new festivals, new occasions for the people to come together (*LE*, 171). The Revolution of February 1848 returned Michelet to his chair but the June insurrection demonstrated how fragile the dream of recapturing unity had been. However, Michelet did not lose heart completely. He continued to believe in education and he planned writing popular works intended to reach those who had not been touched by the saving words pronounced to his predominantly middle class audiences at the Collège de France. Under the Second Republic his courses remained a focus for democratic dissent and in March 1851 he found himself once again suspended. Finally, in 1852, he was officially removed by the Second Empire from his posts at both the Collège de France and the National Archives. Unlike Quinet he was not forced into exile. He returned to his intellectual labours and despite the background of political tragedy he completed his histories of France and of the Revolution. He continued to hope that the revolutionary spirit could be rekindled among his compatriots. Unlike Quinet he did not despair of the people. In 1865, in his study of the French Revolution, Quinet reached the conclusion that the revolutionary attempt to regenerate man had failed because it could not build upon a religious foundation, more precisely on a firm Protestant base. Michelet would have none of this. In his view the Revolution had no need of the symbols of Christianity since it was itself 'a church'.[28]

Although unsparing in his criticisms of aspects of the Revolution, Michelet could never accept Quinet's thoroughgoing dismantling of the revolutionary myth. The two friends quarrelled and the breach between them was never fully healed. Michelet remained loyal to his belief in the goodness of the people and to his conviction that nations, crowds and collective forces made history. The coming together which had taken place in 1789–90 accomplished a general human desire for unity and the ending of division. Michelet's historical work was an ardent affirmation that

a purpose lay at the heart of history. A transforming presence –
but not the person of Jesus Christ – was at work within human
affairs.

7

Conclusion

In most of this book I have taken the failure of the Second Republic as my effective end-date. Where I have journeyed beyond 1851 it has usually been to illustrate how the events of 1848 undermined the authority of history as a grand discourse of legitimation. The body of work which I have been examining took as its point of departure self-reflection upon the fact of the French Revolution. Guizot, Thierry, Quinet, Michelet all viewed 1789 as a boundary marking the emergence of new forms of consciousness and new political arrangements. They brought to their work a sense that they were writing from a privileged position situated near the end of a process of individual and collective emancipation.[1] The destabilising effects of political revolution were felt to have had fertile intellectual consequences for they had opened up a new perspective on the past. History as it had been conceived by the Enlightenment was considered inadequate. It could not provide support for a post-revolutionary identity which, on account of its anxious sense of separateness, desired to be embedded within a different kind of continuity, one which displayed new forms of pattern and purpose. The historical dimension was something that the new generation considered to be essential.

The self-definition of the Romantic historians involved a repudiation of most of the work done by earlier generations. In their desire to put forward a reconstructive agenda they were unfair to their Enlightenment predecessors (on whose erudition they often relied). Having related their own perception of the past so closely to the formative collective experiences of Revolution and Empire it was surely somewhat churlish to charge the Enlightenment with a lack of historical insight. In true Romantic spirit they preferred to align their aspirations with foreign models, with Vico and

251

Herder. Whereas Enlightenment liberalism disdained religion and committed itself to rationality and universal values, the Romantic historians identified with the past as process, as becoming, as a movement of cultures and collective entities. They made history constitutive of meaning in a way which disrupted eighteenth-century ideas of human nature.[2] A gulf separated them from the surviving Idéologues. Romanticism's sense of history as collective and revelatory contrasted with the Idéologue approach which favoured mechanistic models, prized clarity of exposition and looked for explanation in terms of motivation. Grand theories could never inform an approach which was essentially analytical. Hence the difficult relationship between liberal Romanticism and moderate republicanism of the old school.

The impossibility of Ideology producing a readable national history is well illustrated by the example of Amans-Alexis Monteil (1769–1850). Monteil, a friend of Laromiguière and Daunou, had been an active republican during the Revolution. His historical work was known to subsequent generations. (Guizot cited him in his lectures; Michelet used him as a source in the *Origines du droit français*; in the 1830s and 1840s he was taken up by Louis Blanc, a fellow Aveyronnais.) Monteil's aim was to write a people's history. His *Histoire des Français des divers états* came out in ten volumes between 1828 and 1844. It was not a great success, however, and as the years passed Monteil grew increasingly bitter at what he considered the unfair manner in which he had been treated. He felt that his role as an originator of popular history had been overlooked. Had he cause to feel aggrieved? At first Monteil's pronouncements certainly recalled the new history as defined by Thierry. He wrote vitriolic attacks on what he dismissed as old-fashioned 'battle history' and in order to reach a popular readership he employed a number of formal innovations such as choosing to have representative characters tell their tale in the first person. Why then was his contribution not recognised? The real answer lay in the fact that Monteil's text possessed none of the feeling which accompanied the Romantic historians' commitment to the people as collective subject. There was no local colour, no real sense of ideas driving a progressive movement. Monteil wanted to write a new form of history but he himself remained an unreconstructed man of the Enlightenment, hostile to the Middle Ages and uninterested in France's national origins (he considered that what was known about the Celts and the

Franks amounted to no more than conjecture).[3] His history of the French people began in the fourteenth century. His aim was to rehabilitate the producers, the workers, the artisans, but his history never presented national history as an impassioned trajectory of union. He remained loyal to the Enlightenment view of an unchanging human nature responding to better, more reasonable forms of government. Monteil innovated whereas others, such as the sober Daunou or the much respected Sismondi, did not. However, he was unable to transcend the epistemology of the Idéologues and for this reason he could never write a history which answered the demands of the post-revolutionary sensibility. His history was inevitably an anachronism in the world of Guizot, Cousin and Michelet.

The men of the Revolution had deliberately chosen to ignore history in favour of abstract reason. Nineteenth-century thought expressed the opposite view, that adequate knowledge of present reality needed to rest upon knowledge of the processes by which that reality had come into being. As Michelet explained in *Le Peuple*:

> He who wishes to limit himself to the present, to the current, will not understand the present. He who is satisfied just to contemplate the outside, to paint the form, will never even manage to see it: to see accurately, to translate with fidelity, one must see what the form covers; [there can be] no painting without anatomy.

(LP, 63)

Guizot drew a comparison between the historian and the anatomist who cuts open a body in order to discover how the different organs are co-ordinated. Michelet at one point described his historical subjects as marionettes which he could open up in order to draw out meaning. Historical knowledge was transgressive in the sense that it involved getting beneath the surface of events, disrupting and subverting the smooth-running narratives which purported to display the truth about the past. The new history felt that it had emancipated itself from literature.[4] History had become the true science of man. The historian was a serious social scientist, evaluating testimony, selecting documentation, employing his critical faculties, discovering new knowledge. He explained that change was meaningful, that the past displayed purpose, order and direction (the development of freedom, the emergence of individuality, the growth of national communities, the increase in association). The new history was less concerned with discrete historical facts than with the realities which lay behind the unfolding of events. What mattered was the sense of orderly development. In the wake of recent social and political dislocation the discourse of history inspired confidence. It supported ideas of the future which did not seek to identify the idea of order with the desire to replicate the organisation of the past.

We have seen how the Saint-Simonians, emboldened by analogies between history and physiology, considered that their theory of alternating organic and critical periods was proof positive of the law of progress. But clarity and intelligibility on their own were insufficient. History also depended upon the will and the emotions of the historian. The Romantic historians recognised within the collective entities that they studied the passions and desires of the self. The creative dimension of Romantic historical writing involved a merging of the essential qualities of the historian's being with the energies of the people. In the case of Thierry the reconstruction of the past was accompanied by the rehabilitation of the imagination in a manner which eighteenth-century science would have dismissed as confused and imperfect. Guizot, whose own work was largely analytical, none the less reminded his readers that the task of the historian involved going beyond distinction and division, and contained a final stage in which the imagination resuscitated in its living fullness the object of its attention. Thierry spoke of the historian having second sight. Michelet described the past coming alive in his hands as he consulted crumbling documents in the Archives. The historian who brought the past back to life triumphed over time. His word – inscribed in texts or spoken at the Collège de France – seemed to have purchase on the present as well as on the past.

History was important, not because it tried to hold up a mirror to events, but because it distinguished between events as surface phenomena and their deeper causes. The thinkers we have been examining had in common the view that history was the development, not simply of selfhood and subjectivity, but also of the ideas of justice and right which defined social relations. History as the growth of individuality was thus part of a greater history of collective entities. Collective life was organised by ideal forces which were held to be divine in origin. This meant that the discourse of liberty needed to be placed within a religious perspective, a view quite at odds with Enlightenment practice. The Romantic historians differed in the way in which they conceived the divine but they took religion and community to be largely consubstantial. For Michelet, the fraternal Revolution was a real, not a substitute religion. The historians all identified cohesive forms of social life with the power of religious ideas and they consistently looked to intellectual realities – not to the material forces of production – for organising and structuring principles.

However, while it was fine to proclaim in high-minded tones that history was the progressive unfolding of justice, freedom and reason historians were not unknown to disagree when it came to giving concrete meaning to these lofty abstractions. Guizot and Michelet were both centralisers, believers in public authority, law and the power of mind to organise and regulate nature. And yet, by the 1840s, they had developed antithetical visions of the future of France. There was also the question of the relation between the idea and the collective entity which was charged with its actualisation. Did idea and collective subject correspond exactly? Thierry wanted to communicate to the people the optimistic message that it was they who had in reality fashioned the nation's destiny over the centuries. However, when he remade French history it was in the image of the constitutionalist middle classes, and the memory of the insurrectionist Third Estate somehow managed not to compromise the stability of the state. The liberal identity was reconciled with the people constructed as the embodiment of moderate reason. But here the central difficulty arose: who were the people who made history? Was the Third Estate identical with the French people in the broader sense? Behind much of the Romantic fascination with collective forces lay the spectre of the Revolution, of transgression, of regicide at the hands of the people (or their representatives). The liberal historians, happy with a restricted franchise and the constitutional monarchy, had no difficulty in telling the good people from the bad populace. Things were harder for Michelet given his veneration for 'le peuple' and his detestation of class divisions.[5] In his view the best part of the individual was what joined him to others and was externalised in collective action: 'Do not look at the individual in isolation; contemplate him in the mass and in action' (*OC*, II, 254). But what politics could represent the revolutionary masses and what form of writing could adequately display their history?

Romantic history seemed complicit in the myth of its own origination, its revolutionary break with past forms of knowledge.

All the major authors I have discussed – with the exception of the Saint-Simonians – believed that increased individual freedom was the goal of history while recognising that this development needed to be reconciled with coherent notions of civil society and of the state. They were responding to the crisis of post-revolutionary modernity which, in the shape of liberal capitalism and industrialism, left citizens as strangers to one another, alienated from nature and from their fellows. Guizot tried to link the individual sphere of existence to the public realm. Thierry made the idea of the permanence of racial characteristics the unifying factor which determined group identities. Quinet looked to insert the self into a grand synthesis of humankind, nature and God. The wish to recover community was of course no less central to traditionalist Catholicism or to Saint-Simonianism, but they were different because they repudiated the notion of individual rights. The former collapsed politics into religion. The latter ascribed superiority to the social over the political and gambled on being able to pull off a risky alliance between authoritarianism and industrialism. The historians, on the other hand, were all committed to some form of political vision, to liberal constitutionalism or to republicanism within a national framework. They held to the autonomy of the subject and had no intention of going back on the notion of individual rights. This meant that despite their differences they had to accommodate the Revolution in some shape or form. In their writing history was being asked to fulfil two separate but related objectives. First, to validate the autonomous individual as the legitimate end-product of the movement of history; second, to insert the process of individuation itself within a narrative of collective purpose. History was bound up with politics and the writing about the past was inevitably about power as well as knowledge.[6] Within the historical text the elusive reconciliation of public and private, collective and individual, could perhaps be achieved. But history, however much remade and mythologised, could never truly equal the dream of deliverance offered by utopia. In contrast to the transhistorical perfection described in utopian theory and fiction, the world of succession studied by the historian was irredeemably inferior. Even Michelet, in his evocation of the fraternal spirit of 1789–90, could not avoid inscribing disappointment within hope, time within eternity.

The Revolution had failed in its attempt to construct a principle of authority which was not founded upon tradition. In its wake history was called upon to reconcile violence and knowledge by constructing an interpretation of the past which confirmed the superiority of European values (individuality, freedom, civil equality, reason, the worlds of politics and law). All the writers upon whom my attention has focused shared Michelet's sense, derived from Vico, that philosophical truth, the *verum*, needed the support of the *certum*, the collective truth of history and experience. By so doing they all in effect gave a further twist to the Cousinian dilemma of whether religious truth could without loss be converted into philosophical truth: could history now become a reliable site of meaning and provide the locus for a reconciliation of religion and science? The language of history offered a way of reforging links with a spirituality which had been undermined by the Enlightenment's critique of religion.[7] However, reflective nineteenth-century historical writing suggested that the reappropriation of the past by mind was a difficult and complex affair. History, viewed as the purposeful movement of collective forces, seemed to provide a solid foundation for man's moral being. However, as the work of Michelet and Quinet suggested, history represented an ambiguous victory. Was it a tale of triumphant self-assertion or did it mark a fragile affirmation of human meaning against cosmic forces which threatened to destroy value in the name of life?

Notes

1 INTRODUCTION: HISTORY AND THE POST-REVOLUTIONARY CONTEXT

1 David Lowenthal, *The Past Is a Foreign Country* (Cambridge: Cambridge University Press, 1985), 187; R. G. Collingwood, *The Idea of History* (Oxford: Oxford University Press, 1973; first edn 1946).

2 See Ceri Crossley and Ian Small (eds), *The French Revolution and British Culture* (Oxford: Oxford University Press, 1989).

3 See E. J. Hobsbawm, *Nations and Nationalism since 1780* (Cambridge: Cambridge University Press, 1990).

4 Hayden White, *Metahistory: The Historical Imagination in Nineteenth-Century Europe* (Baltimore and London: The Johns Hopkins University Press, 1973). See also Linda Orr, *Headless History: Nineteenth-Century French Historiography of the Revolution* (Ithaca and London: Cornell University Press, 1990).

5 On French liberalism, see L. Girard, *Le Libéralisme en France de 1814 à 1848: doctrine et mouvement* (Paris: Centre de Documentation Universitaire, 1970); André Jardin, *Histoire du libéralisme politique* (Paris: Hachette, 1985).

6 Charles de Rémusat, *Politique libérale ou fragments pour servir à la défense de la Révolution française* (Paris: Michel Lévy, 1875), 2.

7 See Ephraïm Harpaz, *L'Ecole libérale sous la Restauration* (Geneva: Droz, 1968), 246–8.

8 Stanley Mellon, *The Political Uses of History* (Stanford: Stanford University Press, 1958).

9 For further details, see C. Crossley, 'Town–country and the circulation of revolutionary energy: the cases of Bonald and Michelet', in Alan Forrest and Peter Jones (eds), *Reshaping France: Town, Country and Region during the French Revolution* (Manchester: Manchester University Press, 1991), 243–53.

10 For a discussion of the theme of energy, see Michel Delon, *L'Idée d'énergie au tournant des Lumières (1770–1820)* (Paris: Presses Universitaires de France, 1988).

ı1 See Gérard Gengembre, *La Contre-révolution ou l'histoire désespérante* (Paris: Imago, 1989).

12 See Mary Hall Quinlan, *The Historical Thought of the Vicomte de Bonald* (Washington: Catholic University of America Press, 1953).

13 On the Idéologues, see Sergio Moravia, *Il pensiero degli Idéologues* (Florence: La Nuova Italia, 1974); François Picavet, *Les Idéologues* (Paris: Félix Alcan, 1891); Martin S. Staum, *Cabanis: Enlightenment and Medical Philosophy in the French Revolution* (Princeton: Princeton University Press, 1980).

14 See Joanna Kitchin, *Un Journal philosophique: 'La Décade'* *(1794–1807)* (Paris: Minard, 1965).

15 For the philosophical context, see George Boas, *French Philosophies of the Romantic Period* (Baltimore: The Johns Hopkins University Press, 1925); Cheryl B. Welch, *Liberty and Utility: The French Idéologues and the Transformation of Liberalism* (New York: Columbia University Press, 1984); Bernard Plongeron, 'Nature, métaphysique et histoire chez les Idéologues', *Dix-huitième siècle* 5 (1973), 375–412.

16 See Auguste Viatte, *Les Sources occultes du romantisme* (Paris: Champion, 1928), 2 vols.

17 Brian William Head, *Ideology and Social Science: Destutt de Tracy and French Liberalism* (Dordrecht: Martinus Nijhoff, 1985), 120.

18 Emmet Kennedy, *A 'Philosophe' in the Age of Revolution: Destutt de Tracy and the Origins of 'Ideology'* (Philadelphia: The American Philosophical Society, 1978), 49. Cf. Colin Smith, 'Destutt de Tracy and the bankruptcy of sensationalism', in D. G. Charlton, J. Gaudon and A. R. Pugh (eds), *Balzac and the Nineteenth Century* (Leicester: University of Leicester Press, 1972), 195–207.

19 For a detailed exposition of Condorcet's theories and their cultural context, see Keith Michael Baker, *Condorcet: From Natural Philosophy to Social Mathematics* (Chicago and London: University of Chicago Press, 1975).

20 For the French eighteenth-century attitude to history, see the comprehensive study by Jean Dagen, *L'Histoire de l'esprit humain dans la pensée française de Fontenelle à Condorcet* (Paris: Klincksieck, 1977).

21 Kennedy, *A 'Philosophe' in the Age of Revolution*, 140.

22 Ibid., 140.

23 Head, *Ideology and Social Science*, 115.

24 The standard critical work is Jean Gaulmier, *L'Idéologue Volney: 1757–1820* (Beirut, 1951). See *L'Héritage des Lumières: Volney et les Idéologues* (Angers: Presses de l'Université d'Angers, 1988).

25 Constantin François Volney, *Leçons d'histoire* in *Œuvres* (Paris: Fayard, 1989), I, 501–622. Specific page references to this work are henceforward incorporated into the body of my text.

26 Welch, *Liberty and Utility*, 98.

27 Page references incorporated in the text are to Pierre Claude François Daunou, *Cours d'études historiques* (Paris: Firmin Didot, 1849), vol. 20.

28 See Prosper Alfaric, *Laromiguière et son école* (Paris: Les Belles Lettres, 1929).

29 See F. C. T. Moore, *The Psychology of Maine de Biran* (Oxford: Clarendon Press, 1970).

30 Prosper de Barante, *La Vie politique de M. Royer-Collard: Ses discours et ses écrits* (Paris: Didier, 1863), 2 vols. Page references to this work are included in the text.

31 Benjamin Constant, *Adolphe*, ed. P. Delbouille (Paris: Les Belles Lettres, 1977), 247.

32 See Frank Paul Bowman, 'Benjamin Constant et l'histoire', in *Benjamin Constant, Madame de Staël et le groupe de Coppet* (Oxford and Lausanne: The Voltaire Foundation and the Institut Benjamin Constant, 1982), 129–50.

33 See Frank Paul Bowman, 'La révélation selon Benjamin Constant', *Europe* 467 (1968), 115–26.

34 See in particular *De l'esprit de conquête et de l'usurpation* (1814). See Ian W. Alexander, 'La morale "ouverte" de Benjamin Constant', in *French Literature and the Philosophy of Consciousness* (Cardiff: University of Wales Press, 1984), 39–59.

35 Benjamin Constant, *Œuvres*, ed. A. Roulin (Paris: Gallimard, 1957), 1052.

36 See Shirley M. Gruner, *Economic Materialism and Social Moralism* (The Hague: Mouton, 1973).

37 Charles Dunoyer, *L'Industrie et la morale considérées dans leurs rapports avec la liberté* (Paris: Sautelet, 1823). Page references to this work are included in the text. Cf. the review by Benjamin Constant in *Benjamin Constant publiciste 1815–1830* (Paris and Geneva: Champion-Slatkine, 1987), 83–103.

38 See the chapter, 'De l'indépendance née chez les modernes des progrès de l'industrie', in Jean-Baptiste Say, *Traité d'économie politique* (Paris: Guillaumin, 1861; first edn 1803), 375–77.

39 See Frank Paul Bowman, *Le Christ romantique* (Geneva: Droz, 1973).

40 See Alice Gérard, *La Révolution française: mythes et interprétations 1789–1970* (Paris: Flammarion, 1970).

41 For Thiers the best study is J. P. T. Bury and R. P. Tombs, *Thiers 1797–1877: A Political Life* (London: Allen & Unwin, 1986). There is a full discussion of Thiers and Mignet in Jean Walch, *Les Maîtres de l'histoire 1815–1850* (Geneva and Paris: Slatkine, 1986).

42 On Mignet, see the essential study by Yvonne Knibiehler, *Naissance des sciences humaines: Mignet et l'histoire philosophique au XIXe siècle* (Paris: Flammarion, 1973).

43 Page references included in the text are to François Mignet, *Histoire de la Révolution française depuis 1789 jusqu'en 1814* (Paris: Didier and Firmin Didot, 1875), 2 vols.

44 François Mignet, *Nouveaux éloges historiques* (Paris: Didier, 1878), 269.

45 Cousin was probably involved in the movement which led to student disorder in 1820 but he is usually classed as a liberal constitutionalist. See Alan Spitzer, *The French Generation of 1820* (Princeton: Princeton University Press, 1987).

46 References given in the text are to Victor Cousin, *Cours de philoso-*

phie: Introduction à l'histoire de la philosophie (Paris: Pichon & Didier, 1828–9), 2 vols. References to vol. 1 indicate individual lectures with separate pagination.

47 Victor Cousin, 'Discours prononcé à l'ouverture du cours le 4 décembre 1817' in *Du vrai, du beau et du bien* (Paris: Didier, 1881), 9.

48 Victor Cousin, 'De la philosophie de l'histoire', in *Premiers essais de philosophie* (Paris: Librairie Nouvelle, 1853), 315–16.

49 See the illuminating discussion of Cousin contained in D. G. Charlton, *Secular Religions in France 1815–1870* (Oxford: Clarendon Press, 1959).

50 Thomas Carlyle, *The French Revolution* (London: Chapman and Hall, 1894), vol. 1, 184. See C. Crossley, 'English responses to Michelet and French revolutionary historiography, 1830–48', *Franco-British Studies* 6 (1988), 91–104.

51 See E. Hobsbawm and T. Ranger (eds) *The Invention of Tradition* (Cambridge: Cambridge University Press, 1983).

52 For a full discussion of these questions, see Charlton, *Secular Religions in France*.

53 See Arthur O. Lovejoy, *The Great Chain of Being* (Cambridge, Mass.: Harvard University Press, 1973).

2 AUGUSTIN THIERRY (1795–1856) AND THE PROJECT OF NATIONAL HISTORY

1 References to Thierry's works are given in the body of the text. The best critical study of Thierry's writing is Lionel Gossman, 'Augustin Thierry and liberal historiography', *Between History and Literature* (Cambridge Mass. and London: Harvard University Press, 1990), 83–151. The development of Thierry's historical writing is the subject of Rulon Nephi Smithson, *Augustin Thierry: Social and Political Consciousness in the Evolution of a Historical Method* (Geneva: Droz, 1972). See also the penetrating essay by Marcel Gauchet, 'Les *Lettres sur l'histoire de France* d'Augustin Thierry: "l'alliance austère du patriotisme et de la science" ', in Pierre Nora (ed.), *Les Lieux de mémoire: II La nation* (Paris: Gallimard, 1986), I, 247–316.

2 Claude-Henri de Saint-Simon and Augustin Thierry, *De la réorganisation de la société européenne* (Paris: Les Presses Françaises, 1925).

3 Frank E. Manuel, *The New World of Henri Saint-Simon* (Notre Dame: University of Notre Dame Press, 1963), 195.

4 Ephraïm Harpaz, '*Le Censeur européen*, histoire d'un journal quotidien', *Revue des sciences humaines* (1964), 129–259. See also Harpaz's earlier article, '*Le Censeur*, histoire d'un journal libéral', *Revue des sciences humaines* (1958), 483–511.

5 For an exploration of the relations between economic liberalism and industrialism which also includes a discussion of the role of Thierry, see Henri Gouhier, *La Jeunesse d'Auguste Comte et la formation du positivisme* (Paris: Vrin, 1941; repr. 1970), vol. 3, 71–9, 137, 161–3.

6 Smithson, *Augustin Thierry*, 19.

7 'Sur le cours d'histoire de M. Daunou, au Collège de France', *DAEH*, 151–6.
8 Cheryl B. Welch, *Liberty and Utility: The French Idéologues and the Transformation of Liberalism* (New York: Columbia University Press, 1984), 157.
9 Emmet Kennedy, *A 'Philosophe' in the Age of Revolution: Destutt de Tracy and the Origins of 'Ideology'* (Philadelphia: The American Philosophical Society, 1978), 325.
10 For an overview of the historiography of the late Middle Ages, see Bernard Guenée, 'L'Histoire de l'état en France à la fin du Moyen Age vue par les historiens français depuis cent ans', *Revue historique* 232 (1964), 331–60. For an English perspective on these problems, cf. J. W. Burrow, *A Liberal Descent: Victorian Historians and the English Past* (Cambridge: Cambridge University Press, 1981).
11 Gossman, *Between History and Literature*, 97.
12 See George Armstrong Kelly, *Victims, Authority, and Terror: The Parallel Deaths of d'Orléans, Custine, Bailly, and Malesherbes* (Chapel Hill: University of North Carolina Press, 1982).
13 Stanley Mellon, *The Political Uses of History* (Stanford: Stanford University Press, 1958), 7.
14 See M. Seliger, 'Race-thinking during the Restoration', *Journal of the History of Ideas* 19, 2 (1958), 273–82.
15 Marcel Duchemin, 'Six lettres inédites d'Augustin Thierry', *Revue d'histoire littéraire de la France* 4 (1897), 609.
16 See Christian Amalvi, 'Les métamorphoses révolutionnaires d'Etienne Marcel de Danton à François Mitterrand', in *De l'art et la manière d'accommoder les héros de l'histoire de France. Essais de mythologie nationale* (Paris: Albin Michel, 1988), 205–309.
17 A. Augustin Thierry, *Augustin Thierry (1795–1856)* (Paris: Plon, 1922), 221.

3 FRANÇOIS GUIZOT (1787–1874) AND LIBERAL HISTORY: THE CONCEPT OF CIVILISATION

1 The best treatment of Guizot's thought currently available is Pierre Rosanvallon, *Le Moment Guizot* (Paris: Gallimard, 1985). The only full biography is the recent study by Gabriel de Broglie, *Guizot* (Paris: Perrin, 1990). Douglas Johnson's fluent and impressive *Guizot: Aspects of French History (1787–1874)* (London: Routledge & Kegan Paul, 1963) is irreplaceable. It deals with Guizot's life and his ideas and is a model of rigorous intellectual biography.
2 We should remember that Guizot had been educated in Geneva before coming to Paris to continue his studies. In Paris he frequented intellectual circles which favoured recent developments in German thought. (See Henri Tronchon, *La Fortune intellectuelle de Herder en France* (Paris: Rieder, 1920), 430–66.) He published a translation of Gibbon's *Decline and Fall* in 1812. He was appointed to the chair of modern history at the Sorbonne in the same year (his inaugural lecture is

reprinted in *M*, I, 388–404). In the early years of the Restoration Guizot held a number of high administrative positions and was closely involved with affairs of state. He lost his influence and was excluded from government circles in the atmosphere of reaction which set in after the assassination of the Duc de Berry in 1820. He then returned to teaching but his course was suspended in 1822. In the years which followed he devoted his energies to history and journalism. Guizot returned to lecturing in the more liberal climate of 1828.

3 Johnson, *Guizot*, 54.
4 Guizot did not, however, give the industrial dimension the centrality accorded to it by liberal economists such as Charles Comte and Charles Dunoyer. Guizot was more interested in ideas than in industry. See Shirley M. Gruner, 'Political historiography in Restoration France', *History and Theory* 8 (1969), 346–65.
5 See Biancamaria Fontana, *Benjamin Constant and the Post-Revolutionary Mind* (New Haven and London: Yale University Press, 1991).
6 Guizot used his political power and influence to organise and stimulate historical research during the July Monarchy. In 1834 he founded the Comité des travaux historiques. He had begun the vast enterprise of publishing source material under the Restoration. See the *Collection des mémoires relatifs à l'histoire de France depuis la fondation de la monarchie française jusqu'au 13e siècle* (Paris: Dépôt central de la librairie, 1823–35), 30 vols. See Laurent Theis, 'Guizot et les institutions de mémoire', in Pierre Nora (ed.), *Les Lieux de mémoire: II La Nation* (Paris: Gallimard, 1986), II, 569–92.
7 See R. A. Lochore, *History of the Idea of Civilisation in France (1830–1870)* (Bonn: Ludwig Röhrscheid, 1935). See also John Stuart Mill's major essay on Guizot, 'Guizot's essays and lectures on history (1845)', in *Collected Works* (Toronto and London: University of Toronto Press and Routledge & Kegan Paul, 1985), vol. 20, 257–94.
8 See Hans D. Kellner, 'Guizot and the poets', *Journal of European Studies* 7, 3 (1977), 171–88.
9 For a fine analysis of the mood of the times, see Alan Spitzer, *The French Generation of 1820* (Princeton: Princeton University Press, 1987).
10 See Jacques Barzun, *The French Race: Theories of its Origins and their Social and Political Implications* (New York: Columbia University Press, 1932). See also, by the same author, 'Romantic historiography as a political force in France', *Journal of the History of Ideas* 2, 3 (1941), 318–29.
11 The debate on origins had been reactualised by the argument in favour of the nobility advanced by Montlosier in *De la monarchie française* (1815).
12 In *Shakespeare et son temps* (1851) Guizot again attends to the special conditions prevailing in England. He claims that the Roman conquest did not leave on Britain the profound impression it left on Gaul. Successive waves of invaders conquered England but the vanquished did not suffer humiliation at the hands of brutal masters. Consequently England developed a more homogeneous culture than France.

Guizot situates Shakespeare within a community which encouraged transactions between social classes: the landowner who devoted his time to agriculture was no stranger to the humbler pleasures of the people. There is a rosy glow of merry England about much of Guizot's presentation.

13 See Richard R. Chase, Jr, 'The influence of psychology on Guizot and Orleanist policies', *French History* 3, 2 (1989), 177–93.

14 See Vincent E. Starzinger, *Middlingness: Juste Milieu Political Theory in France and England, 1815–48* (Charlottesville: University of Virginia Press, 1965), 110–18.

15 See François Furet, 'Transformations in the historiography of the Revolution', in Ferenc Fehér (ed.), *The French Revolution and the Birth of Modernity* (Berkeley and Oxford: University of California Press, 1990), 264–77.

4 THE HISTORICAL VISION OF SAINT-SIMON (1760–1825) AND THE SAINT-SIMONIANS (1825–1832)

1 See Alan Spitzer, *The French Generation of 1820* (Princeton: Princeton University Press, 1987).

2 Henry-René d'Allemagne, *Les Saint-Simoniens 1827–1837* (Paris: Gründ, 1930), 33–4.

3 Robert B. Carlisle, *The Proffered Crown: Saint-Simonianism and the Doctrine of Hope* (Baltimore and London: The Johns Hopkins University Press, 1987), 89.

4 Frank E. Manuel, *The New World of Henri Saint-Simon* (Notre Dame: University of Notre Dame Press, 1963), 6.

5 Keith Taylor, 'Introduction' to *Henri Saint-Simon (1760–1825): Selected Writings on Science, Industry and Social Organisation* (London: Croom Helm, 1975), 38.

6 Manuel, *The New World of Henri Saint-Simon*, 300–1.

7 For an illuminating discussion of Condorcet, Saint-Simon and Comte, see Keith Michael Baker, *Condorcet: From Natural Philosophy to Social Mathematics* (Chicago and London: University of Chicago Press, 1975), 376–82.

8 For references to works by Saint-Simon, see the Bibliography to this chapter, p. 275.

9 Manuel, *The New World of Henri Saint-Simon*, 152.

10 See Henri Gouhier, *La Jeunesse d'Auguste Comte et la formation du positivisme* (Paris: Vrin, 1933, 1964, 1970), 3 vols.

11 The best treatment of these questions is still Walter M. Simon, 'History for utopia: Saint-Simon and the idea of progress', *Journal of the History of Ideas* 17, 3 (1956), 311–31.

12 Saint-Simon cited by Jean Dautry, 'La Révolution nécessaire d'après Claude-Henri de Saint-Simon', *Annales historiques de la Révolution française* 38, 2 (1966), 41–2. Saint-Simon's writings contain a variety of explanations for the errors of the Revolution. These include: the handing over of power to the unenlightened, the character of Robes-

pierre, the role played by lawyers and abstract thinkers in the unfolding of events.

13 For the history of the Saint-Simonians I am relying upon the works by D'Allemagne, Carlisle and Charléty (see Bibliography). The fullest critical analysis of their ideas remains that proposed by Georg G. Iggers, *The Cult of Authority: The Political Philosophy of the Saint-Simonians. A Chapter in the Intellectual History of Totalitarianism* (The Hague: Martinus Nijhoff, 1958).

14 Quoted in Iggers, *The Cult of Authority*, 78.

15 Philippe Buchez. *Introduction à la science de l'histoire ou science du développement de l'humanité* (Brussels: Louis Hauman, 1834), I, 47.

16 For examples of the high-flown religious rhetoric of the new church, see *Recueil de prédications* (Paris: Aux bureaux du *Globe*, 1832), 2 vols.

17 For some examples of the Saint-Simonian imagination in its relation to the future, see Ceri Crossley, 'Some attitudes towards architecture during the July Monarchy', *French Forum* 8, 2 (1983), 134–46.

18 Abel Transon, *De la religion saint-simonienne: aux élèves de l'Ecole Polytechnique* (Paris: Mesnier, 1830), 5.

19 Ibid., 13.

20 Quoted in Iggers, *The Cult of Authority*, 102.

21 Ralph P. Locke, *Music, Musicians and the Saint-Simonians* (Chicago and London: University of Chicago Press, 1986), 158–61. See also Michel Chevalier, *Doctrine de Saint-Simon: la Marseillaise* (Paris: Everat, n.d.).

22 Gustave Biard, *L'Ami du prolétaire*, I (1832), 10.

23 Frank E. Manuel, *The Prophets of Paris* (Cambridge, Mass.: Harvard University Press, 1962), 184.

5 EDGAR QUINET (1803–1875): HISTORY, NATURE AND RELIGION

1 See François Furet, *La Gauche et la Révolution au milieu du XIXe siècle: Edgar Quinet et la question du jacobinisme (1865–1870)* (Paris: Hachette, 1986); Claude Lefort, introduction to the reprint of Quinet's *La Révolution* (Paris: Belin, 1987).

2 For Quinet's life, see R. H. Powers, *Edgar Quinet: A Study in French Patriotism* (Dallas: Southern Methodist University Press, 1957); H. Tronchon, *Le Jeune Edgar Quinet ou l'aventure d'un enthousiaste* (Paris: Les Belles Lettres, 1937); Albert Valès, *Edgar Quinet: Sa vie et son œuvre* (Vienna: Aubin, 1936).

3 These and other texts are now available in Willy Aeschimann, *La Pensée d'Edgar Quinet* (Paris and Geneva: Anthropos & Georg, 1986).

4 The pages which follow develop some aspects of my argument in *Edgar Quinet (1803–1875): A Study in Romantic Thought* (Lexington: French Forum, 1983).

5 Quinet does, however, compare French revolutionary history with developments in German intellectual life in a revealing manner. Kant's philosophy is likened to the Constituent Assembly's commitment to

reform and the rights of man; Fichte is compared to the sovereign Jacobin will refashioning Europe; Schelling's excursions into oriental mythology are said to recall Napoleon's ambitions in the Middle East; Hegel, finally, is associated with the triumph of the Holy Alliance, with the consolidation of authority by way of a return to the past. See *DLR*, 465–69.

6 See Aeschimann, *La Pensée d'Edgar Quinet*, 607.

7 Quinet had been appointed professor at Lyon in 1839 but he found the provincial life uncongenial and was relieved to obtain the chair of the languages and literatures of southern Europe at the Collège de France in 1841. In published form his lectures were entitled: *Les Jésuites* (1843), which brought together Quinet's and Michelet's lectures on that topic; *L'Ultramontanisme ou l'église romaine et la société moderne* (1844); and *Le Christianisme et la Révolution française* (1845). The lectures of 1842 were published later as *Les Révolutions d'Italie*, which appeared in three parts in 1848, 1851 and 1852.

8 See Frank Paul Bowman, *Le Christ des barricades 1789–1845* (Paris: Cerf, 1987).

9 Nature retained its dominant role in *Le Génie des religions* (1842) which was based upon the Lyon lectures of 1839–40. However, in this case Quinet's subject matter was exclusively pre-Christian religious thought. Quinet's sensitivity to nature is rarely seen in the later lectures. An exception in *Le Christianisme et la Révolution française* is the treatment of Christopher Columbus where once again we find nature in the new world being associated with the possibility of spiritual renewal.

10 See Henri de Lubac, *La Postérité spirituelle de Joachim de Fiore* (Paris: Cerf, 1979 and 1981), 2 vols; Marjorie Reeves and Warwick Gould, *Joachim of Fiore and the Myth of the Eternal Evangel in the Nineteenth Century* (Oxford: Clarendon Press, 1987).

11 See Frank Paul Bowman, *French Romanticism: Intertextual and Interdisciplinary Readings* (Baltimore and London: The Johns Hopkins University Press, 1990), 155–64.

12 Quinet never placed the enfranchisement of the Communes and the rise of the bourgeoisie at the heart of his writing. He made freedom a metaphysical principle rather than the contingent consequence of developments in industry or forms of municipal government. He focused less on events than on the religious ideas which were held to be generative of social change.

13 Quinet exempts himself and Michelet from having subscribed to the view of French history which he is attacking. This is only partially true. We should remember the extent to which Michelet in the 1830s – despite his questioning of Thierry's racial theories – still followed the general line taken by the liberal historians: the defeat of the Gauls by Rome marked a progress in civilisation, the centralisation of power by the absolute monarchy was a step in the direction of national unity.

14 See Simone Bernard-Griffiths, 'Rupture entre Michelet et Quinet', *Romantisme* 10 (1975), 145–65.

15 See Furet, *La Gauche et la Révolution au milieu du XIXe siècle: Edgar Quinet et la question du jacobinisme.*

16 For Quinet's subsequent attempts to insert history into a greater synthesis which accommodated Darwinian evolutionary theory, see my *Edgar Quinet (1803–1875): A Study in Romantic Thought.*

6 JULES MICHELET (1798–1874): HISTORY AS RESURRECTION

1 See Paul Viallaneix, *La Voie royale: Essai sur l'idée de peuple dans l'œuvre de Michelet* (Paris: Flammarion, 1971; first edn 1959). Like all students of Michelet I am deeply indebted to Viallaneix's pioneering work.

2 Quoted by Pierre Citron, *La Poésie de Paris dans la littérature française de Rousseau à Baudelaire* (Paris: Minuit, 1961), II, 253.

3 Michelet cited by Jean Guéhenno, *L'Evangile éternel: Etude sur Michelet* (Paris: Grasset, 1962; first edn. 1927), 39.

4 See the texts collected in *Mother Death: The Journal of Jules Michelet 1815–1850*, trans. and ed. Edward K. Kaplan (Amherst: University of Massachusetts Press, 1984).

5 Guizot, on the other hand, devoted considerable space to Spain.

6 Michelet quoted by Gabriel Monod, 'Michelet professeur à l'Ecole Normale (1827–1838), *Revue des deux mondes* 126 (1894), 901.

7 The sexual polarities which organise Michelet's writing and their origins in his personal life are examined by Arthur Mitzman, *Michelet Historian: Rebirth and Romanticism in Nineteenth-Century France* (New Haven and London: Yale University Press, 1990).

8 See Georges Poulet, 'Michelet et le moment d'éros', *Nouvelle revue française* 178 (1967), 610–35.

9 See Alice A. Jardine, *Gynesis: Configurations of Woman and Modernity* (Ithaca and London: Cornell University Press, 1985); Genevieve Lloyd, *The Man of Reason: 'Male' and 'Female' in Western Philosophy* (London: Routledge 1993; first edn 1984); Carol McMillan, *Women, Reason and Nature* (Oxford: Blackwell, 1982).

10 See Thérèse Moreau, *Le Sang de l'histoire* (Paris: Flammarion, 1982); Ludmilla Jordanova, *Sexual Visions* (New York: Harvester, 1989).

11 See Majorie Reeves and Warwick Gould, *Joachim of Fiore and the Myth of the Eternal Evangel in the Nineteenth Century* (Oxford: Clarendon Press, 1987).

12 See Frank Paul Bowman, 'Michelet et les métamorphoses du Christ', *Revue d'histoire littéraire de la France* 74, 5 (1974), 824–51.

13 See Donald R. Kelley, *Historians and the Law in Post-Revolutionary France* (Princeton: Princeton University Press, 1984), 101–12.

14 See Frank Paul Bowman, *French Romanticism: Intertextual and Interdisciplinary Readings* (Baltimore and London: The Johns Hopkins University Press, 1990), 155–64; Edward K. Kaplan, 'Michelet's revolutionary symbolism: from hermeneutics to politics', *French Review* 50, 5 (1977), 713–23.

15 See the deeply illuminating analysis by Lionel Gossman, 'The go-

between: Jules Michelet, 1798–1874', *Modern Language Notes* 89 (1974), 503–41, and the seminal essays reprinted in *Between History and Literature* (Cambridge Mass.: Harvard University Press, 1990).

16 For a discussion of Michelet's concept of the Renaissance, see Wallace K. Ferguson, *The Renaissance in Historical Thought* (Cambridge Mass.: Riverside Press, 1948), 173–8. Although Michelet lectured on the Renaissance in 1839 and 1840 he did not publish his conclusions until 1855 as the seventh volume of the *Histoire de France*. Here he portrayed the Middle Ages as monstrous and negatively artificial. He asserted that the Renaissance replaced the medieval veneration for virginity with a celebration of maternity and life.

17 Cf. John Boswell, *The Kindness of Strangers: The Abandonment of Children in Western Culture from Late Antiquity to the Renaissance* (London: Penguin, 1988). For information on the relationship between Michelet and his mother, see *Ecrits de jeunesse*, ed. P. Viallaneix (Paris: Gallimard, 1959).

18 See the classic study by John Bowlby, *Attachment and Loss* (London: Penguin, 1981), vol. 3. The best treatment of Michelet over these crucial years is by Michel Crouzet, 'Michelet, les morts et l'année 1842', *Annales* 26 (1976), 182–96.

19 Roland Barthes, *Michelet*, trans. R. Howard (Oxford: Blackwell, 1987; first edn 1954), 19.

20 *Mother Death: The Journal of Jules Michelet 1815–1850*, 95. See also, by Edward K. Kaplan, 'Les deux sexes de l'esprit: Michelet phénoménologue de la pensée créatrice et morale', *Europe* 535–6 (1973), 97–111.

21 See Anthony Zielonka, *Alphonse Esquiros (1812–1876): A Study of his Works* (Paris and Geneva: Champion-Slatkine, 1985).

22 For a development of these ideas within a different context, see my article, 'Town–country and the circulation of revolutionary energy: the cases of Bonald and Michelet', in Alan Forrest and Peter Jones (eds), *Reshaping France: Town, Country and Region during the French Revolution* (Manchester: Manchester University Press, 1991), 243–53.

23 Barthes, *Michelet*, 156.

24 See Michelle Coquillat, *La Poétique du mâle* (Paris: Gallimard, 1982); Naomi Segal, *Narcissus and Echo: Women in the French Récit* (Manchester: Manchester University Press, 1988).

25 Gossman, *Between History and Literature*, 221.

26 Pierre Moreau, 'Michelet', in *Dictionnaire des lettres françaises: Le dix-neuvième siècle* (Paris: Fayard, 1972), II, 156.

27 Gossman, 'The go-between', 540.

28 Quinet, cited by Mme H. Quinet, *Cinquante ans d'amitié: Michelet-Quinet (1825–1875)* (Paris: Armand Colin, 1903), 302.

7 CONCLUSION

1 See Paul Bénichou, *Le Temps des prophètes* (Paris: Gallimard, 1977); Pierre Moreau, *L'Histoire en France au XIXe siècle: état présent des travaux et esquisse d'un plan d'études* (Paris: Les Belles Lettres, 1935); B. Reizov, *L'Historiographie romantique française* (Moscow: Editions

en langues étrangères, n.d.); Jean Walch, *Les Maîtres de l'histoire: 1815–1850* (Geneva and Paris: Slatkine, 1986).

2 See Leon Pompa, *Human Nature and Historical Knowledge: Hume, Hegel and Vico* (Cambridge: Cambridge University Press, 1990); R. V. Sampson, *Progress in the Age of Reason* (London: Heinemann, 1956).

3 Amans-Alexis Monteil, *Histoire des Français des divers états aux cinq derniers siècles* (Paris: Janet & Cotelle, 1828), I, v–vii. See Christopher Warne, 'Aspects of historiography in nineteenth-century France: the politics, poetics and practice of Amans-Alexis Monteil (1769–1850)', unpublished Ph.D. thesis, University of Birmingham, 1992.

4 See Lionel Gossman, *Between History and Literature* (Cambridge, Mass.: Harvard University Press, 1990); Suzanne Gearhart, *The Open Boundary of History and Fiction* (Princeton: Princeton University Press, 1984).

5 See Elias Canetti, *Crowds and Power* (Harmondsworth: Penguin, 1987); Gérard Fritz, *L'Idée de Peuple en France du XVIIe au XIXe siècle* (Strasbourg: Presses Universitaires de Strasbourg, 1988); J. S. McClelland, *The Crowd and the Mob from Plato to Canetti* (London: Unwin Hyman, 1989); Ann Rigney, *The Rhetoric of Historical Representation* (Cambridge: Cambridge University Press, 1990).

6 See Edward Said, *Orientalism* (Harmondsworth: Penguin, 1985); Robert Young, *White Mythologies: Writing, History and the West* (London and New York: Routledge, 1990).

7 For a discussion of the shift from Enlightenment to Romantic views of spirituality, see Charles Taylor, *Sources of the Self: The Making of the Modern Identity* (Cambridge: Cambridge University Press, 1989).

Bibliography

INTRODUCTION

Works of history and criticism

Boas, George, *French Philosophies of the Romantic Period* (Baltimore: The Johns Hopkins University Press, 1925).

Charlton, Donald, *Secular Religions in France 1815–1870* (Oxford: Clarendon Press, 1959).

Collingwood, R. G., *The Idea of History* (Oxford: Oxford University Press, 1973).

Furet, François, *Penser la Révolution française* (Paris: Gallimard, 1978).

Girard, Louis, *Le Libéralisme en France de 1814 à 1848: doctrine et mouvement* (Paris: Centre de Documentation Universitaire, 1970).

Gruner, Shirley, M., *Economic Materialism and Social Moralism* (The Hague: Mouton, 1973).

Hobsbawm, E. J., *Nations and Nationalism since 1780* (Cambridge: Cambridge University Press, 1990).

Jardin, André, *Histoire du libéralisme politique* (Paris: Hachette, 1985).

Lovejoy, Arthur, O., *The Great Chain of Being* (Cambridge, Mass.: Harvard University Press, 1973).

Lowenthal, David, *The Past is a Foreign Country* (Cambridge: Cambridge University Press, 1985).

Mellon, Stanley, *The Political Uses of History* (Stanford: Stanford University Press, 1958).

Picavet, François, *Les Idéologues* (Paris: Félix Alcan, 1891).

Reizov, Boris, *L'Historiographie romantique française* (Moscow: Editions en Langues Etrangères, n. d.).

Spitzer, Alan, *The French Generation of 1820* (Princeton: Princeton University Press, 1987).

Walch, Jean, *Les Maîtres de l'histoire 1815–1850* (Geneva and Paris: Slatkine, 1986).

Welch, Cheryl, B., *Liberty and Utility: The French Idéologues and the Transformation of Liberalism* (New York: Columbia University Press, 1984).

White, Hayden, *Metahistory: The Historical Imagination in Nineteenth-Century Europe* (Baltimore and London: The Johns Hopkins University Press, 1973).

Contemporary sources

Ballanche, Pierre-Simon, *Œuvres complètes* (Paris: Bureau de l'Encyclopédie des Sciences Utiles, 1833), 6 vols.

Barante, Prosper de, *Histoire des ducs de Bourgogne* (Paris: Ladvocat, 1824–6), 13 vols.

—— *La Vie politique de M. Royer-Collard: Ses discours et ses écrits* (Paris: Didier, 1863).

Barruel, Augustin, *Mémoires pour servir à l'histoire du jacobinisme* (Hamburg: Fauche, 1797–9), 5 vols.

Barthélemy, Jean-Jacques, *Voyage du jeune Anacharsis en Grèce* (Paris: Didot, 1799), 7 vols.

Bichat, Xavier, *Recherches physiologiques sur la vie et la mort* (Paris: Fortin, 1844).

Bonald, Louis de, *Législation primitive considérée dans les derniers temps par les seules lumières de la raison* (Paris: Le Clère, 1857).

Boulainvilliers, Henri de, *Histoire de l'ancien gouvernement de France* (Amsterdam, 1727).

Buchez, Philippe, *Introduction à la science de l'histoire ou science du développement de l'humanité* (Brussels: Louis Hauman, 1834), 2 vols.

Chateaubriand, François René de, *Génie du christianisme* (Paris: Garnier-Flammarion, 1966), 2 vols.

Comte, Auguste, *Cours de philosophie positive* (Paris: Baillière, 1864), 6 vols.

Comte, Charles, *Traité de législation* (Paris: Chamerot, 1835).

Condillac, Etienne Bonnot de, *Essai sur l'origine des connaissances humaines* (Amsterdam: Changuion, 1788), 2 vols.

Condorcet, Antoine Nicolas de, *Esquisse d'un tableau historique des progrès de l'esprit humain* (Paris, 1795).

Constant, Benjamin, *Œuvres*, ed. A. Roulin (Paris: Gallimard, 1957).

Cousin, Victor, *Cours de philosophie: Introduction à l'histoire de la philosophie* (Paris: Pichon & Didier, 1828–9) 2 vols.

—— *Premiers essais de philosophie* (Paris: Librairie Nouvelle, 1853).

—— *Du vrai, du beau et du bien* (Paris: Didier, 1881).

Daunou, Pierre Claude François, *Essai historique sur la puissance temporelle des papes* (Paris: Le Normand, 1810).

—— *Essai sur les garanties individuelles que réclame l'état actuel de la société* (Paris: Foulon, 1819).

—— *Cours d'études historiques* (Paris: Firmin Didot, 1849), vol. 20.

Destutt de Tracy, *Eléments d'Idéologie* (Paris: Lévi, 1827) 5 vols.

Dubos, Jean-Baptiste, *Histoire critique de l'établissement de la monarchie dans les Gaules* (Amsterdam, 1734), 3 vols.

Dunoyer, Charles, *L'Industrie et la morale considérées dans leurs rapports avec la liberté* (Paris: Sautelet, 1823).

Dupuis, Charles, *Origine de tous les cultes, ou religion universelle* (Paris: Agasse, 1795) 4 vols.

Gérando, Joseph-Marie de, *Histoire comparée des systèmes de philosophie* (Paris: Henrichs, 1804), 3 vols.

Lamennais, Félicité de, *Essai sur l'indifférence en matière de religion* (Paris: Pagnerre, 1844), 4 vols.

Maistre, Joseph de, *Considérations sur la France* (Lyon: Pélagaud, 1855).

Mignet, François, *Histoire de la Révolution française depuis 1789 jusqu'en 1814* (Paris: Didier and Firmin Didot, 1875), 2 vols.

—— *Nouveaux éloges historiques* (Paris: Didier, 1878).

Say, Jean-Baptiste, *Traité d'économie politique* (Paris: Guillaumin, 1861).

Staël, Germaine de, *De Allemagne* (Paris: Nicolle, 1813), 3 vols.

—— *Considérations sur les principaux événements de la Révolution française* (London: Baldwin, 1819), 3 vols.

—— *De la littérature considérée dans ses rapports avec les institutions sociales* (Paris: Flammarion, 1991).

Thiers, Adolphe, *Histoire de la Révolution française* (Paris: Lecointe, 1828), 10 vols.

Vico, Giambattista, *The New Science*, trans. T. G. Bergin and M. H. Frisch (Ithaca: Cornell University Press, 1984).

Vitet, Louis, *Essais historiques et littéraires* (Paris: Michel Lévy, 1862).

Volney, Constantin François, *Leçons d'histoire, Les Ruines, La Loi naturelle* in *Œuvres* (Paris: Fayard, 1989), 2 vols.

2 AUGUSTIN THIERRY (1795–1856) AND THE PROJECT OF NATIONAL HISTORY

Works by Thierry

Histoire de la conquête de l'Angleterre par les Normands [1825] (Paris: Jouvet, 1882), 2 vols [*HCA*].

Lettres sur l'histoire de France [1827, revised 1829] (Brussels: Gregoir & Wouters, 1839) [*LHF*].

Dix ans d'études historiques [1834] (Brussels: Gregoir & Wouters, 1839) [*DAEH*].

Essai sur l'histoire de la formation et des progrès du tiers état [1853] (Paris: Firmin-Didot, 1883) [*EHFP*].

Récits des temps mérovingiens précédés de considérations sur l'histoire de France [1840] (Brussels: Société belge de libraire, 1840) [*R*].

De la réorganisation de la société européenne [1814] (Paris: Les Presses françaises, 1925). An early work written by Saint-Simon and Thierry in collaboration.

English translations consulted

History of the Conquest of England by the Normans, trans. William Hazlitt (London: David Bogue, 1847), 2 vols.

Narratives of the Mervovingian Era [...] *The Historical Essays*
(London: Whittaker & Co, n.d.).

Critical and historical studies

Augustin-Thierry, A., *Augustin Thierry, d'après sa correspondance et ses papiers de famille* (Paris: Plon, 1922).

Brunetière, Ferdinand, 'L'œvre d'Augustin Thierry', *Revue des deux mondes* 132 (1895), 469–80.

Carroll, Kieran Joseph, *Some Aspects of the Historical Thought of Augustin Thierry (1795–1856)* (Washington: Catholic University of America Press, 1951).

Engel-Janosi, Friedrich, *Four Studies in French Romantic Historical Writing* (Baltimore: The Johns Hopkins University Press, 1955), 88–120.

Gauchet, Marcel, 'Les *Lettres sur l'histoire de France* d'Augustin Thierry: "l'alliance austère du patriotisme et de la science" ', in Pierre Nora (ed.), *Les Lieux de mémoire: II La Nation* (Paris: Gallimard, 1986), I, 247–316.

Gossman, Lionel, 'Augustin Thierry and liberal historiography', *Between History and Literature* (Cambridge, Mass. and London: Harvard University Press, 1990), 83–151.

Jullian, Camille, 'Augustin Thierry et le mouvement historique sous la Restauration', *Revue de synthèse historique* 13 (1906), 125–42.

Smithson, Rulon Nephi, *Augustin Thierry, Social and Political Consciousness in the Evolution of a Historical Method* (Geneva: Droz, 1972).

3 FRANÇOIS GUIZOT (1787–1874) AND LIBERAL HISTORY: THE CONCEPT OF CIVILISATION

Works by Guizot

Du gouvernement de la France depuis la Restauration et du ministère actuel [1820] (Paris: Ladvocat, 1820) [*DGF*].

Des moyens de gouvernement et d'opposition dans l'état actuel de la France [1821] (Paris: Belin, 1988) [*DMG*].

Essais sur l'histoire de France [1823] (Paris: Perrin, 1884) [*EHF*].

Collection des mémoires relatifs à la Révolution d'Angleterre (Paris: Béchet, 1823–5) 25 vols.

Collection des mémoires relatifs à l'histoire de France (Paris: Dépôt central de la librairie, 1823–35), 30 vols.

Histoire de la civilisation en Europe [1828] (Paris: Hachette, 1985) [*HCE*].

Histoire de la civilisation en France depuis la chute de l'Empire romain jusqu'en 1789 [1829–30] (Brussels: Vandooren; Paris: Pichon & Didier, 1829–32), 5 vols [*HCF*].

De la démocratie en France [1849] (Paris: Masson, 1849) [*DF*].

Discours sur l'histoire de la révolution d'Angleterre [1850] in *Histoire de la Révolution d'Angleterre* (Brussels: Meline, 1850), vol. 1, 1–117 [*DHRA*]. Guizot republished this introductory essay with a new title as *Pourquoi la Révolution d'Angleterre a-t-elle réussi?* (Paris: Masson, 1850).

Histoire des origines du gouvernement représentatif et des institutions politiques de l'Europe [1851] (Paris: Didier, 1880), 2 vols. Lectures delivered in 1820–2 [*HOGR*].

Etudes sur les beaux-arts en général [1851] (Paris: Didier, 1860).

Shakespeare et son temps (Paris: Didier, 1851).

Méditations et études morales (Paris: Didier, 1852) [*MEM*].

Trois générations. 1789–1814–1848 (Paris: Michel Lévy, 1852) [*TG*].

Histoire de la Révolution anglaise (Paris: Didier, 1854–6), 6 vols.

Mémoires pour servir à l'histoire de mon temps (Paris: Michel Lévy, 1858–67), 8 vols [*M*].

L'Eglise et la société chrétienne en 1861 (Paris: Michel Lévy, 1861).

Méditations sur l'essence de la religion chrétienne (Paris: Michel Lévy, 1864).

Méditations sur l'état actuel de la religion chrétienne (Paris: Michel Lévy, 1866).

Méditations sur la religion chrétienne dans ses rapports avec l'état actuel des sociétés et des esprits (Paris: Michel Lévy, 1868).

Mélanges politiques et historiques (Paris: Michel Lévy, 1869) [*MPH*]. This contains three important early works: *Du gouvernement représentatif en France en 1816* (1816); *Des conspirations et de la justice politique* (1821); *De la peine de mort en matière politique* (1822).

Les Vies de quatre grands chrétiens français: I Saint Louis II Calvin (Paris: Hachette, 1873).

English translations consulted

Historical Essays and Lectures, ed. S. Mellon (Chicago: University of Chicago Press, 1972), editor's Introduction, xvii–xlv.

The History of Civilisation in Europe (London: Sisley, n.d.).

The History of Civilisation from the Fall of the Roman Empire to the French Revolution, trans. William Hazlitt (London: David Bogue, 1846), 3 vols.

Democracy in France (London: John Murray, 1849).

History of the Origin of Representative Government, trans. Andrew R. Scoble (London: Bohn, 1852).

Shakespeare and His Times (London: Richard Bentley, 1852).

Critical and historical studies

Bardoux, A., *Guizot* (Paris: Hachette, 1894).

Broglie, Gabriel de, *Guizot* (Paris: Perrin, 1990).

Hoeges, Dirk, *François Guizot und die Französische Revolution* (Frankfurt and Bern: Peter Lang, 1981).

Johnson, Douglas, *Guizot: Aspects of French History 1787–1874* (London: Routledge & Kegan Paul, 1963).

O'Connor, Mary Consolata, *The Historical Thought of François Guizot* (Washington: Catholic University of America Press, 1955).
Pouthas, Charles-Henri, *Guizot pendant la Restauration: Préparation de l'homme d'état (1814–1830)* (Paris: Plon, 1923).
—— *La Jeunesse de Guizot (1787–1814)* (Paris: Félix Alcan, 1936).
Rosanvallon, Pierre, *Le Moment Guizot* (Paris: Gallimard, 1985).
Simon, Jules, *Thiers, Guizot, Rémusat* (Paris: Calmann Lévy, 1885), 217–303.
Weintraub, Karl, *Visions of Culture* (Chicago and London: University of Chicago Press, 1966), 75–114.
Woodward, Edward L., *Three Studies in European Conservatism* (London: Constable, 1929), 109–247.

Colloquia

Actes du colloque François Guizot (Paris: Société de l'Histoire du Protestantisme Français, 1976).
François Guizot et la culture politique de son temps (Paris: Gallimard and Seuil, 1991).

4 THE HISTORICAL VISION OF SAINT-SIMON (1760–1825) AND THE SAINT-SIMONIANS (1825–1832)

Works by Saint-Simon

Œuvres (Geneva: Slatkine, 1977), 6 vols [O]. This edition brings together in the form of a photographic reprint works by Saint-Simon from the *Œuvres de Saint-Simon et d'Enfantin* (Paris: Dentu, 1865–78), 47 vols. Unfortunately volumes of the Slatkine edition are not paginated throughout; each volume contains a number of individual texts which retain their original pagination. The page numbers which I provide in the body of this chapter refer therefore to specific texts. However, the individual work to which I am referring is clearly identifiable.
Le Nouveau Christianisme et les écrits sur la religion, ed. Henri Desroche (Paris: Seuil, 1969).

English translation consulted

Selected Writings on Science, Industry and Social Organisation, trans. and ed. Keith Taylor (London: Croom Helm, 1975), Bibliography, 311–12.

Critical and historical studies

Ansart, Pierre, *Saint-Simon* (Paris: Presses Universitaires de France, 1969).
Dautry, Jean, 'La Révolution nécessaire d'après Claude-Henri de Saint-Simon', *Annales historiques de la Révolution française*, 38, 2 (1966), 19–51.

Gouhier, Henri, *La Jeunesse d'Auguste Comte et la formation du positivisme* (Paris: Vrin, 1933, 1964, 1970), 3 vols.
Hayek, Friedrich A., *The Counter-Revolution of Science: Studies on the Abuse of Reason* (Glencoe, Ill.: The Free Press, 1952).
Manuel, Frank E., *The Prophets of Paris* (Cambridge, Mass.: Harvard University Press, 1962).
—— *The New World of Henri Saint-Simon* (Notre Dame: University of Notre Dame Press, 1963). This seminal study which first appeared in 1956 superseded all previous work on Saint-Simon, in English or in French.
Simon, Walter M., 'History for utopia: Saint-Simon and the idea of progress', *Journal of the History of Ideas* 17, 3 (1956), 311–31.
—— 'Ignorance is bliss: Saint-Simon and the writing of history', *Revue internationale de philosophie* 14, 3–4 (1960), 357–83.

Works by the Saint-Simonians

Les Saint-Simoniens (Paris: Microéditions Hachette, 1977), 277 microfiches of books, pamphlets and periodicals. Indispensable.
Doctrine de Saint-Simon: Exposition. Première année. 1828–1829, 3rd edn, revised (Paris: Au bureau de l'*Organisateur*, 1831) [*DSS*].
Doctrine de Saint Simon, ed. C. Bouglé and E. Halévy (Paris: Marcel Rivière, 1924).
L'Ecole saint-simonienne et la femme: Notes et documents pour une histoire du rôle de la femme dans le société saint-simonienne 1828–1833, ed. Maria Teresa Bulciolu (Pisa: Goliardica, 1980).
Buchez, Philippe, *Introduction à la science de l'histoire ou science du développement de l'humanité* (Brussels: Louis Hauman, 1834), 2 vols.
Buchez, Philippe and Roux-Lavergne, Pierre-Célestin, *Histoire parlementaire de la Révolution française* (Paris: Paulin, 1834–8), 40 vols.
Enfantin, Prosper, *Œuvres de Saint-Simon et d'Enfantin publiées par les membres du conseil institué par Enfantin pour l'exécution de ses dernières volontés* (Paris: Dentu, 1872), vols 24, 25, 26.

English translation consulted

The Doctrine of Saint-Simon: An Exposition, trans. and ed. Georg G. Iggers (New York: Schocken Books, 1972).

Critical and historical studies of the Saint-Simonians

Carlisle, Robert B., *The Proffered Crown: Saint-Simonianism and the Doctrine of Hope* (Baltimore and London: The Johns Hopkins University Press, 1987).
Charléty, Sébastien, *Histoire du Saint-Simonisme 1825–1864* (Paris: Gonthier, n.d.; first edn 1896).
D'Allemagne, Henry-René, *Les Saint-Simoniens, 1827–1837* (Paris: Gründ, 1930).

Derré, J.-R. (ed.), *Regards sur le Saint-Simonisme et les Saint-Simoniens* (Lyon: Presses Universitaires de Lyon, 1986). Contains a bibliography updating Walch (see next section, Bibliographies).

Hunt, Herbert J., *Le Socialisme et le romantisme en France* (Oxford: Clarendon Press, 1935).

Iggers, Georg G., *The Cult of Authority: The Political Philosophy of the Saint-Simonians. A Chapter in the Intellectual History of Totalitarianism* (The Hague: Martinus Nijhoff, 1958).

Isambert, François-André, *De la charbonnerie au saint-simonisme. Etude sur la jeunesse de Buchez* (Paris: Minuit, 1966).

—— *Politique, religion et science de l'homme chez Philippe Buchez (1796–1865)* (Paris: Cujas, 1967).

Locke, Ralph, *Music, Musicians and the Saint-Simonians* (Chicago: University of Chicago Press, 1986).

Morsy, Magali (ed.), *Les Saint-Simoniens et l'orient: Vers la modernité* (Aix-en-Provence: Edisud, 1990).

Thibert, Marguerite, *Le Rôle social de l'art d'après les Saint-Simoniens* (Paris: Marcel Rivière, n.d.).

Zuffi, Nerema, *'Le Globe' saint-simonien (1831–1832): Art et société* (Verona: Università degli Studi di Verona, 1989).

Bibliographies

Fournel, Henri, *Bibliographie saint-simonienne* (New York: Burt Franklin, 1973: first edn 1833).

Walch, Jean, *Bibliographie du Saint-Simonisme avec trois textes inédits* (Paris: Vrin, 1967).

5 EDGAR QUINET (1803–1875): HISTORY, NATURE AND RELIGION

Works by Quinet

The standard edition of works published before 1858 is *Œuvres complètes* (Paris: Pagnerre, 1857–8), 10 vols [*OC*].

In addition the following works and editions have been consulted:

Correspondance: Lettres à sa mère (Paris: Germer-Baillière, n.d.), 2 vols.

Introduction and *Etude sur le caractère et les écrits de Herder* as printed in Quinet's translation of J. G. Herder, *Idées sur la philosophie de l'histoire de l'humanité* (Paris: Levrault, 1827–8), 3 vols [*I*] and [*E*].

De la nature et de l'histoire dans leurs rapports avec les traditions religieuses et épiques, published as an appendix to *De la Grèce moderne et de ses rapports avec l'antiquité* (Paris: Levrault, 1830) [*DLN*].

'De l'avenir des religions', *Revue des deux mondes* (July 1831), 117–26 [*DLA*].

'De la Révolution et de la philosophie', *Revue des deux mondes* 4 (1831), 464–74 [*DLR*].
De l'Allemagne et de la Révolution (Paris: Paulin, 1832) [*DLAER*].
'Le pont d'Arcole', *Revue des deux mondes* 3 (1832), 256–62 [*LPDA*].
'Ahasvérus', *Revue des deux mondes* (October 1833), 5–11 [*A*].
La Révolution (Paris: Librairie Internationale, 1865), 2 vols [*LR*].

Critical and historical studies

Aeschimann, Willy, *La Pensée d'Edgar Quinet* (Paris and Geneva: Anthropos & Georg, 1986).
Bernard-Griffiths, Simone, 'Rupture entre Michelet et Quinet', *Romantisme* 10 (1975), 145–65.
—— 'La fête révolutionnaire vue par Edgar Quinet ou l'illusion tragique', in *Les Fêtes de la Révolution* (Paris: Société des Etudes Robespierristes, 1977), 605–19.
—— 'Mythification et démythification de la Révolution dans l'œuvre d'Edgar Quinet', in C. Croisille and J. Ehrard (eds), *La Légende de la Révolution*, (Clermont-Ferrand: Faculté des Lettres et Sciences Humaines, 1988), 431–61.
—— 'Mythe et histoire chez Edgar Quinet ou les chatoiements de l'écriture des temps', *Mesure* 1 (1989), 89–109.
Crossley, Ceri, *Edgar Quinet (1803–1875): A Study in Romantic Thought* (Lexington: French Forum, 1983).
—— 'L'histoire comme objet de croyance: *Ahasvérus* d'Edgar Quinet', in E. Fallaize, R. Hallmark and I. Pickup (eds), *Representations of Belief* (Birmingham: Birmingham Modern Languages Publications, 1991), 121–36.
Furet, François, *La Gauche et la Révolution au milieu du XIXe siècle: Edgar Quinet et la question du jacobinisme (1865–1870)* (Paris: Hachette, 1986).
Powers, R. H., *Edgar Quinet: A Study in French Patriotism* (Dallas: Southern Methodist University Press, 1957).
Tronchon, Henri, *Le Jeune Edgar Quinet ou l'aventure d'un enthousiaste* (Paris: Les Belles Lettres, 1937).
Valès, Albert, *Edgar Quinet: Sa vie et son œuvre* (Vienne: Aubin, 1936).

Colloquium

Bernard-Griffiths, Simone and Viallaneix, Paul (eds), *Edgar Quinet, ce juif errant* (Clermont-Ferrand: Publications de la Faculté des Lettres, 1978).

BIBLIOGRAPHY

6 JULES MICHELET (1798–1874): HISTORY AS RESURRECTION

Works by Michelet

The standard edition for reference is the *Œuvres complètes* (Paris: Flammarion, 1971–) [OC] currently being published under the direction of Paul Viallaneix. This will eventually supersede all previous editions.

Other texts and editions consulted:
Du prêtre, de la femme, et de la famille [1845] (Brussels: Meline, 1845) [*DP*].
Histoire de la Révolution française [1847–53] (Paris: Maron and Flammarion, 1868), 8 vols [*HRF*].
Lettres inédites (1841–1871), ed. Paul Sirven (Paris: Presses Universitaires de France, 1924).
Cours professé au Collège de France: Second semestre 1839 d'après les notes d'Alfred Dumesnil, ed. Oscar A. Haac, in *Revue d'histoire littéraire de la France* 54, 3 (1954), suppl.
Ecrits de jeunesse, ed. P. Viallaneix (Paris: Gallimard, 1959).
Journal, vols 1 and 2 ed. P. Viallaneix (Paris: Gallimard, 1959–62); vols 3 and 4, ed. Cl. Digeon (Paris: Gallimard, 1976) [*J*].
Des Jésuites, ed. P. Viallaneix [1843] (Paris: Pauvert, 1966) [*DJ*].
L'Etudiant, ed. G. Picon (Paris: Seuil, 1970) [*LE*].
Le Peuple, ed. P. Viallaneix [1846] (Paris: Flammarion, 1974) [*LP*].
La Femme, ed. T. Moreau [1859] (Paris: Flammarion, 1981) [*LF*].
Leçons inédites de l'Ecole Normale, ed. Fr. Berriot (Paris: Cerf, 1987).

English translations consulted

History of the Roman Republic, trans. William Hazlitt (London: Bogue, 1847).
The Life of Luther, trans. William Hazlitt (London: George Bell, 1884).
History of the French Revolution, trans. Charles Cocks, ed. Gordon Wright (Chicago: University of Chicago Press, 1967).
Mother Death: The Journal of Jules Michelet 1815–1850, trans. and ed. Edward K. Kaplan (Amherst: University of Massachusetts Press, 1984).
History of France, trans. G. H. Smith (London: Whittaker, n.d.), 2 vols.

Critical and historical studies

The critical literature on Michelet is voluminous. I list below only a selection of the most significant items:

Barthes, Roland, *Michelet*, trans. R. Howard (Oxford: Blackwell, 1987; first edn 1954).
Bowman, Frank, 'Michelet et les métamorphoses du Christ', *Revue d'histoire littéraire de la France*, 74, 5 (1974), 824–51.
Calo, Jeanne, *La Création de la femme chez Michelet* (Paris: Nizet, 1975).

279

Cornuz, Jean-Louis, *Michelet: Un aspect de la pensée religieuse au XIXe siècle* (Geneva: Droz, 1955).

Crouzet, Michel, 'Michelet, les morts et l'année 1842', *Annales* 26 (1976), 182–96.

Fauquet, Eric, *Michelet ou la gloire du professeur d'histoire* (Paris: Cerf, 1990).

Gaulmier, Jean, *Michelet devant Dieu* (Paris: Desclée de Brouwer, 1968).

Gossman, Lionel, 'The go-between: Jules Michelet (1798–1874)', *Modern Language Notes* 89 (1974), 503–41.

—— *Between History and Literature* (Cambridge, Mass.: Harvard University Press, 1990), 152–224.

Guéhenno, Jean, *L'Evangile éternel: Etude sur Michelet* (Paris: Grasset, 1962; first edn 1927).

Haac, Oscar A., *Les Principes inspirateurs de Michelet* (Paris: Presses Universitaires de France, 1951).

—— *Jules Michelet* (Boston: Twayne, 1982).

Johnson, Douglas, *Michelet and the French Revolution* (Oxford: Clarendon Press, 1990).

Kaplan, Edward K., *Michelet's Poetic Vision* (Amherst: University of Massachusetts Press, 1977).

Kippur, Steven, *Jules Michelet: A Study of Mind and Sensibility* (Albany: State University of New York Press, 1981).

Mitzman, Arthur, *Michelet, Historian: Rebirth and Romanticism in Nineteenth-Century France* (New Haven: Yale University Press, 1990).

Monod, Gabriel, 'Michelet professeur à l'Ecole Normale', *Revue des deux mondes* 126 (1894), 894–917.

—— *Jules Michelet* (Paris: Hachette, 1905).

—— *La Vie et la pensée de Jules Michelet* (Paris: Champion, 1923), 2 vols.

Moreau, Thérèse, *Le Sang de l'histoire: Michelet, l'histoire et l'idée de la femme au XIXe siècle* (Paris: Flammarion, 1982).

Orr, Linda, *Jules Michelet: Nature, History, and Language* (Ithaca and London: Cornell University Press, 1976).

Poulet, Georges, 'Michelet et le moment d'éros', *Nouvelle revue française* 178 (1967), 610–35.

Viallaneix, Paul, *La Voie royale: Essai sur l'idée de peuple dans l'œuvre de Michelet* (Paris: Flammarion, 1971; first edn 1959) [*LVR*].

Colloquia and volumes of essays

L'Arc 52 (1973).
Europe 535–6 (1973).
Revue d'histoire littéraire de la France 74, 5 (1974).
Romantisme 10 (1975).
Michelet et 'Le Peuple' (Nanterre: Université Paris X, 1975).

Index

INDEX

282